WOMEN IN THE HISTORY
OF POLITICAL THOUGHT

WOMEN
IN THE HISTORY OF
POLITICAL THOUGHT

Ancient Greece to Machiavelli

Arlene W. Saxonhouse

Women and Politics
General Editors:
Rita Mae Kelly and Ruth B. Mandel

PRAEGER

PRAEGER SPECIAL STUDIES • PRAEGER SCIENTIFIC

New York • Philadelphia • Eastbourne, UK
Toronto • Hong Kong • Tokyo • Sydney

Library of Congress Cataloging in Publication Data

Saxonhouse, Arlene W.
Women in the history of political thought.

(Women and politics series)
Bibliography: p.
Includes index.
1. Women. 2. Social control. 3. Political
science—Philosophy. 4. Civilization, Classical.
I. Title. II. Series.
HQ1122.S23 1985   305.4   85-6369
ISBN 0-03-062202-6 (alk. paper)
ISBN 0-03-062201-8 (pbk. : alk. paper)

Published in 1985 by Praeger Publishers
CBS Educational and Professional Publishing, a Division of CBS Inc.
521 Fifth Avenue, New York, NY 10175 USA

© 1985 by Praeger Publishers

56789 052 987654321

Printed in the United States of America on acid-free paper

INTERNATIONAL OFFICES

Orders from outside the United States should be sent to the appropriate address listed below. Orders from areas not
listed below should be placed through CBS International Publishing, 383 Madison Ave., New York, NY 10175 USA

Australia, New Zealand
Holt Saunders, Pty, Ltd., 9 Waltham St., Artarmon, N.S.W. 2064, Sydney, Australia

Canada
Holt, Rinehart & Winston of Canada, 55 Horner Ave., Toronto, Ontario, Canada M8Z 4X6

Europe, the Middle East, & Africa
Holt Saunders, Ltd., 1 St. Anne's Road, Eastbourne, East Sussex, England BN21 3UN

Japan
Holt Saunders, Ltd., Ichibancho Central Building, 22-1 Ichibancho, 3rd Floor, Chiyodaku, Tokyo, Japan

Hong Kong, Southeast Asia
Holt Saunders Asia, Ltd., 10 Fl, Intercontinental Plaza, 94 Granville Road, Tsim Sha Tsui East, Kowloon,
Hong Kong

**Manuscript submissions should be sent to the Editorial Director, Praeger Publishers, 521 Fifth Avenue,
New York, NY 10175 USA**

To the memory of my father, Hans Warmbrunn

Preface

The title of this book, *Women in the History of Political Thought: Ancient Greece to Machiavelli*, may appear to be a contradiction in terms: apart from the women guardians in Plato's *Republic*, women seem to be strikingly absent from the political thought of this period. However, it is the aim of this work to illustrate that the title is not a contradiction, that women do appear consistently throughout the history of political thought, and that their apparent absence derives from our tendency to limit unduly the meaning of "political" thought. A politics abstracted from the female results from defining politics as the public world of power relationships, of diplomacy, of elections, of wars, of the adjudication of conflict: a world in which, until recently, women have seldom found a place. It is a politics that artificially separates a public world from a private world. The authors discussed in this volume had a much broader conception of political life and did not simply classify their world into these two realms and then choose to ignore the latter; rather, for the most part, they were concerned with the interdependence of these realms of human existence, and thus with the interdependence of the male and the female. While often they may have praised the world of male public action, these authors also recognized that the public world was not the totality of human existence, that the private sphere with its women existed as well, and that that sphere set limits upon and defined the possibilities of the public world.

These authors do not make the error of defining the human being as only male, though much scholarship has made the mistake of assuming that they did. Until we understand what the authors discussed in this book say about the female, whether favorable or not, we will not understand the totality of their thoughts on the problems of political order. Scholarly treatment of these authors has been largely androcentric, focused on the male and male involvement in political life. My argument is that these authors, as much as they may have seen the perfection of the human form in the male sex, did not ignore the female; it is the inadequacies of modern scholarship that have made them appear to have done so.

The task before us, though, is not to draw out those scattered references to women in the hallowed texts of political theory. Rather, it is to show how women are an integral part of an author's understanding of the aims, possibilities, and limits of political life. Acknowledging that role leads to new insights into the study of individual authors, as well as of the history of political thought as a whole. To understand political theory only as the male's reflection on the male's communal life, from which women are excluded, is to have only a partial vision. The authors here considered tried to avoid such a vision. Though most had no place for women in the public expressions of authority, they did grant a certain dignity and importance to the world of women. The structure of the community as a whole depended on how the world of women could be a part of, could support, or could undermine the political world. It behooves us at this point in our own history, when we have become aware that women have been excluded not only from public life but also from the contemporary study of that life, to recover that understanding of the social world that considered women and the private world a part of, rather than just addenda to, political life. The following chapters are to aid in the recovery of such an understanding.

As with any work of the kind presented here, there must be a critical selection of authors and works. I have not tried to be exhaustive, but rather to focus on enough authors to suggest the variety and ubiquity of the treatment of women in the history of political thought. There is no suggestion that the role played by the female throughout the history of political thought is consistent over time, that some overriding theme can capture the significance of her appearance. The variety of expressions of political philosophy is matched and underscored by the variety of perspectives on women presented by the different authors. I have tried in the following chapters to indicate that any understanding of the role of women in the history of political thought entails looking beyond the standard texts and the standard authors considered in the usual history of political thought. Thus, I treat plays and poetry as well as the more traditional Platonic dialogues and Aristotelian treatises. Obviously lacking is any work by a woman. But to flagellate history for what was not, accomplishes little.

Chronologically, this book goes only to the beginning of the sixteenth century with a final chapter on Machiavelli, who tried to redefine the meaning of politics and women's place in the new world he believed he had discovered. Yet, the notion of "woman's place" may be a contradiction for Machiavelli, for his thought denies the assigning of a "place" to anyone, and thus opens the intellectual door for the rise of liberalism in the seventeenth century. He concludes our discussion by rejecting all that went before.

The past decade or so has drawn forth a series of books and articles, written from a variety of perspectives, on women in the history of political thought. I have avoided discussing them in the text for the sake of clarity, and in the notes for the sake of space. They are, however, mentioned in the bibliography. Though my interpretations may differ, I must acknowledge my debt to those who early on took seriously the importance of the questions this book addresses.

In more specific terms, I am indebted to Rita Mae Kelly and Ruth Mandel, who urged Praeger to pursue a series of books on women and politics, encouraged me to embark on this topic, and provided much valuable commentary along the way. I owe much as well to conversations with and critical readings by my colleagues Patrick Dobel, Donald Herzog, and Joel Schwartz, all of whom helped me clarify points—sometimes by listening, sometimes by reading early drafts. The office staff of the Political Science Department at the University of Michigan—Barbara Banbury, Carol Campbell, and Connie Voytas—worked unstintingly and with gracious humor, putting the manuscript into the word processor, making my life ever so much easier when the inevitable revisions needed to be made. Hilary Persky demonstrated her usual intelligence and good sense in compiling the index.

My children, Lilly, Noam, and Elena, endured, often asking engagingly how it was going and offering fond (but unfounded) words of encouragement as summer turned to autumn and then to summer again. If justice is, as Simonides says, giving what is due, I plead guilty to injustice. Sterile words on a printed page can never express what is owed to my husband, Gary, but—as we both know—marriage is not built on justice.

Ann Arbor

Contents

1

The Context: Liberal and Preliberal Views of Political Life

The study of the female in the history of political theory from ancient Greece to the dawning of the early modern period requires casting off certain presuppositions concerning the value, purpose, and origin of political society. Many of our perspectives on these issues define us as children of the liberal era, a period beginning in the seventeenth century with the writings of Thomas Hobbes and John Locke. However, before we can cast off our assumptions, we must understand what they are and how they dominate our vision of political life—and, in turn, the role of the female within that life.[1]

Liberty and Community

As the term implies, our liberal background suggests a primary concern with liberty: freedom from arbitrary rule, from the imposition of the will of others, from a government not agreed to by ourselves. At the base of liberal theory is the assumption of natural freedom. Liberalism originated, in part, as a reaction to patriarchal theory, which also reached its most sophisticated expression during the seventeenth century. Patriarchal theory found the origins of political society and the source of obligation—that is, the reason for accepting the authority of another—in familial relations or, more precisely, in the natural authority of the father. In patriarchal theory one need not question the source of authority, since it belongs to the father through the male act of generation. In opposition to patriarchal theory, liberal theorists posit natural free-

1

dom, which can be limited only by the prior agreement, open or tacit, of those who are governed. By nature no one individual has authority over another: not the father over the son, nor the strong over the weak. Authority, the right to command another's obedience and thus control another's actions, is the result of human choice. Natural processes such as generation or natural attributes such as strength, race, or intelligence give no unequivocal guidelines concerning whom to obey.

The liberal assumption of natural freedom—that we are born with no one appointed to rule over us—forced the early liberals such as Hobbes and Locke to search for a new source of political obligation, new grounds for obeying the commands of a governmental institution. In the patriarchal model, depending heavily on analogical thinking, the king's authority was like the authority of the father within the family and of God the Father within the universe; as the father and God were to be obeyed in the natural order of things, so was the king. King James I of England, writing at the beginning of the seventeenth century, offered these words of advice to his son: "Therefore (my son) first of all things, learn to know and love that God, to whom you have a double obligation; first, for that he made you a man; and next that he made you a little God to sit on His throne and rule over other men."[2] Robert Filmer, writing in the middle of the century, went back to God's original donation to Adam of land and authority, and asserted that there was no natural freedom. We are born into a state of subordination to parents and to kings who ultimately receive their power from Adam:

> I see not then how the children of Adam, or of any man else, can be free from subjection to their parents and this subjection of children being the fountain of all regal authority, by the ordination of God himself; it follows that civil power not only in general is by divine institution, but even the assignment of it specifically to the eldest parent.[3]

While liberal theory posits a natural freedom, it must face a new problem: Why should we, enjoying our natural liberty, listen to the directives of others? Liberal theorists found the answer in consent. We all agree to create an authority whose directives we will accept. That authority exists at our pleasure, not because of any inherent qualities belonging to the possessor of that authority nor because God has defined that person as the ruler over the rest of us. The liberal political system is created by, and finds the source of its legitimacy in, the freely given consent of its members.

We accept the authority of those who rule us because we ourselves have placed them in that position.

Patriarchal theory, in defining the father as the natural ruler, had assumed a natural community as well as a natural authority, subject neither to question nor to rejection. The family, and one's place within that family, determined where one stood in the hierarchical scheme of the world. One exists either as a father or a son, a husband or a wife, in a defined set of relationships. First and foremost, one exists as a social being. One does not exist on one's own. Again in contrast, at the theoretical base of liberalism and its rejection of natural authority is the autonomous individual, free from all constricting relationships that might define his or her place within the world. It is this individual who contracts with other like individuals to create a political authority.

Though such an individual—the possessor of rights, the determiner of values, the judge of the political system of which he or she is a part—can never come into being in such splendid isolation, the early liberals posited such isolated individuals in their theoretical challenge to patriarchalism. For them the community exists not by nature, but is built up by the consent of separate individuals who have joined together to create an environment conducive to the individual happiness of each. Such individuals accept a political community on the basis of an assessment of whether it will make them happy. By nature they are not part of that community. They do not naturally form political communities, nor do they need to form political communities in order to live—as, for instance, they need to eat and drink in order to survive. They are not like the bees or the ants, social animals incapable of survival on their own. Rather, as humans they choose—or, in the language of the early liberal theorists, they contract—to become a part of the political system.

As liberal individuals we make such a contract and enter into the political community in order to pursue individual happiness. The political community arises to provide stability and physical security, which in turn allows "the pursuit of happiness." The nature of the happiness sought is defined by the individuals, not by the state or the city of which he or she is a part. Such happiness is subjective; each individual determines what will bring happiness and what will hinder it. Support for the political community depends on an assessment of whether that happiness will be promoted by being a member of a particular political community. In the patriarchal model, it is not the individuals who define the aims of the polity, but those who rule and have authority.

The happiness pursued in liberal society is often a private happiness, relating to the individual as a private being and not specifically as a member of a political community. Because it is private and subjective, it is a happiness whose pursuit may at times put us in conflict with others. The free individuals of a liberal society often find themselves in conflict with their neighbors. Thus, the political community becomes a mediator, a set of institutions designed to resolve the conflicts between its citizens. John Locke argued that there is no natural authority of one person over another before we enter into political society; we are all judges of our own and others' actions in the condition prior to the creation of the polity. Upon entry into political or civil society, we yield that right of judgment to the government, whose laws establish the guidelines under which we can pursue our private interests. We become members of a community because we believe that the government established by that community will mediate our conflicts with others and thus provide the necessary precondition—security—for our happiness. We are not naturally born into political communities as we are born into families. It is in this way that liberal theorists offer the most fundamental break with patriarchal theorists.

Equality and Inequality

The liberal individuals who comprise the liberal state have one crucial characteristic: They are equal. This does not mean that we all have red hair and blue eyes. Clearly we do not. What it does mean is that there is no clear and irrefutable evidence that could be used to determine which individual by nature has authority to rule over another or to make judgments in another's case. Our natural equality stems from each individual's natural right to rule over himself or herself, not to submit to another's rule except by consent. Thomas Hobbes explained the grounds of our equality thus:

> Nature hath made men so equal, in the faculties of the body, and mind; as that though there be found one man sometimes manifestly stronger in body, or quicker in mind than another; yet when all is reckoned together, the difference between man and man, is not so considerable, as that one man can thereupon claim to himself any benefit, to which another may not pretend, as well as he. For as to the strength of the body, the weakest has strength enough to kill the strongest, whether by secret machination, or by confederacy with others, that are in the same danger with himself.[4]

We each have the capacity to kill our neighbor, and therein Hobbes finds our most basic equality. He thus suggests that we can find no clear foundation, such as paternity, that could distinguish one person from another so as to justify that person's rule. Strength is not adequate, nor wit, nor wisdom. Indeed, in Hobbes's model not even sex justifies the authority of one individual over another:

> Whereas some have attributed dominion to the man only, as being of the more excellent sex; they misreckon in it. For there is not always that difference of strength or prudence between the man and the woman, as that the right can be determined without war. In commonwealths, this controversy is decided by civil law: and for the most part (but not always) the sentence is in favor of the father; because for the most part commonwealths have been erected by the fathers, not the mothers of families.[5]

No criteria exist that enable us to pick out the individual who can demand our obedience and expect our obligation. Paternity does not do this for liberal theorists, nor, for Hobbes at least, does masculinity.

In his *Second Treatise on Civil Government*, John Locke emphasizes, as Hobbes had, natural equality, though more gently and without carrying the argument forth to sexual equality:

> There being nothing more evident than that creatures of the same species and rank, promiscuously born to all the same advantages of nature and the use of the same faculties, should also be equal one amongst another without subordination or subjection; unless the lord and master of them all [God] should, by any manifest declaration of his will, set one above another, and confer on him by an evident and clear appointment an undoubted right to dominion and sovereignty.[6]

Locke suggests that God has not, and will not, confer on another such an "evident and clear appointment"; thus we must begin from our fundamental equality and elect by majority vote those who will rule over us, those who will have the sovereign power. It is the greater number of equal individuals, not their greater birth or status in the society, that grants the exercise of authority. In the Declaration of Independence, Thomas Jefferson captures the basic liberal theme when he asserts our equality founded on those self-evident truths that give each individual inalienable rights, spe-

cifically the right not to be subject to arbitrary rule. He too begins
with the fundamental assumption of equality and concludes that
the authority of one person over another comes not from nature,
but from "the consent of the governed."

We enter the political system as equal individuals and expect
the political system to treat us as equals, with equal duties and,
more important, with equal rights before the laws that have been
created by our consent. As equal creators of the political system
of which we are a part, we expect an equal role in determining the
nature, character, and actions of that system, and an equal opportunity to enjoy its benefits. Our understanding of justice and fair-
ness has come to be based on that equality as expressed in such
notions as equal treatment and equal opportunity. Differential
treatment according to characteristics specific to the individual,
such as sex or race or economic status, is suspect, subject to the
accusation of being unjust. Patriarchal theory was based on just
such differential treatment. The husband differed from the wife;
thus his status and the authority accorded him differed. Similarly,
a king differed from his subject; thus he enjoyed privileges not accorded the subject.

Characteristics such as birth, sex, or age determined one's status in the hierarchical, inegalitarian society about which the patriarchal theorist wrote. Liberalism in its turn had to clarify who
would be included in its community of equals. The definition of
who these equals by nature are has changed radically since the rise
of liberalism in the seventeenth century. At first "equals" were
only those adult males owning considerable property. Much of the
history of political thought since that period, however—indeed,
much of the political practice in liberal states—has entailed the expansion of the term "equality" to include members of various economic groups, of various races, of various religions, and even of the
opposite sex. As Hobbes had suggested, though Locke would have
been loath to admit it, liberalism, carried to the logical conclusions
of its premises, would provide for sexual equality. It is the naturally free, equal individual who is at the base of liberal thought, and
there is nothing in liberalism's premises that says the individual
must be a he or a she, a black or a white, an Anglican or an
Anabaptist.

The participation of the individual in the political system of
which she or he is a part is not determined by characteristics such
as sex, religion, the level of one's IQ, or the strength of one's arm.
The tension we find in much of the contemporary debate about the
place of women in society arises from a conflict between the

egalitarian assumptions of liberalism on which the political system in which we live has been built, and the practices of patriarchal and sexual differentiation out of which our society has grown. Sexual inequality is not an inherent characteristic of liberalism, although it often remains in liberal societies (and thought) as a vestige of an earlier age.

A significant uncertainty in liberalism's theoretical structure is its insistence that by nature we are equal. Equality is a precondition on which we build our political institutions, but it is not a precise or historical description of our condition. Liberalism as first presented by Hobbes and Locke is an abstract, ahistorical political theory; it develops theories of political life that avoid the particularities of specific place and time.[7] Rights are universal; they do not differ from place to place or from time to time. Only those governments based on the consent of their subjects can be called free. The economic, social, and cultural characteristics of a particular state are irrelevant to an assessment along these lines.

Liberalism posits a fundamental equality of all individuals, and attempts to answer the question of political legitimacy and obligation in a world where persons have no obvious place ascribed to them by birth, race, sex, or age. Not only do natural characteristics not clarify where one stands in a liberal society, but they give no clear indication of who is to be a member of the political community and who is to be denied such membership. At what point do we say that the individual is or is not a member of the human species possessing those "inalienable rights" that define him or her as a potential participant in the social contract founding civil society, or a potential consenter to one that already exists? The difficulty inherent in this problem is evident in contemporary political debates concerning, for example, voting age or the status of the fetus. Liberalism, with its fundamental focus on equality and rights, does not show us how to determine who is human enough to be equal. Similarly, it gives no theoretical justification for distinguishing the members of the male sex from members of the female sex with regard to their political status.

The two millennia of Western thought under discussion in this book comprise the preliberal epoch, a period that for the most part did not acknowledge the possibility of an individual existing in isolation from others, did not posit an original natural freedom for all, and did not consider the individual as possessing inalienable rights to anything—much less life, liberty, property, or even the pursuit of happiness. The ancients had no conception of human rights as we understand them.[8] In the preliberal period one individual was not automatically assumed to be the equal of another. Inequalities defined relationships between people and established the grounds of one's obligations. Authority belonged to some because of their natural characteristics. The task of political theory was to discover to whom that authority belonged, who was, in the Latin expression of the term, *capax imperii*, capable of dominion. The discovery of such an individual or set of individuals did not come from the agreement of equals. The judgments of some—philosophers, religious men, the wealthy, the free—were more highly valued than the judgments of others. It was Hobbes's great theoretical innovation, his radical accomplishment, to found his political philosophy on equal individuals, none of whom had any natural authority over others.

The preliberal period also had great difficulty conceiving of the autonomous individual who was separate from a larger whole: from the polity, from the family, from the community of gods worshipped by that family or, in the Christian era, from the order of the universe ruled by God. Such relationships had long before established the lines of authority within which each individual could find his or her place. The individual who was part of such a whole could not indiscriminately be either male or female, for the individual had necessary connections (denied by liberalism) with others; those connections were defined by his or her place within the community and especially, for our purposes, within the family—that is, by the individual's sex and age. The community was considered to be of greater importance than the individuals who comprised it, and the goal of the community was not to provide for the individual happiness of its members. The goal of the community might have been glory; it might have been the transformation of men into truly good, rational beings; it might have been service to the gods or to God; it might have been collective (as opposed to individual) happiness. But most important, the community did not exist to service the interests and desires of isolated individuals.

One's status in the preliberal community depended on one's specific characteristics. Was one intelligent or stupid, born of a king or a serf, a believer in God or an infidel? Was one male or female? The female could not be considered apart from her specifically female traits as reproductive being, just as, for example, one could not see the warrior apart from his strength and possession of arms. In large part because of the reproductive capacity of her sex, the female was seen in the context of her relationship to the family; conversely, because of his capability in war, because of his generally greater physical strength, the male was seen in the context of his relationship to the political unit that needed protection and leadership.

There was, however, an important overlap between the realm of the male and the realm of the female, one recognized by most of the authors we will be discussing. The family has often been regarded as the realm of the female alone, but this view needs to be reassessed. The family obviously required the participation of both female and male. Both men and women were necessary to produce the sons who would be the warriors for the city in the next generation. The male, though not limited by the family as was the female, was nevertheless a part of that family. The female, though she did not freely and openly participate in the activities of the polity, was nevertheless a part of that polity, necessary for its existence and for the production of the children who would ensure the continuity of the polity. The relationship between these realms of existence, between what has been called the public and the private spheres, is one of the topics that will keep arising as we explore the place of women in the history of political thought.

What one finds, then, in preliberal thought is not the emphasis on equality that is so important in our political life today, but the emphasis on complementarity, on differences, on the parts out of which the whole is constructed. Both male and female are necessary for the existence of the whole. Preliberal thought acknowledges the differences between the sexes and attempts to work with that difference, sometimes for better and sometimes for worse, to build coherent, stable political communities.

As we study the authors from this period and their treatment of sexual differentiation, we must take care not to bring in our own preconceptions as we evaluate their thought. The dominant questions in their studies of political life were not the institutionalization of liberty or of equality, nor the alleviation of the tension between the two. Rather, they focused on such problems as the creation of political unity, the attainment of self-sufficiency, the prevention of corruption, the nature of the best (noblest) life for the individual, which could be experienced only collectively through dedication to and participation in the polity. In the context of such questions, the female enters not as she does today—as a potentially equal member of the political community to whom custom and tradition have denied rights in the past assigned to the male—but as a limit on the possibilities of politics or as a member of a coherent whole whose difference from the male must be acknowledged and incorporated.

Universality and Particularity: State and Regime

Today politics is concerned with an equality proclaimed by the laws and enforced by the administrative apparatus of the political system. Laws in liberal society deal with universals—that is, they do not apply to a particular individual but offer general guidelines applicable to all members of the community. There may be laws that apply only to persons who drive cars, but anyone who drives a car is subject to the same laws as every other driver—irrespective of race, sex, economic status, or political status. We are all aware that this equality is not always practiced, but we describe the failure to ticket the mayor's son as a perversion of justice. Laws, thus, can ignore particular sexual characteristics. In contemporary society the expectation is that laws will treat all equally, whether one is male or female, black or white, young or old. Legislation can abstract from such particulars, and liberal theory demands such an abstraction. The Equal Rights Amendment must be understood as an attempt to institutionalize this abstraction from specific characteristics because such abstraction is necessary in a truly liberal society.

For the preliberal authors, the female was not, and could not be, transformed through egalitarian legislation into an equal member of the political community. Rather, the female worked to focus attention on what is private and particular rather than on what is universal, the realm of law and politics. She stood outside the universal activity of legislation. The female, for instance, was seen as caring for a particular child, a particular husband, a particular home. In fighting to defend the whole of the city, the male warrior protected all—all the women, all the children, all the homes—even as he protected his own. In this way he was concerned with the universal at the same time he was tied to a particular female through the family and processes of procreation so necessary to the city's continued existence.

The preliberal authors did not abstract from this relationship between the universal and the particular. Aristotle, for example, begins the *Politics* with a vision of the self-sufficient city directed toward the good (noble) life of its male citizens; he then turns immediately to an extended section on the necessities of household management, the particulars of relationships within the family that must precede attention to the universal realm of the city. The men of the city often overestimate the city's potential for abstractions and universality; the female reminds the early thinkers of the limits of that potential by clarifying the city's dependence on particular bodies, especially the reproductive bodies of its women.

Such limitations, acknowledged by the ancient authors them-selves, often go unrecognized by modern interpreters. The male orientation toward universality blinds such interpretations to the depth of analysis of the preliberal authors who understood the im-portance of the particular within the universal, who saw the female perhaps not as an equal to the male but nevertheless as a crucial part of the political community. Too often in the study of political thought, attention focuses exclusively on the role of the male, who appears as the only participant in political life. The preliberal authors recognized that the female, while she may not have been part of what we call the governmental structure or the political institutions—the assemblies or the armies or the judiciary—was nevertheless a part of the "regime," that which encompasses the entire set of political, social, economic, and religious relationships that characterize any community.

By contrast, the liberals do not encourage the existence of such a comprehensive regime. Politics, in a liberal society, is one demar-cated sphere, one set of institutions among many others. Thus, the logic of politics is different from that of the family, the church, or the marketplace. When American feminists of the early 1970s proclaimed "The personal is political," they were reacting against the theoretical separation of what they saw as closely integrated aspects of human life. The liberal vision insists upon a separation between state and society. The state is the realm of governmental structures, a realm from which women until recently have been al-most universally excluded. Because liberal thought has focused on the state, women have not appeared openly in discussions of po-litical life influenced by liberal presuppositions. In contrast, the role of women had to be discussed within the framework of preliberal thought, since there state and society were melded into the con-cept of the regime.

The way in which a community is governed, the distribution of institutional power, will, of course, influence the character of that community; who participates in the legislative process, who is the executor of those laws will define for any community those who are to be respected, those who set forth for the community its values and its models of behavior. But the distribution of political power is only part of what defines a community. The ancient authors recognized other elements: the native character of a peo-ple, the beliefs expressed in its artistic forms and its religious prac-tices, and the organization of relationships within the family. All these were interdependent. It is this interdependence that defines the regime. It is the regime that gives a particular character to any community—that makes France, for example, different from

Britain—in ways that go beyond the differences in the institutional structures by which communities govern themselves.

In the modern liberal state, with its separation of state and society and its rejection of a concept such as the regime, freedom from arbitrary rule has come to mean the option to live one's life as one likes—"to do one's own thing"—without interference from the state. The separation of government and private life becomes the basis of our understanding of freedom. We each believe that no one can tell us what to do with our lives; the government exists so that we may do with our lives as we will. The dichotomization of public and private, whose origins began, well before the liberal era, early in the Middle Ages with the "two swords" theory and the separation of church and state, is first sharply presented in the modern era in John Locke's *A Letter Concerning Toleration* (1689). Although he introduces certain qualifications, Locke argues that the government of any state has no role in deciding the religious beliefs and practices of its citizens. He emphasizes that governmental power is limited to those areas that affect the public good. Religion, affecting the private good of the individual, is not subject to the power of the magistrate.

> The care . . . of every man's soul belongs unto himself, and is to be left unto himself. But what if he neglect the care of his soul? I answer: What if he neglect the care of his health or of his estate, which things are nearlier related to the government of the magistrate than the other? Will the magistrate provide that such a one shall not become poor or sick? Laws provide, as much as is possible, that the goods and health of subjects be not injured by the fraud and violence of others; they do not guard them from the negligence or ill-husbandry of the possessors themselves.[9]

We must contrast with this quote the classical Greek city-state, the polis, in which the community tended to the moral education of the young and the maintenance of a communal religious life. Aristotle's comments in his *Politics* about the city of Babylon are instructive here. For Aristotle a city was a regime in which everyone must be able to recognize everyone else by sight and, specifically, know their moral character. Babylon was so large that people could not know each other, much less keep an eye on others' moral life. It was, indeed, so large a city that its capture could be unknown two days later in the distant parts of the city, where singing and dancing continued. A city of this size, where people can live their own lives apart from the life of the city as a whole, is for

Aristotle not a city but an empire ripe for disunity and disintegration. In Aristotle's vision, all members of the society must be concerned with the welfare, the health, the religion of the other members—or else we cannot say we have a city.[10]

When Locke wrote *A Letter Concerning Toleration*, his proposal to separate religious and political life from each other was sufficiently provocative for his time that he did not dare publish this letter under his own name; throughout his life he denied authorship. By the time of the founding of the republican form of government in the United States, this separation of society and state was ensured by the Bill of Rights, which set not only religion but also speech, social assemblies, and the news media outside the realm of institutional control by the political forces of the society. The most succinct and famous expression of the principles behind this separation appears in John Stuart Mill's treatise *On Liberty* (1859), in which he, as Locke had done two centuries earlier, argues for the impermissibility of governmental interference in the lives of all individuals, except when their actions may lead to the harm of another. While one may encourage another to behave in a certain manner, Mill argues:

> ...neither one person, nor any number of persons, is warranted in saying to another human creature of ripe years that he shall not do with his life for his own benefit what he chooses to do with it...he himself is the final judge. All errors which he is likely to commit against advice and warning are far outweighed by the evil of allowing others to constrain him to do what they deem good.[11]

While government in liberal society may be the protector of the individual, it is to say nothing about the way in which that protected individual is to live.

Today the contrast with a liberal polity that distinguishes between state and society is the unity of the two in the totalitarian regime, a model that evokes hostility and fear. Yet, the demarcation between state and society has obscured the integration of social, economic, religious, and political relationships that were so much a part of the ancient polities and the political philosophies they spawned. Politics has become a sphere of its own and is recognized only as the institutional legal structure associated with the governmental process; society is distinct from government, a separation we see canonized in any university by the separate academic departments assigned to study them.

Thus, if politics is understood, as it is within the liberal context, only as the public sphere, the realm of the authoritative allocation of power, of legislation, of adjudication, then it is easy to see how and why the female has been excluded from the study of the history of political thought. She has not, until the recent past, participated in this public life. Seldom has she been allocated power or served as a lawmaker or participated in the judicial process. The ancient notions of regime that include both public and private life, that deny the possibility of talking about a government that is distinct from the society in which its citizens live, must include women in the discussions of political life.

Along with the demarcation between the two realms, in liberal theory the public realm loses much of the stature it had in ancient times. Leadership no longer depends on the characteristics of the leader, on that particular person's prowess in war, royal birth, intelligence, or gifts from the gods or God. Rather, the position of leadership depends on the will of the subjects and says little about the personal worth of any leader. Hobbes, in particular, urged his readers to turn away from public life, from the scramble for power and glory. Certain conceptions of human excellence, however noble they might seem, actually produce political chaos. Fearing that conflict for prestige in the public realm might lead to a civil war, Hobbes advocated the search for satisfaction in the private economic realm. Here, pursuit of the commodious life, that of private pleasures and comfort, was to replace the pursuit of glory and public nobility.

Locke, with his theory of property—his contention that the acquisition of property would lead to the increased wealth and happiness of the entire human race—gave a justification for abandoning public life and turning to the private search for wealth. One could be more generous by working to increase the stock provided by nature through the acquisition of property and improvement of nature than by vying for public office.

The term "economics" derives from the Greek words *oikos* and *nomos*, household and law. It is the law of household management. Traditionally, this had been the realm of the female. According to Aristotle, she supervises the use and conservation of those goods that are brought into the household. With the rise of the liberal era and of industrialization, the private world was no longer reserved for the female. Instead, the private realm became the realm of the male displaced from the public life. He was the economic actor as economics left the confines of the household. With this transformation of the male from a public creature to a private one, the female was lost.

As both public and private realms became arenas for male activity in the theoretical perspective of liberalism, the female, whose previous stature had been guardian of the private realm, was denied any significant place in the portrait of society. This is not a fate that confronted the female portrayed by the ancient authors. For these authors the household remained the private realm of female activity. In dealing with the relationship of economics and politics, they automatically had to deal with the relationship of the female to the political life of the community.

Liberal authors, for whom both public (politics) and private (economics) are male worlds, can ignore the female. Our liberal perspective that has defined "politics" as the realm of governmental interactions and administration has blinded us to the place of women in the political thought of the ancient authors. These authors did not fail to see the importance of the female for understanding the nature of political life. With our liberal dichotomization of public and private life, it is we who have failed to recognize how much the female, who was restricted to what we now call the private sphere, was a part of ancient political thought.

Conclusion

As a result of the liberal perspective of modern interpreters, the study of the history of political thought has often been limited to those works dealing explicitly with governmental structure; thus, certain texts have become canonical in the study of the history of political thought. The concept of the regime means we must often look beyond such standard texts. An author's consideration of the female often appears elsewhere than in the works that have become the standard classics in the field. If one reads only Book III of Aristotle's *Politics*, in which Aristotle discusses the political life of the city and defines who is the citizen and how authority is allocated, one might think that he had never heard of the female sex; yet the first two books of the *Politics* deal extensively with the role of women in the political community. Or if one reads only Book I of the *Politics* in addition to Book III, one might conclude that he considered women less important than slaves.

Thus, in the following chapters of this book, several of the works discussed will often be ones not commonly read when one studies the history of political thought; however, they are works that demonstrate the thinker's or the particular age's awareness of the place of the female in any consideration of the political regime and its role in human life. They will, I hope, illustrate how an understanding of the female's place in any society is critical for understanding the nature and aims of the political life of that particular community.

To ignore the impact of the existence of women or the fact that the human species is divided into two sexes is, as it were, to have only half a theory. Though a theory may argue, as does liberalism, that sexual differences are irrelevant in certain circumstances, the grounds for this perspective need to be articulated; they cannot be fully articulated until the differences are acknowledged. My aim in this book is not to take to task the authors of the ancient world for not thinking about women as we do. Rather, it is to illustrate the theoretical importance of recognizing the differences between the sexes and the need for a self-conscious understanding of the implications of such a division in the human species. Women have often been invisible in the texts of political theorists because we have not looked for them. They must be reintegrated into the study of the history of political thought, not only for the sake of historical accuracy, but also because their presence gives us a fuller understanding of the human political experience.

The division of the human species reveals, at the most fundamental level, our basic interdependence on one another and the limitations of a political theory that begins with the assumption of the isolated individual. The fact that there are two sexes denies the possibility of that isolation. Precisely because it introduces the individual without an adequate assessment of his or her sexuality, of what ties one person to another, early liberalism, in its reaction to patriarchalism, tried to abstract from some of the issues raised by those writing in the preliberal period. We look at the authors who follow in this book, not simply to satisfy our antiquarian interest but also because their focus on inequality, community, and particularity illuminates some of the tensions within a society founded on equality and individualism.

Female, Family, aııu
Polis in Greek Literature
before Plato

Variety and the Origins of Political Philosophy

Political philosophy begins in the ancient Greek community known as the polis, a term usually translated "city-state." These communities developed in the middle of the seventh century B.C. and reached their apex in the fifth and fourth centuries B.C., before succumbing to the forces of King Philip of Macedon, who made them part of his empire and thus ended their independence. While the Greeks were united by a common name, common language, common gods, and common customs, they were divided politically; each polis jealously preserved its autonomy. The most famous of these poleis is Athens, and it is from Athens that almost all surviving Greek literature comes. Though we do have evidence about the political and social structure of other poleis, such as Sparta and Corinth, it is primarily to the Athenians that we must turn to find out how the Greeks assessed the value of their political lives—and the place of women in those lives.

The rise of political philosophy is dependent on a self-conscious attempt to evaluate the political society in which one lives—and in which one might live should there be an opportunity for change. A tradition of political thought depends on the refusal to accept the given state of things as natural—or, stated obversely, on a spirit of inquiry that makes one willing to review critically the nature of the political community in which one happens to live, to recognize that the way in which one lives is not the only way to live. In the middle of the sixth century B.C., Athens was beset by a series of conflicts arising from the inequitable distribution of wealth. The Athe-

ve their leader, Solon, the opportunity to change their
onal forms of interaction, to develop a new law code, and
to improve their economic, political, and social life; in other
rds, they recognized that laws did not come from the gods or ex-
st by nature. The human being was capable of manipulating and
changing those laws. However, if one is willing to change the laws,
one must be willing to question them, to ask whether they are
good, or even what might be the best political system and how we
might best be ruled. With their mandate to Solon the Athenians
opened up for themselves the questioning of political systems, both
as they are and as they might be.

The Greek historian Herodotus, in the middle of the fifth century B.C., wrote a history of the Persian Wars, the great conflict between East and West. But his history focused on more than battles and military maneuvers. He included descriptions of the varied
customs and social organizations from all of the known world. To
a people prepared to question the goodness of their own customs,
he offered stories and tall tales from as far away as India and Ethio-
pia, from countries where one honored parents by eating them
when they died and others where burial was practiced, societies
where kings ruled and others, such as Athens, in which men
governed themselves. He wrote about societies where girls of mar-
riageable age waited in the temple of Aphrodite; only after a man
had spent a night with her could she marry. He wrote about other
societies in which chastity was prized above all else.[1] The unifying characteristic of human society for Herodotus is custom,
nomos. *Nomos*, he tells us, is king, though customs differ from one
society to another.

If custom is indeed king and if custom is variable, how can we
define what is truly good? Is all relative, depending on the customs
of the society in which one lives, or can we find a standard of permanent, universal value, of what is good if, for instance, we look
to nature rather than custom? If we make this latter jump, however, another question arises: Where do we find nature, that which,
unlike custom, is true across space and time? Greek political philosophy is based on questioning the meaning of nature and
whether one can say that there is anything that is best by nature.
Can we look to nature as a permanent standard, a guide to our actions, or must we rely on the particular customs we have received
from our ancestors and accept them as universal?

At the same time that such reflection on the social environment began in Greece, the so-called nature philosophers emphasized the difficulty of discovering the meaning of "nature." These

philosophers of the sixth and fifth centuries B.C. saw diversity in the world and searched for an underlying permanent nature; some turned to water, others to air, others to an indefinable "infinite." They suggested that what we see with our eyes is not necessarily what is real. We may see trees and rocks, hair and fingernails, but they are all variations of a fundamental element. Diversity was the result, they argued, of defective vision. We cannot see with our eyes. The stick in water is bent; when removed, it appears straight. Thus, we cannot trust our vision. The diversity of observed custom must be played against the underlying nature of which it is an expression.

The family in ancient Athens was a social institution that, like all the customs of the society, was subjected to scrutiny. The most famous example of this questioning of the foundation of the family will be discussed in the next chapter when we turn to Plato's *Republic*, but throughout Greek literature the family and the females within it continued to raise questions about the order of sexual relations, whether those relations were founded in nature or the result of conventional standards. During the pre-Socratic period— that is, before the latter part of the fifth century B.C. in Athens— the household, the *oikos*, defined the boundaries of the female's life.[2]

Pre-Socratic political thought concerning women focused on the problem of the relation of the household to the city, the inherent tensions and the compatibilities. It is in the period after Socrates, in the fourth century B.C., with Plato and Aristotle, that the question of the naturalness of the household and the sexual relations within it arises. In the earlier period the family was almost universally accepted as an inevitable institution; but precisely because of its inevitability, it put strains on the public structure of the polis. The works of Plato and Aristotle that directly confront the question of the naturalness of the family are attempts to resolve the tensions that arose in pre-Socratic thought when the family was accepted as natural, but was also a threat to political life.

One need only think of the themes of the Greek tragedies to realize how vividly present the family as an institution was in the Greek consciousness. These plays explored, often in terrifying detail, the relationships of various members of a family to each other. The family became the crucible within which all the human passions worked themselves out. However, the relationships within the family were never isolated from the external relationships that comprised the polis. The members of the family, male and female, parent and child, were tied in different ways to the existence of the

polis. The demands of these two communities were often in conflict and there thus surfaced, in many of the Greek tragedies, a fundamental tension between the family and the polis. We find a conflict between the needs of the family as a private world of nurture
and the polis as a public world of war and death. The family with
its fathers, mothers, children, and slaves is set in opposition to the
political community comprised, as the Athenians saw it, entirely
of grown men of free birth, capable of full participation in the military and deliberative life of the city.[3] The family was not forgotten
as the Greeks reflected on their social structure; rather, it served
as a source for alternative values that could sometimes be a
stabilizing or destabilizing element.[4]

Our aim in this chapter is to understand this contrast between
the values of the family and those of the city, as well as their complementarity and interdependence. This will clarify the difficulties
concerning the place of women in political life with which the
fourth-century philosophers had to deal. We will first look briefly
at Homer's *Iliad*, the epic poem providing the Greeks with their
theology and moral system, and at some of the poetry written during the rise of the polis. We will then turn to the classical age, the
fifth century B.C., the age of Pericles, Aeschylus, Sophocles, and
Euripides, the age when the Acropolis was built and its friezes and
metopes sculpted. By the fifth century the structure of the polis
had crystallized and had become an all-encompassing and energetic
community. Civilized existence was defined for the Greeks by participation in the polis; such participation entailed the exercise of
public speech in the assemblies and action on the battlefield. Both
modes of participation were denied to the female. The plays from
this period suggest how the female, despite her exclusion from official participation (except in religious festivals), influenced public
life and raised fundamental questions about its value. While living
in a realm apart from the public, she nevertheless limited its possibilities.

War and the Heroic Ideal

The Greek polis was a small community that treasured its independence from the authority of others. As such, it was continu-
ously faced with the threat of war. Thus, the community of citizens
was a community of warriors. Political leaders were military
leaders, and the heroes presented to the Greek youths were the
great warriors from Homer's *Iliad*, men who slaughtered their

enemy on the battlefield. These heroes gave the Greeks their model of the true man, one who fights well and is fearless in the face of death.

However, in the *Iliad* there is an important difference between the Greek warrior Achilles and the Trojan hero Hector.[5] Achilles fights for fame and honor; when he is not accorded the honor he expects, he withdraws from battle and endangers the success and lives of the Greeks. Achilles is drawn back into battle only by the death of his friend Patroclus. In opposition to Achilles stands Hector, who fights not only for glory but also for the city of Troy and especially for his family—wife, child, mother, and father. His renown comes not only from actions on the battlefield but also from his ability to protect those with whom he has kinship ties.

Homer includes in Book VI of the *Iliad* a tender, indeed romantic, scene between Hector and his wife Andromache. Love and concern are expressed by each—and also the recognition that in order to protect the female, the male must face the enemy on the battlefield. At the same time, as part of the dramatic development of the epic poem, Achilles, the hero fighting for fame, must be made aware that he fights for more than just his own glory, that he too is attached to family and loved ones, that his greatness must be understood within the complex of social relations. Thus, in the final book, Achilles the Greek and Priam, king of the Trojans and father of the slain Hector, weep together at the sorrowful lot of man, for whom the death of some is necessary for the survival of others.

In the *Iliad* there thus develops a tension that dominates all the writing of the Greeks: the demands of war, whereby men gain glory and protect those they love, oppose the needs of the family the warriors try to protect. The warrior brings death to others, and protects his city and family by spilling the blood of those who are outside it. In taking the life of another and putting his own life at risk, the warrior works in opposition to the family, which creates life by giving birth to the new generation. There is, then, the fundamental conflict between the Homeric man as warrior battling on the plain outside of Troy, who brings death to others and to himself, and the female, who, remaining within the realm of the household and the city walls, represents the life force out of which the city grows. Hector reaches his tragic stance as he is caught between the demands of both roles. Achilles grows, through the dramatic action of the poem, into an awareness of these conflicting demands. In this way the poet moves us to an understanding of the nature of social interdependence.

The separation of male and female values is reflected physically by a spatial demarcation: battles occur outside the world of the family, between the walls of Troy and the armed camp of the Greeks. Women do not venture onto the battlefield or into the world of men. Returning from battle, Hector finds Andromache looking for him from the walls of the city. As he bids her farewell, he asks her to understand why he must go, but then admonishes her: "Go into the house and arrange your own affairs, the loom and the distaff, and order your servants to tend to their tasks."[6] Andromache will leave the walls of the city only when she becomes a slave, a concubine to a Greek soldier and no longer the wife of a Trojan hero. The male travels freely between the two realms, fighting in wars, yet also returning to the realm of the family and the private sphere of life. The female does not move freely; a movement across the walls of the city means for her a movement from freedom to slavery.

The Homeric epics were composed before the political life of Greece settled into a society of poleis. The life these poems describe is probably a conglomerate of the society of the Mycenaean age of large palaces and centralized authority and that of the period of migrations and instability. With the rise of the polis in the seventh century B.C. came a transformation in the value system of the Greeks. As the political system became more cohesive, it dominated more directly the affective feelings of its members and replaced the family as the object of one's defensive skills.

At the same time, a transformation in military organization solidified one's attachment to one's fellow soldiers rather than one's family. The phalanx, a military unit in which one man protected the man to his left with his shield and was in turn protected by the man to his right, worked against individual feats of glory such as those described in the *Iliad*. The soldier was part of a cohesive unit; leaving that unit meant death for the soldier and for his comrades. Participation in the city was viewed from a similar perspective. The heroic model of the warrior fighting for his own glory or for the sake of his family was replaced by the warrior fighting for the city, not as an individual, nor as one of a group of warriors moving randomly across the battlefield. Opportunities for individual displays of heroism were limited, and devotion to the group prevailed. Egalitarianism arose among such warriors as they battled a common enemy; the good man was not the man of wealth, the aristocrat, but the one who behaved well as a member of the group.

Tyrtaeus, a poet writing in the seventh century B.C. for a Spartan audience, encouraged the Spartans to fight shield by shield, foot by foot with their fellow warriors: "It is noble for a good man to die falling in the foremost lines of battle for his fatherland." But should such a man fail in his duty in war, his lot is "to wander most miserably with dear mother and old father and small children and wedded wife. Hateful is he to all he encounters."[7] It is clear from this poem that the warrior fights not as Hector did, to preserve his family, which happens to live in Troy. Now, men fight for something more important. The warrior, should he not fight well, is disgraced before the city, and he wanders aimlessly with his family. That the family is protected is insufficient. Manliness is understood in terms, then, of prowess in war for the city. Virtue is a social quality that leads to the protection of the community. Forgotten in the development of this moral code glorifying the polis as the center of one's devotion is the family, an attachment so well captured in Hector's farewell speech to Andromache.

The fifth-century Athenian version of this new attitude is perhaps expressed most effectively in the historian Thucydides' presentation of the funeral oration that the Athenian leader Pericles gave after the first year of the Peloponnesian War between Athens and Sparta (427-04). Pericles praises the men who have died for Athens: so great were their deeds that they can hardly be captured by the words of one man. Pericles concludes with what seem to be heartless words to the families of the dead soldiers. He speaks first to the parents: "Lucky indeed are they who chanced on an ending so complete (though a grief for you), and for whom life has been so exactly measured as to end at the same time that it attains its full happiness." He then encourages those still of an age to have more children to do so, to "serve the city so it will not be deserted of men and so it will remain secure."

To the wives whose husbands have been killed, he offers these words of comfort: "There will be great glory for not being worse than your inborn character: and renown will be hers who is least talked about among the men, whether for virtue or for shame."[8] In other words, the women must not demand attention; they must not detract from devotion to the city. Even good women must be forgotten, for should they be remembered, they will, like Andromache, call forth the conflicting emotions with which Hector fought and died. Pericles indicates that devotion to the polity must override all concern with the private world of the family.

Pericles' speech is that of the general giving a pep talk to the city, asking for total devotion to a city that denies any countervailing interests or affections. The private realm must be forgotten in such a speech; indeed, Pericles claims that whatever a man has done as a private individual pales in significance before his willingness to fight and die for the sake of the city.[9] But in his next speech in Thucydides' history, Pericles must face the impossibility of putting this ideal into practice. Here he recognizes that individuals care about what is their own, about the possessions they own as members of a family. He must therefore appeal to them with a view to their interest in preserving what is their own. He argues that they must protect the city in order to do so. The speech is not entirely satisfying because it fails to acknowledge that preserving oneself and dying for the city are not necessarily compatible. The problems that it ignores are precisely the problems that many of the plays of the Greek stage at this time recognize and present in dramatic form before an Athenian audience.

Warriors and Women in Greek Theater

The Greek plays were part of the religious life of the city of Athens, performed during the festival celebrated in honor of Dionysius, the god of fertility. This festival was also a political event, for religion and politics were not separate in the Greek polis. The polis determined which plays were presented and obliged the wealthy citizens to pay the expenses of production. The theater gathered a large number of Athenian citizens together in one space, not to vote on immediate political issues, such as they confronted when they went to assembly, but to reflect on the theoretical and moral foundations of their lives as members of a community of men and gods. The plays are the authors' reflections on the political, religious, and moral life of the Athenians. However, they are also the authors' opportunity to educate the citizens, to make them aware of the inherent tensions that confront them as a city. We must take care not to see the playwrights only as spokesmen for the values of the city. They are also critics, forcing the Athenians to reflect on the values that the city offers to them.

Debates continue as to whether the women of Athens attended the plays[10]; what evidence there is seems to suggest that they did not, but what is important for our purposes is that female characters appeared on stage—often in major roles, often giving the lie to themes of male potency. We find in the plays a concern with the role of the female in the political, moral, and religious life of the city. And the role that she plays is as a question mark next to the self-assurance of the male devotion to wartime values and to the city as the primary focus of affective feelings—that is, women raise questions about the transformation of Greece from the Homeric model of the *Iliad* to the polis that now dominates the political arena.

The women are not treated as individuals in need of liberation from the truly repressive conditions in which they lived. The dramatists, for the most part, are not interested in them as individual people, but as ones who raise questions about the male devotion to the city and to an everlasting glory that may come from courage on the battlefield. The masculine world view, focused on the polis, forces the individual to abstract from the particular relationships with which each of us has to deal in our everyday lives. The abstraction from particularity, as the men in these plays demonstrate, creates the conditions that lead to tragedy.

While the Greek dramatists often expressed the conflict in terms of male and female, polis and *oikos* (family), the problem that they raised is a central one of political society: the relations between the universal public and the particular private, between what is common and what is one's own. The female is not a particular woman, but part of the human personality that rebels against the glorification of the public realm. In the dramatic form these two aspects of human needs are separated into male and female, and their separation reveals the tragic consequences of valuing one to the exclusion of the other, whether it be the masculine orientation to the universal or the feminine orientation to the particular.[11]

Although these generalizations apply to many of the 47 surviving plays by the three great dramatists of ancient Athens (Aeschylus, Sophocles, and Euripides) and the 11 comedies of Aristophanes, we will look at just a few in some detail to see how these themes emerge. At the same time, we must be aware that the relationship between masculine and feminine is but one theme of these multifaceted works. Though we must study the role of the female in the classics of political thought, we must not make the mistake of assuming that the issues of male and female comprise the totality of these works. I am here looking at what has traditionally been omitted by earlier histories of political thought, but I am not suggesting that what I find in these plays is all that need be said about them.

Aeschylus' Oresteia

Aeschylus' *Oresteia* (458 B.C.) is the one complete trilogy we have from the first of the great Athenian tragedians. It tells the story of murder and revenge in the Argive household of Agamemnon. Orestes, after killing his mother, Clytemnestra, in revenge for her murder of his father, Agamemnon, is brought to Athens to be tried by a jury of Athenians on the charge of matricide. Aeschylus uses Athens as the scene for this trial, to suggest the mythical foundation of the city as the resolver of conflicts among men. Orestes is acquitted as the result of arguments presented by the Olympian gods Apollo and Athene. They stress the insignificance of the ties between mother and son. Apollo speaks: "The mother is not called the parent of the child. She nourishes the young seed she bears."[12] Orestes, however, is unable to convince a majority of the mortals who comprise the jury that we can so easily discard the mother.

Thus, a tie vote must be broken by the virgin Athene in her role as convener of the jury. She sides with the male, making reference to her own birth from the forehead of Zeus: "No mother bore me; therefore I honor entirely the male; except to yield to marriage, in all things my heart defends the father."[13] With these words, Athens is founded on the supremacy of the male and the suppression of the female. The ghost of Clytemnestra and the Furies (the vile female spirits who have pursued Orestes to make him pay for his matricide) are subdued. But, we should note, it is the gods who found the city on these premises, who force the ambivalent humans on the jury to move toward an abstraction from female particularity, from private justice (revenge within the family).

The speeches at the end of the *Oresteia* can be taken as the classic expressions of Greek misogyny, simply confirming an earlier portrait of woman as a threat to the male order. In the first play, *Agamemnon*, Clytemnestra is a monstrous, brutal woman glorying in the blood of her husband as if it were spring rain, promiscuously bringing a lover into her own household, and speaking openly and arrogantly to the people of Argos. With the exoneration of Orestes, Athene also compels the Furies, who had sought vengeance for the murder of a mother, to serve the interests of the polis, as family ties are subordinated to the egalitarian male ties of the democratic polis.

The justice of the Furies had led to constant bloodletting and disorder, as one murder led to another. Therefore, it was necessary to transfer control from the family to the city and, in the process, eliminate the role of the female with her focus on the particular child or particular household. The Furies, who originally existed to keep order through fear and vengeance within families, now, as the result of Athene's threats, are transformed into Eumenides, friendly forces (friendly to the city), with the task of preventing civil strife, conflicts between citizens. The priority of relationships moves from family to city, and with that move the importance of women and the significance of motherhood are denied.

This reading of the play must be qualified, for while Aeschylus reveals the foundations of political unity in the abstraction from the female, particularity, and motherhood, he also uses the earlier plays of the trilogy to suggest what is lost when one transforms particular attachments into universal ones. Orestes' murder of his mother is carried out only with great psychological resistance. He is driven by Apollo to avenge the murder of his father, but he has great difficulty denying the maternal ties that Athene so glibly discards in the last scene of the trilogy. When Orestes learns of his mother's dream of a snake emerging from her womb and sucking blood from her breast, he recognizes himself as that snake. He was born from her and, even in his hatred for her, he acknowledges that he is her son. When Orestes is about to kill Clytemnestra, she bares her breast to remind him of his ties to her. He holds back, debates with her, and kills her only at the strong urgings of a friend who reminds him of the terrors Apollo foretold should he not commit this deed. The rejection of maternity, of particular ties, the abstraction to the generality of the city is done only with great difficulty.

Orestes killed his mother because of her murder of his father, but the first murder was based on yet another death, the sacrifice of Iphigeneia, the daughter of Agamemnon and Clytemnestra. The sacrifice occurred as the Greek army landed in northern Greece, on its way to Troy to bring back Helen, the wife of Agamemnon's brother Menelaus. As they made camp, two eagles devoured a pregnant hare. The army's seer saw in those eagles the omen for the Greek victory over Troy, but he also saw the sacrilege against maternity that that victory entailed. Before Artemis, the goddess of motherhood, would allow the winds to take the Greeks to Troy, she demanded the sacrifice of Iphigeneia. The first choral ode of the trilogy records this sacrifice in searing detail. Agamemnon must make the choice between his war and his family. Aeschylus emphasizes this tension with the description of the daughter crying "Father" through her tears and the father who must close his ears against her pleas and the curses she hurls upon her household. The king, "eager for war," a lover of battles, perseveres in the sacrifice.

After the murder of her husband, Clytemnestra stands before the shocked chorus of Argive townsmen to explain her action. She recognizes their "public curses, their roars of civic hate," but asks

why they did not oppose her husband, "who like a slayer of graz-
ing beasts sacrificed his child, my greatest love born of my pains.
She was for him a charm to produce a Thracian gale. Was it not
he you should have driven from this land?"[14] Clytemnestra
presents to the chorus the conflicting values of male and female.
Agamemnon has been preoccupied with war. The war, however,
which was meant to bring suffering to the offenders who had taken
Helen, comes to destroy the perpetrators of justice as well. The war
fought to bring Helen back to the house of Menelaus is to end with
the destruction of the family of Agamemnon. According to Clytemnestra's perspective, the perspective of a woman, Agamemnon
deserves the greatest execration for putting war above the interests
of the family, for putting masculine pride and vengeance over the
sentiments of the family for which he claims to fight.

At the end of the trilogy, the female values of birth and particularity (Clytemnestra had talked of *her* daughter, whom *her*
pain had brought forth) are subsumed under the universal city established under the guidance of the gods. The humans in the play
have difficulty denying their ties to the family. Agamemnon does
not easily sacrifice his daughter for the sake of the war, nor does
Orestes easily kill his mother to avenge the death of his father. In
this trilogy Aeschylus in no way denigrates the establishment of
the city. It is, indeed, necessary to transcend the particularistic society that preceded the polis, a society in which individuals were
responsible for just punishments and in which family members
meted out bloody vengeance to each other.

The individual who had been punished by those closest to the
deed is now to be punished by those distant from the deed: the wife
no longer is killed by the son for the murder of her husband, nor
is the husband killed by the wife for the sacrifice of the child. The
murderer may even be acquitted, as Orestes was, should the interests of the whole, the city, demand it. But Aeschylus points out
to his audience that something important is lost when the city is
built and the responsibility for giving to each his or her due is
taken away from those most directly involved in the case. The female Clytemnestra has stood throughout the plays to remind us
of this.

Sophocles' Antigone

Despite the dark undercurrent of what has been forgotten in
the founding of the city, Aeschylus' trilogy ends on a happy note.
Order has been restored, the family no longer threatens the politi-

cal interests of the city, and men have been raised by the gods to a universal view of the city that overcomes the particularistic limitations of the family. As Aeschylus portrays it, for the city to come into being, the family and the female as the mainstay of the family must be subordinated. City and war demand the covering of one's ears when the sacrificed daughter calls "Father" through her tears.

In Sophocles' the *Antigone* (441 B.C.) these tensions burst forth, and the conflicting demands of the city and the family tear both apart. Once again the female represents the family and once again the female representative becomes masculine in her defense of the family's value in opposition to the masculine interests of the city. Both figuratively and literally, the female must step outside the bounds of the household in order to protect it. Antigone becomes a male warrior similar to those who defend the city as she protects the religion of the family.

As the *Antigone* begins, two women are on stage. Ismene, Antigone's sister, hesitates at Antigone's suggestion that they bury their brother Polyneices, who was killed during an attack on Thebes. They would have to defy the decree forbidding burial of the traitor. The decree was issued by Creon, current ruler in the city and their uncle and guardian according to the religious laws of Athens. Ismene emphasizes her weakness before the male city and the unnaturalness of such participation in men's affairs: "But it is necessary to keep in mind in the first place that we were born women, not to carry on battle with men and because of this we are ruled by the stronger. . . I am forced in these things and I shall obey those who are set in authority."[15] She equates the male with power, and power with the city. Antigone is not threatened by masculine power, nor does she fear the decrees of the city. Neither does she associate political power with righteousness. Rather, her defense of her brother, her kin, is her act of righteousness against the unholy decrees of the city.

Antigone differs from Clytemnestra and the *Antigone* from the *Oresteia*, for Antigone associates the values of the family with the universal, at the same time that she puts the city on the level of the particularistic realm. The burial of her brother is demanded by the gods, by what is holy at all times and in all places, by the divine order of things. The decrees of Creon relate only to one city. Antigone flaunts her devotion to the gods of death as she notes that she will have to please them far longer than she has to please the men of the city. Ismene wishes to do those gods no dishonor, but "I have been born unable to act against the force of the city." She has no illusions about the legitimacy of the city. She recognizes that it is based on force and not on universal right, but does not find in that acknowledgment the strength to reject it.

As Antigone defends the family, she destroys the foundations of the city. The city needs to define who is friend and who is traitor. That definition may, as it did in this case, overlook familial ties, for Polyneices did attack Thebes and did fall in combat with his own brother, who fought for the city. In her devotion to the religion of the family, and the universal decrees of the gods, Antigone ignores the definitive demands of the city and ultimately ignores the family as well. She ignores Polyneices' role in the death of her other brother. She opposes her sister, virtually disowning her. And then Antigone denies her marriage to Haemon, Creon's son, a marriage prescribed by the religious laws of the family, by insisting on her death, the punishment due the burier of Polyneices' corpse. She is willing to destroy the city, and ultimately the family within it, to preserve what she defines as the divine law of that family. In her devotion to righteousness, she refuses to recognize the city's role as protector of the family. Ismene's physical weakness parallels the family's weakness to protect itself; neither can withstand the strength of the city, and both depend on that strength for their survival. Thus, Antigone dies along with her betrothed Haemon. In her excessive devotion to the family, she marries death.

Creon, in his devotion to the preservation of the city, in his conception of it as free from questions of piety, as an organization devoted to law and order, ignores the needs of the family to pursue its religious life. His focus on the political and economic dimensions of life obscures any vision of the family's or religion's demands, and how the city in its turn may need to depend on the security and preservation of the family. This one-sided perspective leads to his downfall in the city he tries to defend, and more tragically, with the death of his wife and son, to the destruction of the family he had chosen to ignore.

In this drama, the realms of city and family stand in tragic opposition. Aeschylus' play had ended with the universal city as superior to the particular family and with the justice of the city, ignoring particular ties, as superior to the justice of the family. Sophocles' play offers no such easy solution. The values of the family had been denied by Creon; he learns to recognize the validity of those claims, but in the process of being taught this fundamental truth, he brings into question the foundation of the unified city that has to clarify who is traitor and who defends it. The isolation of the two realms and their opposition, as captured in the conflict between Antigone and Creon, lead to the tragedy of this play. The greater tragedy, though, is that Sophocles in no way suggests any resolution.

Euripides' Trojan Women

The Peloponnesian War between Sparta and Athens during the last third of the fifth century B.C. was long and drawn out, catastrophic in its impact on the Greek cities. Apart from the lives lost, the fabric of society crumbled as the war came to control the consciousness of the Athenians. The admiration expressed in the Homeric poems for the savage warrior lessened as the meaning of that savagery was brought home to the civilized polis. Euripides' *Trojan Women* (416 B.C.) illustrates the tarnishing of this ideal by using vulnerable women, captive women, to evoke our horror at the violence of war and our pity for those who must suffer the consequences of the male's devotion to great deeds on the battlefield. The female stands in this tragedy to remind the audience that the destructiveness of war spreads far beyond the battlefields, to the intimate relationships between men and women.

The women in this play appear strong only in their capacity to endure suffering. For defense they had depended on their husbands, sons, and fathers, but now their protectors are dead. Andromache, trying to resist the guard who is to take her child, is told: "Being weak, do not seem to be strong. . . . Your city and your husband are destroyed. You are in our power. We are able to do battle with one woman."[16] The play is a succession of scenes in which the captive women learn their fate at the hands of the murderers of their husbands. Each scene brings a fate worse than the one before, and in each case the treatment of the women is related to their dependent role within the structure of the city. They are defined exclusively by their relationships to the men in their lives. When those men are killed, they are defined by their captors. Andromache is encouraged by her mother-in-law, Hecuba, to forget her dead husband: "Honor your present husband and give him loving enticements of your charms."[17] Other Trojan women, those still young enough, will be forced to share the beds of the conquerors of Troy and to breed their children. As the chorus says: "The bedrooms, desolate of slaughtered youths, give brides to the Greeks to be bearers of their children."[18]

As slaves, the Trojan women will perform the same tasks at the loom and in bed that they performed in Troy. Their station relative to other women in the society has changed, but they do not lose their role in the community. The men, in contrast, must be killed. They cannot be transferred from one city to another. The Trojan warrior cannot become a Greek warrior. The play ends as the body of the young son of Andromache and Hector is buried by his grandmother. The male depends on the city for a meaningful existence, and thus, no matter how young he may be, must die when the city is destroyed. The female, defined by her relationship to the male, but not to the city, need not be killed, only transferred.

Nevertheless, Hecuba, weeping over the death of her grand-child, mourns that he was unable to become a man and thus have the chance of dying for the sake of the city, thereby gaining glory. She, whose laments throb through the entire play, hints that the fame her city will get from this war may answer for all the pains that she has suffered. The Trojan maid Cassandra, given the powers of prophecy, says in one of her mad speeches that while Hector's fate may cause grief—as indeed it does in this play—yet, if the Greeks had not come "though he was great, none would know."[19] The masculine focus on war and glory is shown by Euripides to have become a part of the females' self-assessment. We mourn for the suffering of those women on stage, and yet, as they mourn for themselves, they do not escape the value system that has made war a part of their lives. For Euripides the tragedy is not only the specific acts committed against each of the captive women we see on stage. It is the mentality that allows these women to accept self-definition in male terms, and thus accept the pursuit of military glory and its consequences.

Aristophanes' Lysistrata *and* Ecclesiazusae

The comic poet Aristophanes wrote a play in opposition to the prolonged Peloponnesian War, but while the tragedian turned to classical myths to express his anger at the devastation and dehumanization of this war, Aristophanes uses fantastical contemporary images to suggest his concern. In the *Lysistrata*, it is a sex strike by the wives of the Athenian, Spartan, Corinthian, and Boeotian warriors. The women refuse to sleep with their husbands until peace is declared. Aristophanes does not offer a particularly favorable portrait of women. They are primarily interested in recapturing their husbands for their own sexual gratification. They do not evoke our pity, as do the Trojan women waiting before the Greek tents, so much as our laughter, at the same time that we are made to appreciate, or at least feel sympathy for, their claims to private happiness.

The women in the *Lysistrata* rely on their traditional crafts as they work in the world of men, for in order to fight the masculine attention to war, they must not only deny the men sex, they must leave the home and take over the acropolis, where the public treasury is kept. In the process, they transform the city into a family and obscure the conflicting demands each makes on the other. In response to the magistrate who tries to resist the women's attempt to take control of Athens' treasury, with which the war was financed, they respond that war is not necessary. They suggest that the city can be run as if it were a household, and they solve political problems with analogies to household activities such as weaving and spinning. By eliminating war, the women try to eliminate the distinction between household and city—that is, to end the tension that characterizes so much of the tragedy of the Greek stage.

This tension, however, remains as Aristophanes points throughout the comedy to the demands that public action places on the private lives of individuals. The women are not eager to join together in this plot; no one shows undue haste to attend the organizational meeting, each offering a different domestic excuse. They would rather enjoy their wine and what husbands are there than become part of the unified sex strike. Once they have taken possession of the acropolis, they make up excuses so that they can join the men outside. Their leader, Lysistrata, must teach them that public action at times requires the abandonment of private pleasure. Women who focus on private pleasure in Aristophanes' plays may fail to understand the need for war and the reasons their husbands may have to depart from their beds. Aristophanes clearly opposes war in this comedy, but he is not insensitive to the demands that any public enterprise must make on private lives. Except for Lysistrata, the women have difficulty recognizing the validity of these demands, both in their attempt to influence the public policy of the city and in the grander sphere of Athenian international relations.

Despite these problems, Lysistrata's plan succeeds because the men have no pleasure without women. Lysistrata assumes that war is not enough to sustain the men, and that their public lives must be supplemented by their private lives. The sex strike forces an awareness of what they have ignored in the mindless, as Aristophanes sees it, pursuit of war. They are men unlike Hector; they have failed to understand the close connection between private and public. However, whereas in the tragedy of the *Iliad*, Hector must die, on the comic stage it is possible for the men to escape death on the battlefield in order to enjoy their wives in bed.

The women of the *Lysistrata*, who have no sympathy for the

war, also work as expressions of Aristophanes' Panhellenism, his desire for unity among the Greeks. The male, centered in the public sphere of a particular polis for which he fights, is unable to transcend the confines of the polis. The female, not tied to the city for fulfillment, is able to exist beyond the city as well as within it. The conspiracy of women to stop the war is itself Panhellenic. They can join together because their interest in sex does not tie them to Athens or to Sparta. The men of the cities engage in war against other Greeks because they are attached to a particular political regime. For the same reason, in Euripides' tragedy the women could become slaves, but the men had to be killed.

In his play the *Ecclesiazusae*, Aristophanes explores the consequences of a lack of interest in the particular public regime and the consequent transformation of the polis into the household, leading to a denial of difference between public and private, between male and female, between good and bad. The comedy was written after the end of the Peloponnesian War and portrays a city at peace. The public no longer demands the sacrifice of male soldiers, and thus no longer presents the tensions we noted earlier in such literature. This time the leader of the women is Praxagora. She plots the takeover of the Athenian assembly by women. The women are to become legislators and administrators, replacing the apathetic males.

With language drawn from the household, the women appropriate the political machinery, and once they have taken charge, they create a radically new city where there is no family and no private wealth. The naturalness of the traditional family is brought into question. The polis takes over all the functions of the family: it will distribute clothing and food; it will use the harbors as wine cellars; it will transform the courtrooms into dining rooms. Praxagora envisions a society in which there are no poor, no trials, and no adultery. There will be neither private property to steal nor marriages to corrupt.

At the same time she must eliminate all political elements: legislation, judging, and foreign policy. The polis can become the family only by abstracting from these concerns. The entrance of the women into political life here has to be understood in the context of its full radical implications. By liberating the female and destroying the tension between public and private, all that Greek society had previously been based on is destroyed. The men are denied their realm for public honor and become sybarites ready to enjoy banquets and sex, but not much more.

After Praxagora institutes her reforms, she leaves the stage and the rest of the comedy traces the implications of her proposals. It does not present a very happy picture. She has taken away a public goal, and the city almost falls apart as men eager to continue enjoying private property see no need to give their own objects to the communal treasury. More important, though, is that the women establish certain rules governing the distribution of handsome young men among the sexually eager women of the city. They demand that sexual pleasure be distributed according to age, with the oldest and ugliest receiving gratification first. Thus, before the final joyous dance as the characters exit for their communal banquet, the comedy offers a grotesque scene in which the three ugliest hags fight over a youth who wishes only to pursue the young woman he has come to woo. There is no concern with public welfare in this scene. Rather, it offers a vile attempt to act against nature by making the ugly take precedence over the beautiful. Or we might see it as Aristophanes' distaste for a community where women have come to take precedence over men.

Aristophanes has in this comedy given women the opportunity to transform the political system, but he has not given them power to transform private concerns into public ones, or to unite the private love of one's own with the love of what is common. The *Ecclesiazusae*, written at the end of Aristophanes' career and well into the fourth century B.C., sounds the death knell of the masculine Homeric hero who fought to protect the public world. One sees elsewhere the dangers of the masculine focus on glory achieved in war. The *Ecclesiazusae* illustrates what happens when men are home from the war and, in effect, yield to the women in their lives. The radical proposals of Praxagora do not create the beautiful political system of order and stability that she at first predicts. Her politics lie ultimately in the private sphere, rather than in the public realm of a devotion to something greater than oneself. Though women need be no more self-interested than men, Aristophanes in his comedies generally, and specifically in this one, uses the female as the representative of the private and the opponent of the public. When she comes to dominate the city, it dissipates into a realm of sensual satisfaction.

This brief analysis of a few plays from the corpus of Greek drama is certainly not complete, nor is there any suggestion that any unified conception of the female in the political life emerges in these plays. The playwrights use the female for varied purposes, but it is precisely this variety that is important, for it suggests the importance of the question of the female in the Athenians' portrait of themselves. They could not describe their city, their relationship to their gods, and the universal order without a reference to the women of their city. They recognized the female's claim to be a part of human reality. At times that claim may have been seen as a threat, at others as a sign of the inadequacy of the male's vision of himself, but the female as a concept was not kept indoors as easily as were the Athenian women, who most likely were not allowed to attend the plays in which they were portrayed.

Conclusion

As noted at the beginning of this chapter, political philosophy begins when one questions the laws, traditions, and customs of one's society. The Athenians of the classical age lived in a political community that was all-encompassing, where the city was the central focus of man's existence. Pericles had demanded of his Athenians that they become lovers of the city. However, while the city made such complete demands on the individual, there were those, such as the playwrights considered above, who were not willing to accept in an unreflecting manner the laws, the traditions, the regime in which they lived.

In order to reflect upon the city in which they lived, in order to question whether devotion to it could be based on the city's foundations in nature, the Greek authors often turned to the women of the city as those whose all-encompassing devotion could not be, or was not, to the city. At times their role in the ancient community put them at odds with the demands of the polis. Their existence and their status within the family posed a variety of problems; they indicated the duality of human nature, the tension of conflicting loyalties, the significance of the abstraction from particularistic ties to a more general orientation. Women thus forced men to question the natural status of the city by suggesting contradictions within its structure. Was the inherent incompatibility between the city and the family a sign of the permanent tension inherent in nature, or could laws be found that might overcome all such tensions? The playwrights faced these issues head-on and turned them to tragedy or to comedy.

In the next chapter we meet the author who tried to resolve the problem, as Aristophanes had in the *Ecclesiazusae*, by making the polis the same as the family. The question that will confront us as we consider the significance of Plato's writing on the female is whether he thus introduces comedy or tragedy into his best city.

3

Plato: Philosophy, Females, and Political Life

In 399 B.C., Socrates was executed by the Athenians for corrupting the young and introducing new gods into the city. Athens, reeling from its recent defeat at the hands of the Spartans and from the violent oligarchy established by the Spartans, had recently reestablished the democratic regime that it had enjoyed from the beginning of the fifth century. Athens' security had been shaken, and through all this tumult there had been one who, though serving his city in war when called upon, had devoted himself not to questions of politics, to the problems of Athens as democracy or Athens as oligarchy, but to questions relating to the nature of the soul and its perfection, to questions of personal virtue rather than political success.

This, of course, was Socrates. He taught that in order to perfect the soul and be virtuous, one must engage in questioning the beliefs, the traditions, the *nomoi* on which the city was founded. He did not wish to destroy those traditions, and the city with them, but to indicate that all citizens needed to be able to explain what was worthwhile about the city. For many, such explanations were not easy. Tradition praised virtues that were difficult to define, and it failed to give precise guidelines on how to act in specific cases. Socrates the questioner led others to such confusion that they were no longer able to defend adequately the city they wanted to defend. As harmless as he pretended to be, the city recognized the threat his questioning posed to the stability of old, if inadequate, values and executed him.

Plato was a follower of Socrates. Socrates had no students, for he claimed not to teach and had no school such as Plato was to establish when he founded the Academy. What Socrates gave to his followers was training in a way of life that treated all human experience critically and measured that experience against what might be. It was a way of life that valued the health of the soul over the health of the body, the pleasures of the intellect over the physical pleasures; that moved individuals beyond the city in their search for values and standards. Plato, as a young man tied by family relations to the Athenian leader Pericles and about to embark on a political career, rejected politics so as to continue the life he had come to admire in Socrates. To do so, he wrote dialogues, many of which had Socrates as the major character.

With these dialogues, Plato gives us the Socrates with whom the Western world has been enamored for centuries. However, he also forces the reader to question the role of Socrates within the city. Socrates, except for the few battles and the public service required by the Athenian regime of all its citizens, withdrew from political life. Plato questions whether such withdrawal is really possible. He recognizes the dangers inherent in the questioning of a society's values. In his dialogues he allows Socrates to engage in such questioning, but he also reveals the consequences. For this reason, Plato's dialogues are not a simple presentation of the views of his mentor; rather, they force us to reflect on the passion for knowledge and the limits that the city places, and needs to place, on this passion.

As the Athenians recognized when they executed Socrates, the pursuit of philosophy can threaten the stability of the political community. Plato, as much as he admired Socrates, recognized this too. For this reason, the philosopher stands outside the city. In Greek society, so did the female. Throughout Plato's work, as we shall see, the philosopher and the female share a common alienation from the city as well as a common devotion to the processes of generation, one intellectual, the other physical. Thus they both work within the Platonic corpus to raise questions about the value of the polity. Plato is establishing an opposition between philosophers and the city, between women and the city. The problem facing him as he reflects on the nature of political society is whether this opposition can ever be overcome. In the *Republic* he tries to resolve this tension by making both philosophers and women part of the city. We, however, must question whether he suggests that the problem is ever susceptible to resolution.

The *Republic:* Sexual Equality and
Its Role in the Dialogue

Plato is unique among the authors under consideration in this book. While the playwrights discussed in the last chapter encouraged a sensitivity to the demands of the female, to the realm of the private, Plato alone, through the person of Socrates in the *Republic*, proposes introducing women into the realm of public power in the best city and having them participate equally in the guidance of such a city. The argument, though it must be qualified on many counts, is startling on two levels. First, Socrates suggests that men and women are equally capable of being the philosopher-rulers who govern in his city; sexual differences are irrelevant. In answer to one of the central questions of the ancient political philosophers, asking who is capable of rule, Socrates argues that the answer, at least for the city of our dreams, need not be sex-specific. Second, Socrates suggests that the role of the female in the reproduction of the young can be made inconsequential with regard to her participation in public activities. The fact that she carries the fetus, gives birth, and nurses need have no implications for public roles in the city.[1]

The *Republic* is a work in which the initial question confronting the participants concerns the nature of justice. At first the answer seems obvious, though different, to the various persons gathered at the home of Cephalus; but under Socratic questioning the easy definitions disappear and Socrates himself is asked to define the nature of justice and to explain why it is good. He suggests that the pursuit of justice will be easier if one looks at what is large—the city—rather than at what is small—the individual; thus, he founds a city in speech to find at what point justice comes into the city.

The process of founding the city and discovering the nature of justice present in it take up most of Books II through IV of the *Republic*. In Book IV, after he has proposed a tripartite division of workers (artisans), warriors, and rulers, with each class performing that task for which it is suited by nature, he claims to have found justice in the performance by each person or class of the task assigned by nature to each. In the midst of this discussion, he casually comments that the ruling classes, which include the warriors and the rulers, will, like friends, have all things in common, meaning, at this point, women, children, and property.

At the beginning of Book V, as Socrates is about to discuss the disintegration of the just regime, the interlocutors in the dialogue stop him and ask him to explain his offhanded, radical proposal. In response he offers an even more radical proposal, for he suggests the inclusion of women in the ruling class: bringing the female, who had been totally excluded from political life in Athenian society, into the public realm as a full participant. Before, such thoughts in Greek literature had called forth visions of monsters such as Clytemnestra or laughter, as in the comedies of Aristophanes. The setting for the dialogue in the *Republic* is Athens' port city, a place open to new and foreign ideas. Socrates' proposals here are indeed new and foreign.

Book V is divided into three waves, as Socrates calls them, each about to drown him in a sea of ridicule. First, he must argue for including women in the public life of the city; next, he must argue for the destruction of the family, since all that had been private, from one's clothes to one's wife, was to be made common; finally, he must deal with the question of possibility, the question that introduces the philosopher-rulers—a proposal as comic as, if not more comic than, the one to include women. The first wave threatening Socrates is the most important for our immediate concerns, but his arguments for the equality of men and women are closely related to his arguments for the community of property— or, put another way, the destruction of the family. Similarly, these arguments are related to his discussion of the possibility of such a city. But let us understand his argument concerning equality first, and then consider how it is integrated into the political philosophy expressed elsewhere in this work and in Plato's other dialogues.

The Argument

Socrates' first argument relies on an analogy with animals as he begins to talk about the inhabitants of this city as if they were animals to be trained and bred, to be treated as if they lived in a barnyard rather than Socrates' best city.[2] Socrates begins by acknowledging that they had tried in the argument "to set up the men as the guardians of the herd."[3] He then poses the crucial question: "Do we believe that the females among the guardian dogs are to guard along together just as the males guard and to hunt together and to do all the other things in common?"[4] Glaucon, Plato's half brother, who often, in his enthusiasm for founding this city, fails to restrain Socrates when he makes some of his

questionable statements, agrees that we make no distinction between male and female guardian dogs, though he does make a
qualification concerning the relative strength of the sexes, a qualification that comes back on occasion to haunt the argument for sexual equality. But Socrates continues to argue that equal participation in the guardianship of the city (or the herd) entails an equal
nourishment and education.

Socrates' initial argument leading to the startling suggestion
of an equal education is one based on an analogy with dogs. On the
comic stage men were turned into animals such as frogs or wasps
or birds, whereas in tragedy men tried to become like gods and
their humanity was displayed by their distance from those gods.
Here, when talking about sexual equality, Socrates reminds us of
comedy, not of tragedy, and we must ask ourselves whether for Socrates, watchdogs and humans are to be compared on such an issue. Are we to learn from animals how to act in the best city that
Socrates creates in order to discover justice—or should we be looking to the gods for our model? None of the interlocutors who
caught Socrates on the initial problem of the community of women
and children catches him on this question. Instead, they allow him
to proceed with his suggestions concerning the gymnastic exercises in which both men and women engage—naked, whether
young or old.

This flies in the face of the experience of the Greeks, whose
wives for the most part stayed in the women's quarters and were
unseen by most men—even their close relatives. Socrates himself
comments on what is most laughable of all, old men and women
exercising together, "their bodies wrinkled and not pleasing to the
eyes."[5] With these suggestions Socrates is here, I believe, trying
to offend the sense of beauty and of shame of these young men,
who come from a culture in which the youthful and smooth human form was godlike and idealized in the sculpture of sacred
buildings. In contrast, he specifically alerts them to the unattractive, all too human, sight of wrinkled bodies, both male and female,
engaged in exercise—a sight as unattractive for most men of his
generation as a woman dressed in armor on the battlefield would
be.

In the gymnasiums of Socrates' best city there must also be an
absence of erotic desire; in this city where men are to be the same
as women, eros is ignored and the bodies whose differences would
turn attention to sexuality are made irrelevant. The education of
the warriors described in the earlier books of the *Republic* had
been directed explicitly toward the denial of bodily desires—for

food, for sleep, for drink, for any form of sensual pleasure. The warriors were to rise above their bodily demands in order to create a most austere city. Having so abstracted from such bodily needs, Socrates, in his proposals for the equality of men and women, now abstracts from sexuality. Bodily differences do not matter, and thus eros disappears. This is the price that must be paid for sexual equality.

However, so swayed are the interlocutors by Socrates' talk of animals and of men, that they fail to respond to the cues he has been giving them. Instead, Socrates himself must introduce the skeptic, the one who is ready to hold him back from his flights of fancy. He questions himself through this fictitious opponent, who refers the group back to Socrates' initial arguments in Book II, where he built up the just city by assigning each person the task for which he or she was most fitted by nature. The man who by nature was a farmer would farm, and the man by nature a cobbler would cobble. Aren't, this skeptic asks, men and women different by nature? And if they are, shouldn't they be assigned different tasks in the community? This had been the guideline earlier in the founding of the city, and it had become central to the definition of justice in Book IV. Why should this guideline and principle be ignored here?

The argument presented by this fictitious skeptic is an important one, and we must attend to the assumptions that Socrates must make to overcome it. By nature we are suited to do certain things—such as farm or cobble or fight in wars. Our abilities in these areas are dependent on a variety of factors, not the least of which is our body. We need certain physical attributes in order to farm or cobble or fight in wars. But we also have souls that enable us to learn quickly or slowly, to be magnanimous or stingy. We are suited by the nature of our bodies and of our souls to do some things, but not others.

Socrates' response to his critic is that we must attend to the relevant natures or characteristics in determining that for which we are suited by nature, and he finds these relevant natures only in the soul. Having long or short hair, curly or straight hair, being stout or lanky makes no difference with regard to one's ability to be a cobbler; one merely needs a cobbler's soul to be a cobbler. On an analogous argument, the male and the female physicians do not have distinct natures with regard to being a physician. They have, as Socrates phrases it, "the same nature of soul," whereas two males—one a cobbler and the other a farmer by nature—do not.

Then if the race of men and women seems to be different with regard to a particular craft or other pursuit we shall say that it is necessary to assign that craft to one or the other. But if it seems to differ in this only, that the female gives birth and the male mounts, we shall say that in no way has it been shown that a woman is different from a man concerning that about which we have been talking, but we shall still believe that it is necessary that our guardians and their women should engage in the same pursuits.[6]

Socrates continues to elaborate on these points in the succeeding passages, using arguments that at times are strikingly similar to those used by contemporary advocates of sexual equality. With regard to the establishment of the city, is there any craft or skill that belongs peculiarly to the male or to the female? No answer is easily given by the interlocutors. The differences between male and female in the past were the result of different education, not of different natures. Socrates affirms that it is not nature that keeps women out of the public life of cities. It is custom. "We are not making laws which are impossible or similar to prayers, as if we set down a law which contradicted nature. Rather, those practices which exist now are in opposition to nature, as it seems."[7]

One must transcend custom, which is something we can do. Socrates had told us earlier in Book V about the possibility of changing customs. He recalled how the practice of exercising naked had only recently been accepted by the Greeks. When this custom was first introduced in Crete and Sparta, the Greeks considered it worthy of ridicule. Now it is a fully accepted practice, once it was discovered that during exercises "it is better to strip than to cover all such things."[8] The inclusion of women in the public life of the just city will come to be as accepted, as the custom of exercising naked had been. The exclusion of women from public life is simply convention, not dependent on the demands of nature at the basis of the just city.

This distinction between nature and culture weighs heavily in discussions of the place of women in contemporary society. However, if Socrates offers the same theoretical framework for the discussion of the question of the proper place of women in public and private life, he nevertheless maintains a definite position asserting the superiority of the male over the female. For instance, despite his earlier claims, he asks Glaucon:

Do you know of any craft practiced by humans in which the race of men is not entirely superior to that of women? Or shall we speak at length by mentioning weaving and the concern with baking and boiling in which the female race seems to be the best and where being bested is most ridiculous of all.... Then, dear friend, there is no pursuit concerning the ordering of a city which belongs to a woman because she is a woman, or to a man because he is a man, but the natures are dispersed in both animals and a woman partakes in all pursuits according to nature and similarly a man, but in all things the race of women is weaker than that of men.[9]

Socrates thus concludes that though women *may* be included among the guardians of his city, they will always be physically weaker—and this is for a group of leaders composed mostly of warriors, individuals for whom strength of body is crucial. Any area in which women might have a natural superiority—such as weaving and baking—is one assigned to the lower class of this society where sexual equality is not proposed. Again he must base his sexual equality on the total abstraction from body.

Socrates, getting the nod of approval from the other participants in the dialogue for his arguments concerning sexual equality, gives a big sigh of relief: "This point then we shall say we have escaped, as from a wave, in our discussion of the law concerning women."[10] The interlocutors are now ready to move on to the next wave, one that will make the first wave look moderate in comparison: wives and children shall be common, no woman is to live privately with any man, no parent shall know his or her child, and no child shall know his or her parents. Marriages are to be called sacred, but are to last only as long as necessary to impregnate the woman, and are to be arranged so as best to serve the interests of the city—that is, to produce the best children through eugenics. Matching and mating are determined by the rulers, and only a temporary encounter for the purpose of procreation is allowed. Once the child is born, he or she immediately leaves the mother for a common rearing "pen." The mother heavy with milk will come to nurse a child, but she will know not whether the child to whom she gives the breast is the one she bore. Nurses, both male and female, take the burden of parenthood from the mother. Glaucon comments: "It is a most easy child rearing that you describe for the women of the guardian class."[11]

We must, however, look, as Glaucon does not, at the obverse side of this liberation from child rearing that Socrates offers to his women. While the creation of the monogamous family may over-come paternal uncertainty, the female knows that she is the mother without relying on the conventions of the family. She feels the child move within her and she experiences the child leaving her body. Male participation in the creation of the child is limited to a brief moment in time. The family offers the male the intellec-tual association between the father and the child that nature gives only to the female.[12] Socrates' proposals, by destroying the family and taking the child away from the mother at the moment of birth, create both paternal and maternal uncertainty. That neither the mother nor the father knows her or his own child is something that must be legislated and does not come from nature. Thus, the liber-ation of the female into the male sphere of political life also liber-ates her, in Socrates' model, into ignorance. By becoming the equals of men, women, like the men, lose a sense of what is their own.

Participation in the political community, according to Socrates in the *Republic*, demands an abstraction from the love of one's own. If women are to become part of the political community and part of its leadership group, they too must be deprived of what is their own through legislation. The equality that Socrates offers to his females is a double-edged gift. They participate in the public realm denied them by the traditions of Athenian society, but they do so only by giving up what is peculiar to them, the certain knowl-edge concerning maternity. The abstraction from the private, from the family, is necessary for the male to become truly a part of the public space. For the female, this abstraction is even more difficult to achieve, for it means specifically ignoring the peculiar charac-teristics of her body. The plays discussed in the previous chapter showed the tensions this abstraction created for the men of the city. In the *Republic*, Socrates now creates this tension for his women.

The Contextual Significance of the Argument

Socrates' proposals for his two laws about women, while they appear to us to be radical departures from Greek practice, were not unique. As we have seen, at the beginning of the fourth century B.C., shortly before the composition of the *Republic*, Aristophanes had written his *Ecclesiazusae*, in which the women, upon becom-ing the legislators in the assembly, transformed the community of separate households into one big household, with all private goods changed into public goods and all sexual relations released from the restrictions of the traditional private family. Similarities of language between Plato's work and Aristophanes' comedy[13] strongly suggest that Plato intended for us to recall Aristophanes as we read Socrates' proposals—and recall the comedy of the situation that arises when women rule.

Plato makes the comedy less explicit, but Socrates' qualifications on what he says and the examples he puts forth (particularly those using birds and dogs as models for his eugenics and his inadequate attempts to avoid incest) undermine any notion that Socrates seriously envisions the full participation of women in the political life of his best city, or the possibility of ever establishing a communism as complete as he proposes in the middle wave of Book V. Nevertheless, Plato has frequently become the darling of contemporary feminist theorists for his foresight, his daring, his willingness to go against custom to suggest the possibility of removing women from the private sphere and placing them in the public world.

We, however, must question why Socrates makes these proposals, how such arguments fit into the aim of his work as a whole. We must understand why Plato, writing 2,500 years ago, cannot be used simply as an early advocate of women's rights, a concern totally alien to his conceptual framework and one that obscures the more vital and comprehensive implications of his proposals. The laws about women are introduced to explain the nature of politics and not to advocate any particular political role of the female.

First, we must recognize the relationship between the first two proposals, one for sexual equality and the other for communism among the upper two classes of his city. Scholars have debated which proposal has priority, whether sexual equality necessitated the communism subsequently described or whether the communism left us with a large corps of unemployed women whom Socrates had to keep in the polity in one fashion or another. The direction of the causality, though, is unimportant for our immediate concern. Rather, we must attend to the complementarity of the two proposals, for what Socrates achieves with both is the elimination of the private sphere of life for those members of his city who are to be its rulers and warriors, for those who deny themselves as individual beings for the sake of the city.

Traditionally, as we have seen, women were restricted to the private activity of birth and engaged in those activities necessary to maintain the internal functioning of the household, the *oikos*. When Socrates proposed introducing women into the public sphere and eliminating the traditional family, he boldly destroyed the private realm, leaving it to the workers and to the appetites. The plays discussed in the previous chapter demonstrated the inherent tension between public and private that plagued Greek life. Socrates' proposals, by eliminating the private for both men and women, try to overcome those tensions and destroy the attachments of the individual members of the society to anyone or anything that might separate them from the whole of the city.

"Do we have any greater evil," Socrates asks, "for a city than that which tears it apart and makes it many instead of one?...Does not the community of pleasure and pain bind whenever, as much as possible, citizens similarly delight or grieve over the same things coming into being and dying?...The privacy of such things destroys the community."[14] Socrates' explicit aim is to make of the city, or at least two parts of the tripartite city he has created, one individual rather than many, with the unity of experience that a single individual feels.

In order to achieve this unity, he introduces the communism of the second wave, but at the same time he must work to destroy any differences that may exist between individuals, any differences that might cause them to experience pleasure and pain differently. The finger of one person becomes the finger of all, so that the cut on one person's finger gives pain to all. The child of one person is the child of all, so that the pious inhibitions that prevent one from striking a parent will prevent one from striking all who could be a parent. What separates and isolates people in cities—those not founded on Socrates' principles of justice—is their private existence. It draws them away from the public unity. To allow that private, distinct existence to flourish is to encourage selfishness, difference, and division—and to endanger the stabilty of the community.

The communism Socrates proposes makes every pot a collective pot, belonging not to one but to all. His communism obscures any and all distinctiveness, including differences between the sexes. Socrates here is suggesting that the most important threat to the survival of the city is the divisiveness fostered by a sense of what is private, which comes from seeing oneself as different, separate from others. That leads to a special care for what is one's own—be it a child or a pot or a finger. We tend to care more about what is close, what is our own, who is our father or our daughter, than we do about those who are more distant.[15] The unified city that Socrates tries to build cannot acknowledge a greater care for one than for another, and so it destroys the possibility of there being one who is not close, who "belongs" to someone else.

Sexual equality is tied to the destruction of what is separate, what is other. On the one hand, in Greek thought the female had always stood for what is private and other. By equating the male and the female, the public and the private are made one. There is no "other." But, more basically, the female suggests the divisiveness of the human species, that we are indeed not all the same, that there *is* something that is other. In order to create the unified city, Socrates must destroy the female as female, the female as a threat to the unity of the human species. She is integrated into the political community not as herself, as one with distinctive talents or distinctive experiences, but as an inferior male, a physically weaker male. The sexual equality that Socrates proposes with a view toward unity is concerned not with the integration of the female into public life, but with the destruction of the female, the representative of a private life and that which is different, who undermines the unity necessary for a just city.

The process of childbirth within the city of Socrates' dreams is made as peripheral as possible for the female; we hardly know that she bears the child, for Socrates moves immediately from the mating to rearing the child in the "pen" by nurses living apart in a certain section of the city. The reproductive differences between male and female are virtually ignored. Thus, the female is removed from her reproductive tasks, which in ancient times distinguished her most from the males to whom she must now be assimilated. We should note here that Socrates, in order to eliminate that which separates people from one another, must abstract from the body, and in the particular case of women, from the erotic nature or the sexuality of the female.

This abstraction from the body is necessary because it is the body that emphasizes isolation, that points out to the human being who is "other." Despite Socrates' claims, we can't pretend that the finger of another is ours. The absolute unity of the political community that Socrates seeks is denied by body. Sexuality specifically emphasizes bodies, and thus must be overcome or rejected in order to create the artificial unity of the city that Socrates proposes. His denial of body here allows for the sexual equality and the communism characteristic of his city, but it also ignores his conception of the human being as a composite of body and soul, a unity he acknowledges throughout Plato's dialogues. When he talks about natural capacity as the basis for sexual equality, he appears to suggest that the only relevant criterion is the soul, but a soul cannot farm or cobble; a soul must work in conjunction with the body. Similarly, the soul cannot fight in wars; fighting is done with bodies. This explains why, despite his emphasis on equality, he remarks frequently on the physical weakness of the female in battle.

There is, however, one realm in which the body does become irrelevant, and it is for the sake of this realm, I would argue, that Plato has Socrates introduce the notion of sexual equality. Philosophy depends on the soul, not on the efforts of the body. Socrates uses the example of the philosophic Theages,[16] whose sickly body kept him from engaging in politics but did not keep him from philosophy. Similarly, advantages of strength and weakness or the apparent disadvantages of reproductive responsibilities have no effect on the activity of philosophy. Whereas politics for the Greeks before Aristotle entailed the use of the body in war, philosophy, as its opposite, did not require the body.

By introducing the female into his political community in Book V of the *Republic*, Socrates is asserting the superiority of philosophy over politics. The city he is proposing becomes possible, he says in his famous speech in response to the third problem of Book V, when philosophers become rulers or rulers become philosophers; by bringing the female into a public life and suggesting the irrelevance of the body, he sets up the groundwork on which such a proposal, so preposterous for the ancient Greeks of Socrates' time, is offered. Though the response of generations of readers has been to take him seriously, the reaction of the interlocutors is to laugh at him. A philosopher-ruler is even funnier than a female ruler.

The female in this context becomes the instrument for Socrates' opposition to politics as practiced among the Greeks. She is opposed to values that the Greek city placed on military valor and physical prowess. Socrates is less concerned with the status of women than with the status of philosophy. The female stands in opposition to the male as the philosopher does to politics. In the book in which he is to make politics the same as philosophy, he must also make the male the same as the female. However, the difficulties that are entailed in making the sexes the same are reflected in the difficulties entailed in making philosophy the same as politics. The philosopher must be transformed from a being who is concerned with the ascent to the highest truths to one forced to descend into a world of darkness, a world of lies and shadows.[17] The opposition between philosophy and politics is the opposition between up and down, truth and falsehood, female and male.

By elevating the feminine principle to the level of philosophy over the political, Socrates reveals much about his conception of philosophy, which is important for our understanding of his notion of politics. The activity of philosophy for Plato is very much like the sexual activity of conception and birth. In Book VI, Socrates makes an analogy between sexual desire, conception, and birth and the pursuit of philosophy.

> The philosopher naturally struggles to obtain what is, and not tarrying by the many particulars which are thought to be, but goes and is not dulled nor ceases from his love until he has laid hold of the nature of each thing itself which is with the part of the soul that is suitable to seize hold of such a thing. It is suitable for that which is akin to it. Being near to it and joining together with what really is, having begotten mind and truth, he both knows and lives truly and is nourished and thus ceases from the pangs of labor, but not before.[18]

The language in this passage is explicitly sexual and bears a close relationship to language and imagery found in Plato's dialogue the *Theaetetus*. There Socrates frequently portrays himself as a midwife to philosophical ideas.[19] This metaphor gives Socrates frequent cause to describe the philosophical process in terms of labor and birth, images that constantly call to mind the biological function of women.[20] Though most of the fetuses that Socrates brings forth turn out to be "wind eggs," the relationship between the intellectual and bodily processes of labor and birth ties Socrates and his activities to biological woman. The activity of philosophy is a life-giving force, one that parallels the creation of life. The activity of politics is a death-directed power; it killed Socrates and several of the interlocutors in the *Republic*, including the host and his son.

Thus, the equations Socrates makes between philosophy and politics in his proposal for a philosopher-king and between male and female in his wave of equality introduce new and parallel tensions. They turn the philosophers (pursuers of truth) into political tellers of untruth (as in the famous noble lie or the falsehoods the philosophers must utilize as they arrange the matings intended to appear as random couplings), and they turn women into men. In each case, there is a distortion, a disregard for what is by nature characteristic of each, at least according to Socratic and Greek perspectives.

In order to create "the best city"—that is, to rely on political life as the basis of justice—Socrates must do the worst to philosophers. He must make them "live worse lives."[21] Similarly, the women are denied the peculiar traits of their bodies and are

made to live inferior lives as weaker men for the sake of the city—
prepared and educated to pursue war (and thus death) rather than
life. Both women and philosophers fit awkwardly into Socrates'
city, the women emphasizing the distinctiveness and the private
that remove attention from the general needs of the city, the
philosophers emphasizing a concern with universal truths that go
beyond the particularity of the city.

In Book VI of the *Republic*, the philosopher and the female are
united through a series of images. In addition to the one cited
above, where the philosophic endeavor is compared to procreation,
there are others in which philosophy is explicitly compared to a
young girl ravished by unworthy suitors[22] or wed to an inferior
man and thus bearing weak and inferior offspring.[23] The compatibility between the two is captured by images that keep returning to the female. Socrates' integration of the female with the activity of philosophy tells us much about his conception of
philosophy in its opposition to politics. In the Greek tradition
women are private individuals belonging to the world of the *idios*,
the idiot or one who is not part of the community. Similarly, the
philosophers in the Platonic corpus are private individuals. Women
stay in seclusion in their homes; the philosopher must insulate
himself from opinions of the city. He must not allow the beliefs, the
dogmas, of the city to control his search for a knowledge existing
above and beyond the beliefs of the city. He must remain independent of the demands that the city makes upon his intellect.

To be a member of the city, one must sacrifice one's private
knowledge and accept the views of the city. This is something the
philosopher cannot do. He asks his questions without regard to the
political consequences or the political needs of the community;
women likewise perform their functions privately, irrespective of
political circumstances. Women bear children whether they live in
Athens, Thebes, or New York City. Philosophers pursue knowledge
wherever they may live. But the political individual behaves differently, depending on the political conditions of his or her particular community. The female and the philosopher, for Plato, live
apart from the political world. In the *Republic*, he forces both into
politics.

The philosopher like Socrates may become dangerous to the
city, but more often, again like the woman, he is simply useless.
When one of the interlocutors accuses the philosopher of being useless,[24] he recalls the words of Pericles in Thucydides' history:
"We alone think of one who does not participate in [public] affairs
[the *idios*] not as a quiet man, but as a useless one."[25] The Greek

polity had no place for the *idios*. Thus, the tensions that surround the introduction of the female into political life are the same as those that surround the introduction of the philosopher. Both naturally belong to the world of the private.

Yet the aim of Book V, in which both enter political society, is to make public all that previously had been private—from sexual intercourse to a hurt finger. In the process of becoming politicized, the female and the philosopher are removed from their natural environments. To become political creatures, both the feminine and philosophy are destroyed. The equation of the female and philosophy here is not to elevate the female, but to suggest the opposition of both to the political realm. Sexual equality in the city of the *Republic* foreshadows the philosopher-rulers. According to Socrates, both notions elevate the political over the natural; this was a sacrifice Socrates, who chose to die rather than respect the demands of the city that he stop questioning its values, could not make, as much as he might experiment with the idea in speech.

The Female Teachers of Socrates

Though we usually think of Socrates in terms of the questioning philosopher, the one provoking those around him to anger at him and to anguish in themselves, Socrates twice admits to having teachers who were women. One teacher was a (perhaps fictitious) prophetess from the city of Mantinea; the other, the mistress of Pericles. The former, Diotima, whose name means "one who honors god," teaches Socrates about love at the expense of political life; the latter, Aspasia, tries to educate Socrates in the political art of rhetoric as understood by the woman associated with the most important political leader in Athens during much of Socrates' life. Let us look at the prophetess first and then consider what the political female tries to offer Socrates.

Diotima in the Symposium

Diotima appears as Socrates' teacher in a dialogue in which the participants celebrate the playwright Agathon's prize for the best tragedy presented at the festival of Dionysius. The participants are all luminaries in the sophisticated life of the Athenian intelligentsia. They decide to forgo the usual drinking and instead compete with one another in speeches in praise of love. For the most part the speeches offered by these men praise homosexual love and scorn heterosexual attachments, including those of the family.

Phaedrus, a poet, is the first to speak; his praise of love centers on its ability to make men brave. He proposes armies comprised of homosexual pairs. The lovers would be ashamed to show cowardice before their beloveds; therefore, they would fight bravely in the face of death. Love has political benefits, but only when used properly in military endeavors. Phaedrus includes one reference to a woman in his speech when he tells the story of Alcestis: she so loved her husband that she was willing to die in his place. Again, love led to courage. In contrast, Orpheus tried to use his music to charm the gods of the underworld to get back his Persephone, but had been unwilling to die to be reunited with her. He does not earn the name of lover. We should note here that in his praise of love, Phaedrus sees love as leading to death. Orpheus, unwilling to face death, is not a true lover.

The Socratic vision that is presented through the speech of Diotima later in the dialogue emphasizes the role of love as creating life, especially the life of the philosophic vision. Before that, though, the dialogue takes us through a series of speeches denigrating the female. Pausanias, a student of comparative legal systems, praises love by excluding what Phaedrus had shown to be the only unambiguous example of love. He separates out the love of and by the female. It is sordid, characteristic of the common people; the heavenly love, in contrast, leads to a love of the male. Within his speech he offers no justification for the separation, but chooses to talk of the moral advantages of political communities that allow and encourage homosexual liaisons.

Aristophanes is also present at this celebration. He speaks of our original nature, when we were spherical beings with four arms, four legs, and two faces; when there were three sexes: the male-male, the female-female, and the female-male. Because of our arrogance we were split by the gods, and now spend our lives searching for the other half with which we were originally united. The original male-males seek out the male, while the original male-females seek out members of the opposite sex. Aristophanes describes the latter as adulterers, entirely ignoring the status of the legitimate family. Instead, he talks about the true men, those sprung from the original male-male, who choose a political life and are the lovers of other men. These men are forced by custom into marriages. Laws, not nature, move such men to participate in the engendering of children. Sensual involvement with women is the sign of our falling from an earlier golden age of omnipotence when generation was not necessary.

In stark contrast with this negative attitude toward the female expressed throughout the dialogue is Socrates' insistence that he had learned about love from a woman, a seer who understood the will of the gods. In the speech he repeats the words of this woman, words he supposedly heard as a young man, rather than speak in his own voice. He tells of love as a longing, as desiring to be united with what will make one complete.

To explain the nature of this love, Diotima uses a parable: The feast to celebrate the birthday of Aphrodite is attended by the male Plenty, who, heavy with wine and food, falls asleep. The female Poverty comes to the feast, finds Plenty asleep, and, lying down beside him, contrives to have a child by him. From this union of Poverty and Plenty, Love is born, incorporating into his person the traits of both parents. Many of the details in this story are contrived to make us associate Socrates with Poverty and the traits that she passes on to her child Love—for instance, they both go barefooted, they both hang around doorways and porches, neither is ever satisfied, and each is always scheming to get more. We should note that it is the female, the mother Poverty, with whom Socrates associates himself, as he had done with the midwife imagery of the *Theaetetus*.

This association with the female goes on as Diotima continues to describe the nature of love. It is the desire to appropriate beautiful things, not for a short time but forever. However, since we are mortal, love forces us to search for immortality—and we do this through the process of procreation. However, rather than describing love and procreation from the male perspective of engendering in another, Socrates appropriates the imagery of pregnancy for the male. In a startling phrase Diotima suggests that all humans are pregnant. She does not distinguish between males and females; indeed, she presents the male as transformed into the female, as capable of being pregnant. The virility, the strength, the courage of the father pale before the capacity to become pregnant, the sign of humanity and of being a true lover. Unlike Pausanias, who scorned the generative love, and Phaedrus, who found love only in the willingness to die, Socrates' Diotima sees love only in the processes of birth and generation.

Diotima describes a hierarchy of loves; on the bottom rung is the creation of human children, the immortality possible for the many. As we move up this hierarchy, though, and the models become poets and lawgivers and philosophers, the feminine imagery of birth and generation does not yield. We hear not of bodies pregnant, but of souls pregnant as the ascent moves from children to fame and finally to the beautiful. The bodies are forgotten as the seer describes the different levels of engendering, but always the language is that of reproduction. Thus eros is associated in Socrates' speech with creativity and the feminine. In this speech the female is not vulgarly associated with the body, as she had been by the previous speakers. The emphasis of the previous speakers on the male had led to a focus on political life, and thus a focus on death, the death of the battlefield or the absence of generation characteristic of Aristophanes' "true men." Socrates, rejecting that world, turns to a female teacher whose education in love matters moves him beyond and outside the city in his philosophic pursuit of true beauty. That beauty for Socrates is found neither in the city nor in the love of the male.

Aspasia in the Menexenus

In one of Plato's most baffling dialogues, Socrates claims to learn the art of rhetoric from Aspasia, the mistress of Pericles. Near the beginning of the *Menexenus*, Plato has Socrates suggest that the real author of Pericles' renowned funeral oration was this woman. Such speculation on Socrates' part certainly is not meant seriously, but with this outlandish suggestion he undercuts what has been seen by many, both ancient and modern, as one of the noblest panegyrics ever presented. Such a speech could not come from the mind of a woman—one who, according to the Greeks, could not understand the glories of war or of the city so praised.

But in the preface to the discussion of the *Menexenus*, Socrates had described the task of the funeral oration as an easy one. To praise Athens among the Athenians is no great challenge. To praise the Athenians among the Peloponnesians or the reverse would be an example of the rhetorician's skill. (Or we, having read the *Republic*, might think, to praise the philosopher among political men, or women among the men at the dinner party of the *Symposium*, is a task worthy of a great rhetorician.) Thus, while he learns the art of rhetoric from a woman, he denigrates the art of rhetoric here.[26] At the same time that he praises her, he endeavors to undermine the activity in which she supposedly excels, and thereby undermines even the efforts of the male who really stood behind the funeral oration.

The dialogue of the *Menexenus* begins as the young man of the dialogue's title, about to enter political life, asks Socrates if he could give a funeral oration if requested to prepare one hastily. Socrates replies that it would be easy. He was recently taught one by Aspasia so that he could recite it by heart. The one he learned earlier would satisfy the needs for a speech for tomorrow, since such speeches are never specific and have no special relation to the deeds that may have been performed—that is, they are abstracted from the actual activity of war. Socrates admits that he learned the speech by heart because Aspasia was a harsh teacher, ready to strike him whenever he forgot his lines.[27] Rhetoric, the political art of persuasion, is taught by force. Unlike the prophetess Diotima, the one close to the gods teaching about love matters, Aspasia, located close to the center of power, uses the force of politics even though she is a woman.

However, though she educates through force, she transforms the funeral oration from one dealing with the death of young men for the city to one concerned with life—specifically the birth process. The beginning of her speech nicely parallels Pericles' speech, but where Pericles had turned to the ancestors and their feats against the Persians at Marathon and Thermopylae, Aspasia turns to the one ancestor, the earth, the mother from whom the Athenians sprang. She describes the soil as a mother who bore and nourished her children, continuing the metaphor for several pages. The milk of the mother is like the fruit of the earth. Indeed, the human mother appears only as an imitation of the earth, not the earth of the mother.[28]

The myth to which Aspasia is referring is the Athenians' view of themselves as autochthonous, sprung from the earth. Traditionally, however, the autochthony myth excluded the female. Men could be born without the benefit of the human mother. The male seed was simply planted in the soil, and thus the woman could be left out of the origins of cities.[29] Aspasia insists that we recognize the place of the female, without whom there would be no political community. Hers is not the masculine speech of Pericles, and it is hers that Socrates is willing to learn by heart.

At the end of the funeral oration, Pericles advises the women of his Athens to seek a virtuous life in which they are least talked about, whether for good or for evil. Aspasia obviously does not allude to those famous comments, but Plato has his Socrates do so. After Menexenus marvels at the speech of one who is only a woman, Socrates warns Menexenus not to tell on him; Aspasia's education of Socrates must not be talked of, not be part of the public discourse. If Menexenus promises, then Socrates will tell him many other fine political speeches. Menexenus promises, and the dialogue ends.

Pericles, having urged silence and invisibility for women, perhaps recognized their subversive force. Aspasia educated Socrates in an alternative view of politics that focused on maternity rather than paternity. Diotima trained him to search for fulfillment in a realm beyond politics. The two female teachers of Socrates, as different as they might be, offered him a view of political life that did not conform to or exalt the virile world of homosexual love, which dominated the other speeches of the *Symposium*, and the original funeral oration, which had removed women from the realm of speech and action.

The *Laws*: Women in the Second-Best Regime

Plato's final dialogue, the *Laws*, is a massive work in which an Athenian Stranger prescribes laws for a city to be founded in southern Crete. The discussion is carried on with Kleinias, an old man from Crete, and Megillus, another old man from Sparta, both from cities famed for their *eunomia* (good laws). The Stranger rejects both the Spartan and the Cretan models, and offers his own. However, here the communism found in the *Republic* is reserved for a community of gods; the Stranger claims that such communism is impossible among humans. Instead, the laws for this new city— to be called Magnesia—are the guidelines one would set forth for the second-best political regime, one that takes men and women as they are, as they arrive from various communities around Greece.

The Stranger compares the founding of this city to the creation of a single hive with members from a variety of hives joining in Crete to engage in the creation of this Hellenic city. In the *Republic*, the founders planned to send away all except children under the age of ten. There human nature had to be so reshaped that after the age of ten such training would be impossible; thus parents were to give up their children for this adventure in utopia building. The inhabitants of the *Republic* had to forget that they had ever had parents, that they had had anything or anyone that was peculiar to them, that might separate them from others. The city of the *Laws* is not so harsh in its demands or transformation of human nature. The adults arrive knowing full well the meaning of possessing what is one's own. There is no attempt to take away what is their own once they become part of the city. They retain their property and their sexual identity as male or female. The Stranger aims to describe a city that is possible.

Along with possibility and the absence of communism, though, come the inequality of the sexes and the inferiority of the female. There come as well the family and extensive legislation about all matters having to do with the family, specifically about women as the bearers of children, something Socrates chose to ignore in the *Republic*. The assumption of the inferiority of the women and the focus on reproduction necessitate a quite different treatment of the role of women in this work. Here, they are so inferior to the males that lack of attention to their education leads to more than double the problems for order within the state. The Stranger criticizes the regimes in Sparta and Crete for their failure to attend to the education of women, precisely because the women are inferior. After praising the common meals for men in both cities, the Stranger says:

> But the arrangements concerning women are not at all correctly established, as they are without any established laws and never has the practice of common meals for them come to light; especially that race of us humans which is born more prone to secrecy and thievery, on account of its weakness, that is, the female race, was not correctly allowed this disorder because the lawgiver yielded. . . . For it is not only half, as it would seem, which is disorderly when the things concerning women are overlooked, but by however much the female nature for us is worse with regard to virtue than the male, by so much does the harm become more than double.[30]

The argument is just the opposite of that found in the *Republic*. There, equality had demanded an equal education. Here, difference with regard to virtue demands the same education and common meals.[31] The Stranger acknowledges that making women equal to men is opposed to the natural way of things, since by nature women are prone to "secrecy and thievery," but he suggests that this equality can be instituted by education. There is no argument that women are by nature the potential equals of men, only that they can be trained—and need to be trained—to engage in the same pursuits. This, he claims, is possible but requires considerable effort. The Stranger uses the example of the women called Sarmatians, "for whom there is a community with the men in practices having to do with horses, bows, and arms and who practice equality besides."[32] If one looks across cultures and historical time, one can find women able to handle the equipment of war and hunting, even if these are skills not natural to the feminine temperament and physical attributes. Women can be educated to overcome their limits.

In an extended section of the *Laws* (794d–795d), the Stranger discusses the importance of developing ambidexterity, so that one does not lose the advantage of using both hands with equal skill. This, on the surface, might appear to be an argument meant to parallel the arguments for including women in the same activities and educational processes as the men. However, we should reflect on this call for ambidexterity and the effectiveness of training for it. Is not Plato suggesting that the Stranger is ignoring nature, which makes some of us by nature right-handed and others by nature left-handed; the attempt to make both hands equally skilled, in opposition to nature and through training, lessens the ability of the naturally stronger hand. Once again we must consider the parallels with the uniform training for men and women, and the qualifications that Plato appears to suggest for this proposal by his discussion of ambidexterity. As the naturally stronger right hand is made weaker by the emphasis on training in ambidexterity, so would the sexes be turned away from attention to their natural strengths in the efforts to make them equal.

The Stranger, unlike Socrates in the *Republic*, does not try to make the females the same as the males of the city. Rather, he views their education from the perspective of the interests of the city. The educational process is to limit their inferior tendencies; thus the females, prone to "secrecy and thievery," must be trained to care for the city to the same degree as the men. We have already noted this as a persistent problem in the Greek understanding of the political role of women and one that dominated the Greek stage. If women were simply left to care for their own things and bring up children, the Stranger says in the *Laws*, "they would not partake in war, so that if ever chance should force them to fight for the city and their children," they would not be able to take to the battlefield "like Amazons."[33]

Traditionally, the female cared more for the family than for her city.[34] In the *Republic*, Socrates took that family away from her in order to make her part of the city. In the *Laws*, she is prepared psychologically and physically to defend the city should it be attacked. She is not transformed into a male warrior. The family remains and the female continues to tend to it as she did in Greek society generally, only now she is made a part of the city rather than left behind as a threat to its stability.

At the same time that the preliminary education is to be similar for the sake of defending the city, the different roles for each of the sexes with regard to procreation is emphasized. Before marriage, females participate in the physical activity of games and races that train children in gymnastics; after marriage they join the males at the communal meals—perhaps not at the same table, but at least nearby. There is no suggestion, we should note, that this is a special gift that in some sense frees women from the confining walls of their homes and allows them to enter the blessed public sphere. Rather, the Stranger suggests, "There is nothing that is more difficult than this for the race of women to endure, for it is accustomed to live within in darkness. The women will resist in every way being dragged by force into the light, and will be far stronger than the lawgiver."[35]

This early integration of the sexes by the city does not last. Once pregnancy occurs, the regimens for the father and the mother differ. Even before children are born, they need to be rocked to develop strong bodies; thus pregnant women must walk daily to the temple—they are no longer training for war, but devoting themselves to the religious life of the city. Similarly, "It is necessary that the legislator take especial care of those women carrying children. . .so that the pregnant woman will not experience many lewd pleasures or pains, but will live through that time honoring what is gracious, even minded and gentle."[36] In the *Republic* the women were like watchdogs, going out with the men, irrespective of whether they were pregnant or not. The status of the pregnancy was ignored. In the *Laws*, in contrast, the lawgiver offers a host of prescriptions and restrictions for pregnant women—for instance, women of childbearing years are not to attend funerals[37] nor to participate in wrestling matches or in combat with heavy armor.[38] These restrictions are tied to a concern for the welfare of the fetus.

In the *Republic* details of the process of procreation are avoided; the only reference to the difference of experience between the male and the female parent is that the female bears and the male mounts,[39] and that the female breasts produce milk for the child. In every way there is an emphasis on the similarity between parents. For example, Socrates says: "There is a need for the best men to have intercourse with the best women, and the reverse for the most ordinary men with the most ordinary women."[40] In the *Laws* the Stranger proposes just the opposite; now complementarity is the rule:

> It is necessary that the one who knows himself to be more reckless and swift in all his affairs than needs be be eager for more orderly parents [by marriage]. The one born with the opposite orientation should be eager to make the opposite his kinsman through marriage.[41]

Procreation is based on the differences between the partners; and the emphasis on differences, rather than similarities, is carried forth during the period of childbearing as the roles of the male and the female with respect to the polity remain distinct.

Nevertheless, the Stranger proposes that women, once past the age of childbearing, can again become similar to the males in both the public and the private spheres—that is, the different roles with regard to the polity are based on the differences of male and female bodies with regard to reproduction and limited to that time during which reproduction is relevant. The Stranger puts women into public office at the age of 40 and adds, "As for the woman whom it would seem necessary to use in military affairs when she has completed giving birth, she would be assigned to what is possible and fitting for her until the age of fifty."[42] Perhaps more startling is the passage in which adultery is proscribed for both males and females during their reproductive years, something quite contrary to Athenian practice, where male sexual liaisons outside the family were commonplace. In Magnesia, once past the reproductive period of their lives, "the man and the woman who show moderation with regard to such things should be allowed to retain an entirely good reputation,"[43] so long as they do not have intercourse with one still capable of producing children.

From attention to equal education for the sexes because of differences, and then to sexually differentiated roles during child-producing years, the Stranger moves to a period in which sexual roles and differentiation become irrelevant. During adulthood it is the potential for becoming pregnant that separates the female from the male; the Stranger's laws acknowledge this difference when it is relevant and ignore it when it is no longer relevant. In the *Laws* differences are acknowledged and necessary, but are also to be compensated for through education. The political structure of the city and its educational aims adapt to these differences and treat them in diverse fashion.

In the *Republic*, Socrates, in the interests of unity, had tried to abstract from the differences between male and female and to allow women to become philosophers. In the *Laws*, the Stranger takes no chances on ignoring those differences: women are different from men, their childbearing bodies determine what they can do. Nevertheless, he sees that they are necessary for the city. The answer for the Stranger is not the suppression of differences, but integration; not ignorance, but adaptation. The female is no longer a model for philosophy as she was in the *Republic*, but neither is she here abstracted from her nature as understood by Plato and the Greeks of his time.

The second-best city, unlike the regimes in Crete and Sparta, recognizes the need to account for women, but in so doing it attends to the female body as Socrates in the *Republic* refused to do. The second-best city that is possible recognizes that politics must account for bodies. In the *Republic*, Socrates had tried to ignore bodies and the erotic desires of bodies. His treatment of women there had illuminated the defects of such a politics. In the *Laws*, attention to bodies is indicated by the Stranger's concern with the female's reproductive role. By understanding the role of women in each dialogue, we come to a fuller understanding of the conception of politics, its limits and its possibilities, presented in each.

Conclusion

Plato is not interested in the social and political status of the Athenian women of his time. He has found in women—those who give birth, those who are different from the males, those who are closer to the private realm—a symbol that becomes useful for his critique of an Athenian society devoted to the political life of ambition, money, and war. Women stand apart from the world that Plato too has rejected as the result of his association with Socrates. In his fantasies of possible political regimes that overcome the problems he sees inherent in the world of the Athenian polis, Plato must consider the place of women just as he considers the place of the philosopher. Neither women nor the philosopher can, in Plato's vision, ever fit comfortably into the world of political activity. His aim is in part to suggest to his readers why this is so and how political regimes might adjust to this tension. However, from his perspective, the tension never can be fully resolved.

4

Aristotle: Defective Males, Hierarchy, and the Limits of Politics

In 367 B.C., the young Aristotle came to Athens from the kingdom of Macedonia to study at Plato's Academy. His twenty years at the Academy set the framework for his own analyses, and the Platonic impact is never to be forgotten in considerations of his thought. Two decades of interaction between these two founders of the tradition of Western philosophy left a lasting imprint on the thought of the younger student. Yet, Aristotle's philosophy is distinctive in its form of presentation,[1] in its organizational focus, its emphases, and its methods of analysis. It is also distinctive in the way it treats the relations of the female to political life.

Indeed, Aristotle appears to be almost the polar opposite of Plato in this regard. While Plato, at least in the *Republic*, seems to offer a radical critique of the contemporary exclusion of women from the political leadership of the city, Aristotle comes across as the conservative defender of the status quo, with statements suggesting the natural inferiority of the female, both intellectually and morally, and the natural subjection of the female to the superior male in a patriarchal household. Such summary comparisons, though, are too simplistic. The teacher's impact on the student is not missing in just this area. As with Plato, we must not look at isolated claims, but understand whole arguments to find in Aristotle thoughtful reflections on the role of the female in political society, as well as a criticism of a society satisfied with its male superiority. With careful scrutiny of the language, and particularly the context within which Aristotle makes his misogynist comments about women, and with attention to the direction of his thought as a whole, we find that his reflections on women and the

63

political world are not so far from Plato's as abstracted half-quotations have often made them appear.[2]

Teleology and Nature

Aristotle was a Greek by birth; that is, he was born to Greek parents and spoke Greek, not the Macedonian language of the country in which he was raised as the son of a Greek physician serving at the court of the Macedonian king. Whether or not Aristotle's interest in scientific questions can be traced to the influence of his father, the study of the natural world plays a central role in the development of his thought, as it never did in Plato's. Aristotle's stay at the Academy ended with Plato's death in 347 B.C. He left Athens for twelve years, staying in Asia Minor and in Macedonia. During his time in Asia Minor, he spent long hours observing the marine life of the area. Out of this study came classifications of species and generalizations derived from his careful observations, all incorporated into his several works on animals.

The study of the physical world, of which animals are a part, is for Aristotle the study of nature, *physis*; and for him the study of nature is the study of how things grow. The Greek term *physis* derives from the verb *phueo*, which means "to grow." The questions Aristotle asks as he analyzes the natural world have to do with growth and change over time, according to set patterns of development. We understand living things, according to him, by understanding their patterns of development, whether we are talking about a flower, an earthworm, a woman, a family, or a political community. Growth as we see it in the natural world is not indiscriminate. There are certain patterns of growth in nature for each class of things. A maple sapling does not suddenly become an elephant; if the maple sapling follows the course prescribed by nature, it becomes a maple tree. Every living thing, including ourselves, possesses a certain potential. We have the capacity to grow into something, and it is that something at the end of our growing process that defines what we are—for instance, a human being or a tree.

Aristotle's study of living things is based on the apprehension of the end toward which each thing directs itself. The sapling has the potential to become a maple tree when it has come to the conclusion of its growing process. This process may not be the usual or normal pattern followed by all maple saplings. Indeed, most die. But, according to Aristotle, in order to fulfill its nature, the maple sapling *should* become a maple tree. It is this focus on the normative end that defines Aristotle's work as teleological. Each plant and animal, including the human being, has an end, a telos, a point at which it attains its final form, toward which it is directed from the moment of generation—that is, from the moment it is put into motion. If it fails to reach that end, it has not fulfilled its potential, it has not become what it can become under normal conditions.

Behind this teleological view of the world is an implicit, though obviously not articulated, rejection of the principles that underlie modern liberalism's abstraction from the notion of an end or a final fulfillment of one's nature. Hobbes proclaimed in Chapter 11 of *Leviathan*: "For there is no such *finis ultimus* [utmost aim] or *summum bonum* (greatest good) as is spoken of in the books of the old moral philosophers."[3] With these words he gave the modern world the principles at the base of the notion that we all can develop as we please, that neither God nor nature nor the state defines who or what we should be. In the jargon of our own time, the rejection of teleology allows for the possibility of "doing one's own thing," of rejecting the judgments of others, whoever they may be, concerning the worth of one life rather than another.

Aristotle's teleology does not allow for everyone to do as he or she pleases. There is an end toward which each must aspire by nature. This "must" is implanted by nature, and with the acceptance of nature as an end becomes a moral "must." In order to be good, that end must be pursued. Not to attain that end is a deformity, a deviation from natural patterns of growth. For the human being, that completion is attained when, as a fully grown person, one exercises one's reason to make the right choices concerning good and bad, right and wrong actions. The end for the human being is not a static condition but one of activity, specifically the activity of choices according to reason, which, for Aristotle, is the source of human happiness.

In order to attain this end, the human being must live in the polis—that is, the human being is a political animal. The individual must associate with others in the political realm and benefit from the educative processes of the polis and its laws. The natural end of the human thus does not come simply from nature. For other animals, the end, their perfection, is determined by nature; if they arrive at the perfection of their nature, they do so whether they chose to or not. If nature succeeds, they reach that point. If nature fails, which is often the case (the sapling dies, the acorns rot), then they do not. But for humans this is not the case. Human actions work with nature. The human being must employ convention, the laws of the city, in order to reach a condition of completion. Life must be ordered through the creation of the polis and its law. There must be human activity directed specifically to the creation and preservation of the realm of the city, the realm of reasoned choice, speech, and education.

The human being is different from other living creatures because of the possession of reason (*logos*), a term that in the Greek also entails speech. To exercise our reason-speech is the fulfillment of our natures, but in exercising our reason we must engage in discourse with others and must make choices according to the evaluations that derive from our reasoned consideration of potential actions. We must be able to explain to others the choices we have made. These choices and the grounds we have for making them determine the kind of lives we shall lead. In order to make the right decisions—those decisions appropriate to our status as human beings with the capacity of *logos*—we must be educated. Specifically, we must be educated in the political community that we have created to fulfill our potential.

Although by nature we all have a specific end, characteristic of our class, toward which we move, much may happen to prevent the fulfillment of the potential that each living thing has. If we go back to our maple sapling, nourishment may be lacking and it may die. Storms may knock off some of its branches and its growth may be stunted. A gardener may decide to train its branches into odd shapes, and it will have a form different from the form intended by nature—or, in a language that, though more cumbersome, avoids any obvious personificiation of the forces of nature, that to which it would have grown if there had not been some external interference with its growth process. The human being who does not develop reason within the structure of the polis has not completed or fulfilled the human potential. The forces of nature have been undermined and a perverted human being emerges. (This may be a god or an animal, but in either case not human.) Or the polis that does not provide the conditions conducive to the development of the rational human being has not fulfilled its potential. It becomes a defective form of organization or a deviation away from what should be, according to the natural patterns of growth.

The difference between the maple sapling and the human being is that the human engages in choice; the maple sapling is influenced by external factors: the weather, the gardener, the soil conditions. The human is self-moving, making decisions and choices concerning how to live. These choices allow for a certain openness, but they also allow for mistakes. The plant does not make mistakes.

All natural phenomena can be studied according to Aristotle's model of growth and teleology. In his biological works he applies this mode of analysis to the female. When we look at his analysis of the female as a natural biological creature, however, what we find is not particularly congenial to our notions of equality. For Aristotle the biologist studying the generation and the growth of living things, the female of the species, human or otherwise, is the defective male. She arises when the growth process is not completed according to its natural pattern.

The duality of the sexes, Aristotle explains, is necessary:

> To be is better than not to be and to live is better than not to live; on account of these causes there is the generation of animals. Since it is impossible that the nature of one born is to be everlasting, it is everlasting according to the way open to it, that is, generation.[4]

In order that there be this generation that keeps specific classes of beings in existence, it is necessary that there be both the male and the female principle.[5] However, though both are necessary for generation, Aristotle continues, it is also necessary that the male and the female be kept separate, "for the better and the stronger are to be kept apart from that which is inferior."[6]

The male is better in this context because he gives to that which is generated both the final cause, the telos, the reason for existence, and the form, the shape that being will take when it has reached its completed state. The female provides only the matter. Aristotle offers an elaborate comparative analysis of semen and menstrual fluids to support his observations, which include the notion that the female's body is incapable of concocting the necessary heat, the "pneuma," which transfers to the generated being both reason and form.[7] He does not deny the necessity of the female's participation in this process. Conception must take place between the male and the female of the same species. The human being as embryo cannot take nourishment from the matter of a cow. Aristotle thus does not see the female simply as the flowerpot within which the seed of the male grows. Both male and female contribute "residues," the difference being that the male's residue is "concocted" through the presence of heat, while the female's is not.[8]

Behind his attempts to offer scientific presentations of the processes of generation lie Aristotle's biological assumptions concerning the physical inferiority of the female because she cannot "concoct" the "pneuma" that gives form to matter. This failure on the part of the female comes from a disruption at the point of conception. Aristotle begins Book IV of *The Generation of Animals* by noting that the distinctions between male and female arise while the animals are still incomplete (*atelon*), then adds that there is disagreement as to whether these distinctions occur before they are obvious to our senses. After reviewing other theories, he presents his own: the female arises when the male principle, the semen, fails to gain mastery over the female principle. The case for the weakness of the male principle is the absence of heat. Aristotle then proceeds to support these speculations with evidence: young parents produce more female offspring, and more female offspring are conceived when the wind is in the north or when the moon is waning. All these conditions are characterized by reduced heat and lead to the birth of females and deformed children.[9]

At the same time that he insisted that nature needed to create both male and female in order to keep the race of beings in existence, Aristotle also claimed that the female is a male who is unable to reach the full state of completion because of certain inferior conditions that were present at the moment of conception. The growth pattern of the human being normally leads to the full-grown male; the existence of the female suggests that the pattern was not fully followed. Throughout his work on the generation of animals, Aristotle compares the female to a child or a boy. The female is understood as an infertile male, but whereas the child has the potential to continue to grow and to become the fertile male, the female's growth has already been diverted and she retains no such potential.

With analyses such as these from his biological works. Aristotle has easily become the bête noire of ancient philosophy, the classic male chauvinist who assumes the natural inferiority of the female, she who failed to become male. Could this be the student of a Plato who wrote Book V of the *Republic*, whose Athenian Stranger in his *Laws* proposes opening political offices to women who had passed their childbearing years, whose Socrates reveled in comparing himself to a woman and swore by the goddess Hera?

Hierarchy and the Limits of Observation

Aristotle uses his teleology as an analytical tool; he understands the world around him by understanding the causes and ends of what comprises it. We all have ends toward which we move by nature, and all our actions are motivated by the desire to reach an end. Our motion is purposive, not chaotic nor anomic. In his very first words of the *Politics*, Aristotle reminds us: "For all act in all cases for the sake of what seems to be the good."[10] When what "seems to be the good" is not, mistakes are made and the fulfillment of one's potential is not achieved. To understand the ends, Aristotle suggests, we must also understand how the ends of different organisms relate to other ends—that is, whether and how some things exist for the sake of others. Aristotle's teleology entails an orderly, structured perspective on the universe, and part of this order is the relation of things to one another, specifically in terms of better and worse.

The world for Aristotle is hierarchically structured. For the human being this hierarchy begins on the most basic level: the soul is superior to the body. In an ordered individual, living according to his nature, the soul rules the body. If this is not the case, that individual is in a condition of disorder and exists in opposition to nature. Hierarchy, like teleology, gives meaning to the world, for it establishes the priority of what is highest, what is the best. What is, exists for the sake of the best; without hierarchy, the world would lack meaning and nature would be chaotic. This hierarchy is crucial if life on earth is to continue. The mind must rule the body, or the body could not be fed and clothed and housed.

According to the natural hierarchy of the better ruling over the inferior, the soul should have control over the body; and, according to Aristotle's analysis of the generation of the female as the defective, incomplete male, the male is superior to and should have authority over the female. As he states frequently throughout his works, the better must rule over the inferior, and thus the soul must rule the body; similarly, the male must rule the female—*if* all works according to nature *and if* the intentions of nature are clearly understood and capable of being implemented.

Reading Aristotle's comments concerning teleology and the processes of generation, and his justification of hierarchy might easily lead (and has led) to a view of him as a simple supporter of the society of ancient Athens, where the female was indeed considered an inferior being entirely subject to the males around her, incapable of making appropriate choices in marriage or in monetary affairs. But all this would assume that the society of ancient Athens is the society that comes from the natural growth processes that Aristotle emphasized elsewhere in his works, that nothing similar to the absence of heat in the generation of the female hindered Athens' growth, that all the choices entailed in the "growth" of Athens were correctly directed not to the apparent but to the true good.

This was not the case. Athens is not the regime according to nature. At the very end of Book III of the *Politics*, Aristotle tells us that the regime according to nature is that in which the best rules; he who is most able by nature must be left to rule over those who by nature are inferior.[11] We are reminded here of Socrates' proposals concerning the necessary rule of philosophers if cities are to be saved. However, after ending Book III on this note, Aristotle turns in Book IV to the cities that are possible—especially those he finds in his own time, such as the democracy at Athens or the oligarchy at Chalcis in Euboea; there the best do not rule. Athens as a democracy is one of the defective regimes. It makes equal those who are not and acts in the self-interest of the many against the interest of the rich. Along with the oligarchies found elsewhere, it does not allow for the rule of the best. Indeed, Athens has even instituted ostracism to remove the best from the city.[12]

The hierarchies that have been established in the regimes Aristotle sees around him are not based on the natural hierarchical structure of the better over the inferior. Nature has not brought these cities to completion, since they are deviations from the natural relationships that would establish the priority of the better over the inferior. The choices of men during the growth processes of the city have led to the deviant rather than the best regime. The openness of human choice has led not only the barbarians but also the Greeks away from the best.

The disjunction between what is and what should be in a world organized around the principle of the superior having authority over the inferior is particularly apparent in Aristotle's discussion of the problems presented for Greek society by slavery. He begins by noting that the slave is an animate piece of property; the problem, however, occurs when the question is asked as to who is to be this piece of animate property and who is to control it. Can such a relationship between human beings be based on nature? Immediately, what is not sufficient for the subordination of one individual to another is clear: "It is necessary to look to that by nature which obtains according to nature rather than to those [relations] which have been corrupted."[13] In the corruption of Aristotle's society we find slaves who exist in such a condition according to the laws of the society but not necessarily according to nature. By looking at slavery in ancient Athens, one is looking at a condition of corruption rather than one existing by nature.

The slaves in Athens are those whose cities have been conquered by the stronger forces of the Athenians. Though some would argue that such strength would justify the enslaving of those conquered, since the stronger are the better by nature, Aristotle does not agree. Nevertheless, even if one were to grant *this* position, Aristotle further argues that we cannot take the children of slaves as slaves as well. The enslaving of the children of slaves assumes that "just as humans are born from humans, and beasts are born from beasts, so too the good are born from the good." Aristotle demurs: "But while nature may wish to do this often, it is not, however, always able to do so."[14]

As a consequence, Aristotle suggests, those who are not worthy by nature to rule over others remain masters while those not worthy by nature to be subjected remain slaves. The society of the Athenians, with its reliance on traditions and conventions, often acts against what would be demanded by nature, and thus places the inferior over the superior. The order of nature has been confused, and human relationships do not achieve the perfection of which they are ultimately capable. Force rather than friendship, therefore, is necessary to preserve the hierarchical structure of slavery.[15] The pattern of growth within the city has been perverted, and slavery is but one example of this problem.

What holds for the master-slave relationship may also be true in the case of the male-female relationship. According to nature the male is superior to the female. The history of generation described in the *Generation of Animals* explains this; because the superior must rule over the inferior, and under normal circumstances the male is closer to human perfection than the female, the female must be subject to the male. But in the cases where nature has not fulfilled itself, which are outside or against *physis*, the female may be superior to the male; and when she is, then it is against the natural hierarchy that the male rule over the female. In this case, the inferior rules over the superior. Aristotle does not state that all males are better than all females, only that this is natural. We cannot be assured that nature is in control at all times.

At the end of the first book of his *Politics*, Aristotle discusses fleetingly the relationships within the family. He had begun his discussion of the city with reference to the three hierarchical relationships that exist within the family: husband-wife, father-child, and master-slave. He then turns to a more detailed discourse on the basis of slavery in nature and to a discussion of the human activity of acquisition of goods by which one nourishes and sustains oneself. Finally he distinguishes between the rule of the master over the slave and that of the husband and father over the wife and children. The latter two forms of rule he defines as political, while the former is despotic. Rule over the child and the wife is rule over free individuals, though in the case of the child it is rule over one who has not yet reached a condition of completion—that is, the reasoning powers have not matured.

In other words, wife and child are free and to be treated as one treats fellow citizens—or potential fellow citizens. Aristotle's understanding of the political relationships that he attributes to the husband-wife relationship entails the process of a rule among equals, those who are equal in taking their turns to rule. In the case of the wife, though, what he sees around him is that the rule of the male is permanent, whereas in other political relationships the process is one of taking turns to rule and be ruled. Later, he will say of political relationships: "In the largest number of states the ruler and the ruled exchange positions, wishing to be equal in nature and differing in nothing."[16]

In order to explain the nature of this relationship between the ruler and the ruled in marital and political situations, in the midst of his discussion of the husband-wife relationship Aristotle offers the example of a king of Egypt, Amasis, who had been a private person before he ascended to the throne—that is, he had been no different from those who were to be his subjects. He had a golden pan in which he and his guests often washed their feet. He melted down this pan and refashioned it into the shape of a god. The Egyptians then worshiped the former pan. The substance of the pan had not changed, but its appearance and the honors accorded it did. Being in a position of rule does not change the individual, but it does change the nature of the honors accorded the individual. The same happens in the case of the male and the female, but in the family the male is always in the position of rule, receiving the external honors due to a ruler, though in fact he may be no more worthy of reverence than Amasis' pan. The male is marked off from his wife less by a difference in nature than "by a difference in appearance and speech and honors."[17]

Men retain authority by the conventions of the society even if this authority is not always justified by nature, just as the Athenians make slaves of the children of slaves even if this mastery is not justified by nature.

Aristotle brings home the ambiguity of the ascription of power according to sex or birth with an allusion to a play by Sophocles. Concerned with the problem of whether the virtues of the ruler and the ruled are the same, he turns to the question of the unity or multiplicity of virtues: is virtue the same for all, ruler and ruled, master and slave, male and female? He rejects the ascription of virtue to function: for instance, it is necessary that a child grow, but to grow is not enough to assign virtue to the child. The child must grow in a certain fashion and, once he has grown, must satisfy different demands concerning the attainment of his completion. The surrounding conditions are crucial. Similarly with women. Aristotle quotes Sophocles to show the common assumption concerning the virtue of the female: "Silence brings orderliness to a woman."[18] These words are spoken by Ajax to his wife Tecmessa in Sophocles' tragedy the *Ajax*. Ajax is angered that Achilles' shield has been given to Odysseus rather than to himself. This brings on his madness, his slaughter of the cattle of the Greeks, which he mistakes for the heroes of the Greek army. Tecmessa tries to calm him, urging him not to put on his armor in his rage.

It is in this context that Ajax speaks the words concerning the appropriateness of silence for women. In this context they are entirely inappropriate, an indication of his madness and failure to see the truth in what she says. Had he listened to her words, he would not have acted so destructively. He would have maintained the order that he claims Tecmessa's silence would preserve. The natural hierarchy of the male over the female has been reversed, and it is the failure of Ajax to recognize this aberration in the natural way of things that leads to disaster. Virtues are not easily assigned to a class of people or things. The context and the particularity of the situation must be taken into account if what is natural is to be preserved. To treat all those who lived in conquered cities as slaves, or all those born female as lacking sense, is to fail to recognize the diversity of nature and to limit oneself to a functionalist perspective.

The problems for women in Aristotle's model of society and sexual relations does not come from their reproductive role, as some have suggested,[19] but from the perception of women as controlled by their emotions rather than their reason (*logos*). The Tecmessa story should suggest, though, that this perception is not always justified; in the story of Ajax it is the male who lets his emotions and his anger rule, while the female retains perspective on the situation. The subordinate position of women comes from their being inferior by nature, but the problem with society—and precisely where Aristotle is critical of the hierarchical relations in the society in which he lived—arises when it is unable to determine when the female, and which females, may have something to offer to the males to whom society has given authority. The failure to recognize such times and such women is a sign of the defects of the society, a sign that it is not ruled by the best.

At the end of Book I, when Aristotle is trying to clarify the differing relationships within the family, he does so at one point with reference to the deliberative power (*to bouleutikon*) of each member of the family. The deliberative power gives each individual the capacity to choose actions and to be able to express in words the justifications for such choices. The activity of the city is deliberative—that is, it debates courses of action as participants justify to each other one policy or another. The *boulé* was the administrative council in the Athenian assembly, in which the citizens deliberated about the activities of the city. Natural slaves, Aristotle maintains, do not have any capacity for deliberation. They have no capacity to choose what will benefit them; therefore, it is in their interest to be the subjects of those who can choose. In a child the deliberative capacity is not yet fully developed, and thus the child must be educated so as to mature into an individual who can make the appropriate choices and be able to justify his actions to others. In the female, the deliberative power, Aristotle maintains, is *akuron*, without authority.

Here there is a problem with translation: often *akuron* is translated as "inferior" and *kuros* as "superior." In the Greek, though, *kuros* is associated with the possession of authority or the right to rule over another. When the male is described as being *kuros* over the female, Aristotle is not saying that he is superior, only that he has authority. Thus, the deliberative power in the female lacks authority. The problem of translation goes further, though: Does Aristotle mean authority within the soul, or in the female's relationships with others? If we are meant to take this only as referring to relationships within, then women would appear to be emotional cripples, unable to control their desires through rational choice. On the other hand, if we see *akuron* as referring to relations between people, we can see that Aristotle is suggesting that the female lacks authority with the males around her, who would refuse to listen to the advice of a woman just as Ajax refused to listen to the advice of Tecmessa. The actual meaning of *akuron* here is ambiguous, but this ambiguity is crucial because it leads to an ambiguity concerning who should rule and who should have authority in situations that arise in opposition to nature, such as those in which the female may be more "deliberative" than the passionate male.

The failure of Athenian society to understand when the female *bouleutikon* should and should not have authority leads to the indiscriminate exclusion of the female from all deliberations, and thus fails to take account of the natural (rather than the conventional) hierarchy, which sets the superior over the inferior. The city has had to rely on an inadequate criterion, sex, in order to determine that hierarchy, and thus the actual regimes give precedence to those who are inferior (the many) rather than the superior, just as within the family the Athenians always give authority to the male rather than the female.

The problem arises because the city needs some external standard by which to distinguish between people, by which to decide who shall rule and who shall be ruled, who shall participate in government and who shall not. These standards rely on external criteria such as the body, birth, and wealth. Yet, when Aristotle turns in Chapter 13 of Book I of the *Politics* to issues concerning virtue or goodness, he claims that we must turn to the soul, for that is where virtue is located. But a problem arises: We cannot see the soul, and thus it is difficult to recognize the goodness of one individual in contrast with another. How do we know that the virtue of one man's soul is such as to justify authority over the soul of the female who happens to be his wife? The problem that Aristotle sees us facing is how to discover who is better when the evidence for such judgment is not readily apparent. Though nature has decreed that the superior must rule over the inferior, as in the hierarchy of the soul over the body, she has not done much to make it obvious to us who is superior and who is not. Pursuing conventional standards, one would assume that Ajax was superior to Tecmessa. The problem is particularly acute for Aristotle in the case of the slave.

> Nature wishes to make the bodies of free men and of slaves different, the latter strong for the sake of life's necessities, the former straight and useless for such work, but useful for the political life. . . . but often the opposite happens and slaves have the bodies and souls of free men. Since this is clear, if in body alone men would differ so much as the statues of the gods, then all would agree that those who are inferior are worthy of being enslaved to them. And if this holds concerning the body, then by so much more justly is this said with regard to the soul. But it is not entirely easy to see the beauty of the soul as of the body.[20]

We can't see the souls of the individuals who are placed in a position of authority because nature does not always relate the beauty of the soul to the beauty of the body. Thus, the soul of an Ajax, wonderful fighter that he may be, is deformed, while an orderly soul may exist in the defective body of the female. The problem of political life, for Aristotle, is how to discover superior and inferior, who should rule and who should be ruled. Nature has not made it easy for us to answer this question, since observations of what exists do not give us information about the worth of the individuals who have power. Nature, not always giving us these important clues to the proper hierarchical relationships, has left us to choose, but consequently often finds herself deformed and distorted as the result of the choices of misinformed individuals.

The task of politics, for Aristotle, is how to deal with this problem of distortion. The answer is not to install the best in positions of power, since we cannot know the best. Therefore, observing the problems in the society in which he lives—the instability of the political regimes in which men disagree about who should have power, since they cannot see the best—Aristotle turns to the question of stability: "For the good of each thing preserves that thing."[21] It is not simply preservation for preservation's sake, but that stability ensures the leisure that is necessary to pursue the higher things in life. In Book VII he elaborately develops the point that war is for the sake of peace and that the polity, giving us leisure to become full human beings exercising our capacity to make reasoned choices, must be preserved. But how can the political system that is not directed by the best preserve itself? Although much of Book V, on revolutions, is devoted to this question, it is in Book II that we learn how women specifically help or hinder the preservation of order and stability in the political realm.

The Family, the Female, and the Problem of Political Stability

At the beginning of Book I of the *Politics*, Aristotle explains the genesis of the political community and expresses the view that the growth of the city entails the transformation of the human concern with mere life into a concern with the good life. The polis provides the condition for the good life, the life of moral choice; but before we can live the good life, the necessities of the body must engage us. We must live in order to live well. Thus, Book I of the *Politics* quickly becomes a compendium of ways to ensure life itself on the most basic levels of reproduction, manual labor, and food gathering. Even on this level, Aristotle assumes social interaction, cooperation between individuals to draw forth from nature that which creates and supports life. He presupposes that there must be families. They exist by nature and are the expression of our most fundamental drives. Even more basic than our life in the polis is our life in the family. The move toward the family comes initially from an inclination no different from animals' inclinations to reproduce themselves. There is no choice for animals but, according to Aristotle's conception of the development of human reason, the human being moves beyond simple inclination, to choice.

Inclination also leads us to participate in the city, but through our participation we legislate and control the structure of the regime we live in. Similarly within the family; be we Athenians, barbarians, or Spartans, we are drawn naturally into families, but the organization of the family is not determined by nature. Aristotle notes at the outset of the *Politics* that the barbarians have an inferior model of intrafamilial relations. They treat women as if they were slaves. This is a mistake, he says, because women and slaves are different types of human beings and therefore must be treated differently. Women do not exist, as does the natural slave, simply to be used to satisfy the ends of others. To treat them as if they were the same as slaves is to choose actions that are in opposition to the natural integrity of each individual capable of making judgments concerning benefit and harm. Slaves, incapable of performing this intellectual task, need masters; women are capable of making such judgments, and thus must not be ruled as if they were slaves.

To fail to make the proper distinctions within the family between the treatment of women and that of slaves leads to improperly ordered cities such as the barbarians have. We must understand the character of the basic relationships within the family before we can reflect on the relations within the city as a political institution, and we must understand how those relationships influence the survival of the city over time.

Book II of Aristotle's *Politics* is a catalog of the attempts of men, philosophers and lawgivers, to envision and to create the best political regimes, those conducive to the best life. Characteristic of all their dreams and constitutions is a concern with the family. Without attention to this, there can never be the good life. The social organization of the family, unlike the social organization of the ancient city, includes both the female and the male, the slave and the master, the child and the parent. How does the female fit into the society dedicated to the preservation of life, and how does the organization of this association affect the polis' problems of stability? If the barbarians ordered their private life incorrectly, what is the right way?

The answer is clearly not just submission to the husband's authority. Even as defective male, the female is not a slave, nor is the difference between male and female so great as to lead to slavery for women.[22] But where does the difference that does exist lead? What solution is possible? In Book II Aristotle discusses several very different solutions, two of which are presented below. On the one hand, he explains the Spartan answer, license for women of the city: freedom from laws and constraints, and little contact with their husbands. On the other hand, he offers for consideration the solution that Socrates in Plato's *Republic* proposes: a community of wives and children in which anything that is private is destroyed among those, including women, who are to be the rulers in his city.

Freedom for Women: The Case of Sparta

> The freedom given women [in Sparta] is harmful concerning the aims of the regime and the happiness of the city. Just as the man and the woman are a part of the household so it is clear that it is necessary to think of the city as divided into almost two equal parts, that of men and that of women, so that in existing regimes which hold as trifling matters the affairs having to do with women, it is necessary to think of one half of the city as being without laws and legislation. This is what has happened [in Sparta] for the lawgiver wishing to make the entire city strong, has done so clearly among the men, but was unconcerned with the women.[23]

The result in Sparta, according to Aristotle, has been a regime that, though directed toward military superiority, the expression of virile power, is in fact ruled by women. The women, uncontrolled by the traditions and the laws of the society, live a life showing no restraint, dedicated to the pursuit of luxuries. Thus, the regime from which we get our term "spartan" is one that honored wealth. The principles of the Spartan regime had not been directed toward women, and thus the polis was divided within itself—on the one hand ascetic and martial in its aims; on the other, luxurious and effete. When Sparta was attacked, Aristotle notes, the women offered no help; they had not been trained in the art of courage, and thus they created more commotion than the enemy did.

In this brief analysis of the Spartan constitution, Aristotle goes against the conventional wisdom of his time, which had commended that constitution for its good laws, its *eunomia*. Tradition had it that these laws had survived 700 years. They had provided for a strong military city considered the model of orderly existence for the Greek world.[24] In the *Laws*, Plato had had the Athenian Stranger criticize the Spartan regime because it had been dedicated to war and military victories, had emphasized the virtue of courage to the exclusion of other virtues. The end of the regime was misguided, according to the Athenian Stranger. Aristotle here does not criticize the aim of the regime[25] but, rather, its failure to recognize the distinction it unwittingly made between male and female. The men of the city came to understand the demands of a social life from their experience on military campaigns. There they had learned to submit to the discipline required in a political community. They had thus been willing to submit to the authority of the laws that governed their lives off the battlefield as well as on it. But the women, having been left home to do as they liked, were free from the exigencies of the military life and did not learn the art of submission to authority. They resisted the restraints of political authority even within the city, and pursued private rather than communal aims.

In his critique of the Spartan regime and its failure to take seriously the political education of women, whether it be through military campaigns or otherwise, Aristotle recognizes the importance of the female in the political life of Greece. Precisely because he recognizes her importance, he rejects the common opinions of the Greeks concerning the virtue of the Spartan regime, a regime not attendant to its women. In the *Rhetoric* he also criticizes the Spartans: "Whoever treats the affairs of women as worthless, as the Spartans do, lacks one half of happiness."[26] He sees not only the license and lack of courage that came from the failure to deal appropriately with the women, but also the avarice of the society as a whole. The women are greedy and, as rulers over their men, they make the city as a whole one that is governed by greed. The stability of any city depends on the role of women within it. Sparta had failed to attend to this problem, and thus suffered internally; even as success greeted the male warriors, the seeds of internal decay were growing.

The passage cited at length above, taken out of context, might lead to the view that Aristotle saw women as naturally weak and licentious. Nevertheless, there are two important points to note here: the men were not as weak nor as lascivious as the women because they were taken out on military campaigns and thus learned the art of submission, while the women were left free at home; and the problem is not insoluble, for since men had learned to submit to political and military authority, so could the women. The latter were lacking in discipline because the male lawgiver had forgotten them. The female must be part of the city, part of its educative process. The city is to train men to make them part of the community, to make choices that correspond to the needs and the interests of that community; and if it forgets about the education of women, it creates within itself a destabilizing force. Unlike the slave, who submits because he cannot do otherwise, the female is capable of choices and must be trained, like the male, to make right rather than wrong choices. When women make the wrong choices, such as those governed by greed do, the whole city is likely to fall.

Political life must attend to the problem of stability because it cannot discern who is best; thus, such a disregard for the education of the females in the city undermines the entire political endeavor. Socrates' city in the *Republic*, with its education for women and its inclusion of the female in the city's army, seems to answer Aristotle's reservations about the Spartan regime. But Socrates adds the notion of communism, a community of wives and children, which in Aristotle's mind undermines Socrates' whole endeavor and becomes a destabilizing force.

The Community of Women:
The Case of Socrates' City

When a modern reader turns to Plato's *Republic* and the utopian scheme therein, the most striking suggestion for many is the proposal that women be allowed to participate along with men of equal talents in the political and military life of the city. Aristotle, when he evaluates Socrates' proposals, ignores the issue of sexual equality. Rather, he finds the most novel proposal to be the community of wives; the question of equality would arise only if there were such a community. If one looks back to the section of Plato's *Republic* that Aristotle is analyzing, one notes that Socrates introduces the question of the equality of the sexes in response to the objections presented to his proposals for the communism of wives and property.

Though he offers the two issues as two separate waves of his argument, they are clearly related. The community of wives frees the female for consideration for equality with the male, but for Socrates the issue of equality must be discussed first as creating the conditions that lead to the communism. For Aristotle the community of wives assumes the equality of the sexes, while the preservation of the family entails the maintenance of sexual inequality.

Aristotle had dealt with the issue of sexual equality at the end of Book I of the *Politics* when he described the hierarchical relations within the family and the different virtues appropriate to the different classes of people within the structure. So long as there continue to be females to keep the race in existence, there will be, for Aristotle, hierarchy, authority, and inequality—the family.

The problem that Aristotle poses for himself as he begins to consider Socrates' city is how much should be held in common in the political association: some, all, or none? Clearly some, since without something held in common there is no city. At the most basic level the land on which the city is located must be shared. But Socrates goes to the other extreme and says that all must be held in common. His arguments for this communism are varied, but behind them all lies the concern with the stability of the political system that comes from unity.

The female and the family exist within a private realm that focuses on what is particular rather than on what is universal; thus they work, as Socrates presents it, in opposition to the interests of the community, which must emphasize a devotion to the universal. When Socrates discusses the decline of regimes in Book VIII of the *Republic*, he traces the increasing concern with the private, from the concern for private honor in the timocratic man to the uncontrolled self-interest that characterizes the life of the tyrant. By destroying the private realm through the destruction of the family and its particularistic orientation, Socrates aims to leave the self open to the complete devotion to the public such as we saw in Pericles' funeral oration in Chapter 2 of this volume.

This had been possible in Socrates' city because Socrates had abstracted from the body, which ties one to the procreative and nutritive aspects of the family. He had worked through education in poetry to train his warriors to scorn their bodies and their bodily needs. The abstraction from the body had removed a concern with the private and the particular. The bodies of Socrates' citizens did not define who they were, and thus the female body could be ignored in the communism of the city and the equality of the sexes introduced at the beginning of Book V. In Socrates' city the family was replaced by the community of rulers, among whom "my own" and even "my own body" had no meaning.

Aristotle does not abstract from the body; instead, he emphasizes how the body works against Socrates' proposals, how nature turns our attention to our bodies, what is particular about them, and how, by nature, we love our own bodies. Socrates abstracts from difference by avoiding bodies. Aristotle emphasizes bodies and, thus, difference. For instance, he finds support for the ties between children and specific parents in the natural physical resemblances between parent and child. He suggests that the people in Socrates' city would be driven to discover their own relations. "Furthermore, it is not possible to escape some form of guessing about who are brothers, and children, and fathers and mothers."[27] Socrates' citizens will engage in this guessing precisely because it is possible to recognize similarities between children and parents. Our bodies indicate these connections.

Aristotle supports his argument concerning inherited physical characteristics with reference to Upper Libya, where communism of wives is practiced. Paternity is determined some time after birth by the physical resemblance between the children and the men of the city. Indeed, he comments that there are certain females, among both women and animals (such as cows and horses), who by nature produce offspring especially similar to their parents. Such a one is the mare of Pharsalus that they call "The Just," presumably because she gives back what is due to those who have been coupled with her—that is, children who look like their fathers.[28]

Bodies, by revealing these connections, accomplish what intellects, particularly Socrates' intellect, may wish to ignore. Denying such connections, as Socrates tries to do in the *Republic*, is, according to Aristotle, to act against nature. Acting against nature leads to unholy and impious deeds that are offensive even in the contemplation of them. In referring to such deeds, Aristotle moves from violent acts against one's parents to the sexual liaisons that would occur between the members of one's own natural family: fathers with daughters and even, what he considers the most horrendous and unnatural of all, brothers with brothers. The anonymity imposed by Socrates' scheme, and thus the lack of shame to restrain human actions, opens the door for all these acts against nature. The restraint that had come from a knowledge of these who are close is removed. Oedipus, knowing that Jocasta was his mother, would not have wed her. Without the knowledge that she is his mother, nothing stops him from his unholy deeds— neither shame nor piety. Later he must pay for his impiety.

Aristotle finds further problems with Socrates' city, for it fails to take account of the natural love of oneself and of what is one's own. "Not in vain," he says, "does each have a love of oneself. This is according to nature."[29] We love ourselves and we love what we create. We exist through activity, and since we love our existence, we love what that existence has brought into being, be it our children, our handiwork, our writings. We act in accordance with a love of ourselves and of what we have created.[30] Socrates' community eliminated that natural love of oneself and one's creative activity. This distortion of our natural drives, Aristotle claims, will cause instability and lead to the demise of the city. He uses the example of household slaves to support this point: If too many slaves are assigned a particular task and no one feels that the accomplishment of that task entails his or her creative activity, the task will not be performed. The many, having no particular attachments to the task, having no sense of seeing themselves in the accomplishment of that task, will leave the work to others. "There is the least concern for what is common, but the most care for what is private."[31]

The female, as the symbol of what is private, of the home and what is particular, as the source of children who are one's own and recognized as such by the city at large, is a vivid expression of the need all humans have to tie themselves to that which is particular and one's own. To communalize the female is to destroy the private and to overemphasize the public and its universalistic aims; for Aristotle this is the same as destroying the moral and psychological bases of the city. The community of women, so opposed to the demands of nature, cannot support the city as an institution arising from the natural drive of men to perfect themselves.

There are other problems with Socrates' city. By removing the family and ignoring the difference between male and female, Socrates destroys the diversity, multiplicity, and interdependence at the core of the city. Aristotle argues that diversity is essential for the city; we need cobblers as well as doctors. To make the cobblers and the doctors the same, to ignore what is different about them, and to expect the same expertise from each is to change the city into an individual. By nature we are different and have different abilities. Socrates himself had stressed this as he began to found his city in the city of pigs.

By nature the male is not the same as the female. Though in Aristotle's biological works these differences are often expressed in terms of defects, in the "practical" pieces he focuses on the differences in virtues. "The virtues of a youth are moderation and courage in the soul.... The virtue of a girl is beauty and greatness of body, and in the soul moderation and a love of work without slavishness."[32] That diversity must be retained on the private level, or the city—lacking cobblers and doctors, men and women—will die. Socrates' abstraction from the private realm casts doubt on the survival of his city. In contrast, on the public level, the realm of political life, there must be an equality, a focus on what unites through similarity. All are citizens, all are capable of ruling and being ruled. The particular differences between individuals defined as equal become irrelevant. But we can reach this state of equality only when the necessities that demand differentiation have been met.

The problem with Socrates' model, as Aristotle sees it, is that Socrates, in proposing sexual equality in the political realm, had done so through ignoring the diversity demanded in the private realm, through ignoring that the public must build up from the private. As shown in Book I of the *Politics*, Aristotle cannot discuss the good life until he has discussed life itself. In Book V of the *Republic*, Socrates tries to ignore life in order to jump headlong into the good life. As a result, as Aristotle understands it, Socrates destroys the potential for both.

Aristotle on the Family and the Female in the Polity

> There seems to be a friendship between man and woman by nature. For the human being by nature is more disposed to live in pairs than in the polis, insomuch as the household is prior in time and more necessary than the polis, and the creation of children is more common with other animals. Among other animals, the community extends only this far [to the creation of children], but for the human being, living together is not only for the sake of reproduction, but also for various aspects of their lives. Immediately, the work is divided, and there is one task for men and another for women. So they assist one another, putting their individual talents into the common good. On account of these things, there seems to be both usefulness and pleasure in this sort of friendship. This friendship also exists in accordance with virtue, if they are both good. For there is a virtue of each, and they are pleased by this. . . . It seems that children are a bond, wherefore marriages without children dissolve more quickly. For children are a common good for both and what is common holds them together.[33]

This passage offers a picture of human involvement in the family often forgotten as one turns to the Aristotle of the famed "man is a political animal" quote. Here he portrays the human being as an economic being, in the true sense of the term. We see in this passage a concern with the community that is the family, the pleasure that both members, male and female, derive from a friendship devoted to what is common and their individual talents exercised in their attention to what unites them. The family here is not a dark recess of subordination and domination, but a prepolitical condition incorporating into itself many of the elements of unity and friendship that the actual cities of Greece in Aristotle's time failed to exhibit.

Neither the Spartan lawgiver nor Socrates recognized the special value that Aristotle attributes to the family, a value that takes it far beyond the process of reproduction that ties the human species to other animals. The Spartans with their men at war all the time and Socrates with his communism ignored the family and the female who was a part of it. Aristotle wants to reassess the stature of the family, and his criticism of the utopian and the practical regimes is a major part of that reassessment.

In Socrates' city Aristotle had found a community with no family to educate in a love that goes beyond the self, a community where the door had been opened for the common practice of impiety. Socrates' city left no room for liberality. If one identified the city as being the same as oneself, to act for the city could not be called a liberal act. Thus, the communism of his city destroyed all the potential for virtue. The Spartan regime had failed to educate women in the art of submission to authority that all regimes must entail. The failures of others are captured in Aristotle's attempt to justify and resuscitate the family. The polis arises, in his view, to help complete what the family ultimately cannot do successfully: educate the young. It is to continue the process begun in the family, not to make the family irrelevant, as the others had tried to do.

Throughout all the criticisms of Socrates' city and the Spartan regime, Aristotle never focuses on the inherent deformity of the female that had been a part of his work on the biology of animals. His arguments against communism do not come from arguments about the inequality of women, that women need supervision, as does the natural slave. The value of the family for Aristotle is not that it brings about subordination, but that it provides the orderly community of love and friendship, the natural hierarchy whose stability offers the preconditions for the pursuit of virtue. Though the family may not always conform perfectly to the rule of superior over inferior, it appears to order itself naturally, to be founded on a natural hierarchy that the city composed of supposed equals can only pretend to approximate.

Because of the problems with observation noted above, it is difficult within the context of the city to determine who is equal, who should rule, and who should be subject. The justice of the city in distributing offices is artificial rather than complete. It is dependent on an inequality that cannot be secure. All polities depend on this justice. Within the family the hierarchy in operation is closer to the natural way of things. The family is the model of the natural aristocracy. By this Aristotle means an association in which the man rules according to his worth "and about those things that it is necessary for a man to rule, but whatever fits well with a woman, he hands over to her."

If the man chooses to rule in those areas where he is not suited by nature to rule, he transforms the aristocratic relationship into one that is oligarchic, one in which he rules in his own self-interest and not in the interests of the community. A few lines before the passage just cited, Aristotle had suggested that an oligarchy is a regime in which the rulers do not distribute the affairs of the city according to worth, but give all the good things to themselves.[34] The well-structured family recognizes the differences between the members and takes these differences into account as they all work toward the common good. Within the city that is based on equality and a sharing in the process of rule, the differences between those who are citizens must be ignored and each has the same tasks as everyone else. With all citizens determined by artificial criteria of equality, there can be no distribution of offices or tasks according to worth, since all must share in the activities of the political community.

When cities are threatened with revolution and instability, it is because there is disagreement about the meaning of equality, who is to be equal and who is to be subject. In Book V of the *Politics*, Aristotle notes that in all cases, "on account of inequality, there is internal conflict."[35] While men agree that justice is simply distribution according to worth, "they differ nevertheless with some saying that if they are equal according to one attribute, then they are completely equal, while others claim that if they are unequal in one attribute, then they are worthy of unequal treatment."[36] In families in which the difference between the sexes and the generations at the base of the distribution of tasks is more readily observed, the distribution of tasks and authority is more easily accepted.

The city's inequality and equality are not precise. They therefore remain constantly subject to debate and are an incentive for internal strife. The city becomes, in a sense, only an imperfect reflection of the natural hierarchy of the family, and the order of the family is only inadequately captured by men's attempts to set up barriers among themselves, barriers for which nature has offered no clear signposts. Even within the patriarchal household, where differences are more subject to observation, mistakes can occur, as in the case of Ajax and Tecmessa. Thus, even within the smaller unit of the family, true justice is not always at work, because the criterion of differentiation is not always adequate to justify differential treatment. At the beginning of the *Ethics*, Aristotle asks that the same level of precision not be sought in all forms of speech nor in all realms of inquiry. Precision concerning equality is not possible in political life, nor is precision concerning inequality possible in the family. In the family, though, according to Aristotle, it is somewhat more accessible.

The portrait of the female within the family may not earn much admiration from contemporary students of women in the social sphere, but Aristotle's analysis of the family, as a cooperative adventure in which the friendship between the members comes from a common concern for the welfare of the unit, goes far beyond the view of the family in ancient Greek society that many have offered to us. Students of the Greek legal system trace a set of relationships in which the female is little more than the instrument for transferring property from one family to another and for giving birth to future protectors of the religious rites of a particular family. Aristotle's understanding of the family goes beyond such "uses" for women and suggests that the family must be understood as a set of associations and relationships from which the grander and more important polis derives.

Within the family, the role of the female, that task assigned to her because of her special abilities, is the same one taken up by the statesman within the city—preserving what has been acquired, providing for stability. Nevertheless, however important the female may be in the family, Aristotle never envisions her as part of the public realm of the city. Again this view derives from his understanding of the notions of equality and inequality. The family as a realm of hierarchy stands in contrast with the city as a realm of equality. Within the family the male retains authority over the female, the father over the son, the master over the slave. Inequality of authority or power derives from differences with regard to sex, age, ability.

The family, unlike the city, is characterized by its differences; and in order for it to continue over time, it must incorporate these differences. The male must be different from the female if there is to be sexual reproduction. The master must have the intelligence that the slave lacks, and the slave must have the physical capacity that the master need not develop. The relations of difference within the family maintain the unit. Within the polis, the criterion must be one of equality: Citizens must be equal in their possession and exercise of reasoned speech, of discourse about the just and the unjust, and they must be equal in their leisure to engage in such speech. Thus, as workers captured by the necessities of existence, lacking the leisure to participate in such discourse, cannot be part of the citizen body, neither can the female, who, because she is nourishing the young with her body, lacks such leisure.

For Aristotle, then, the exclusion of women is based in part on their unequal leisure time, their role as the preservers of the household and the bearers of the young. In responding to a proposal for a community of wives with the retention of private property, Aristotle asks, "Who is to guard the household?"[37] with the further note that the analogy that had been used in the *Republic* in the discussions of sexual equality was strange indeed, for "animals do not have households (families)."[38] However, more significant for Aristotle's exclusion of the female from the public realm is the lack of authority of her reasoned discourse. Since the polis is to be a realm of activity for the *logos*, the female, in whom that *logos* is not predominant, cannot participate fully.

In being so excluded, women are not alone. Slaves obviously are excluded, but so are workers, not because Aristotle the aristocrat rejects the lower classes, but because his conception of political life requires the participation of those who engage in the reasoned discourse of the complete human being. Workers lack the leisure for this engagement. In contemporary society, where political participation is not defined by the activity of reasoned discourse, the restrictions that Aristotle established appear meaningless or downright unjust, but his concern that the public realm serve as the arena for the highest human activities (after philosophy) led to his demand for such an intellectual engagement.[39]

In the last two books of the *Politics*, Aristotle discusses the city of his dreams.[40] Having found the regimes of his own day and the proposals for better ones so inadequate, he offers his own visions. Women figure here only very briefly as he considers the issues of reproduction and the earliest stages of the child's life. The legislator must have the best material with which to work, and that means the healthiest population. To ensure this health, he must attend to the laws governing matrimony and reproduction. Aristotle is particularly concerned that reproduction not begin at too young an age, when deformed offspring (including women) are likely to be born.

But Aristotle slips from these biological considerations to psychological ones. Picking up on the themes in the *Ethics*, he maintains that the legislator must also be concerned with the community that is created within the family and must ensure that there is a compatibility of sexual life for the married couple. This means that the ages of husband and wife must match, so that one will not be able to be reproductively active when the other can no longer function in this capacity. Thus, since he sees 70 as the age for men's declining sexual potency and 50 for women, he suggests that the man be 20 years older at the time of marriage.[41] Not marrying at too young an age ensures that offspring will be conceived by those in the prime of their reproductive life; when the parents are old, their children will take over the maintenance of the family.

Once conception has taken place, the female is to exercise her body, but not her mind, for her body must be strong in order to give strength to the growing child, just as something growing draws from the earth.[42] If we look only at these last words comparing the female to the soil, Aristotle could justly be accused of seeing only the material role of the female. She is the matter out of which the citizens grow, but the earlier comments expressing concern for the compatibility within marriage suggest that Aristotle has a deeper understanding of the female's place in the polity. Though she is not a part of the public community, the private community depends on a nonexploitive, communal relationship between the male and female.

Again, however, the student of Aristotle must go further to understand fully the place of the female in his analyses of the best city. Specifically, one must note the persistent hostility to the city as an armed camp composed of virile warriors, spirited in their desires to acquire dominion. As Aristotle expresses it at the beginning of Book VII, the best city, the one that need not worry about stability, is the one that promotes the individual happiness of its citizens. The task for Aristotle is to explain the conditions that would provide this happiness. The mistake of the many, according to him, is that they equate happiness with what is external, with the excessive accumulation of goods. For these men conquest, war as the means to acquire goods, becomes the source of happiness. Aristotle argues that the city must not be structured to facilitate the continual pursuit of more goods, but the limitless pursuit of virtue. And how does one pursue virtue? Not through conquest, but through education, through attention to the arts.

In Chapter 7 of Book VII, Aristotle attacks regimes dominated by a spirited love of war. He associates such regimes with the cannibalism practiced by the Cyclops. The most choiceworthy life, with which Aristotle's investigation into the best regime began, is not one of domination—one country over another, the male over the female, the master over the slave, all of which are based ultimately on war and inequality—but one of the processes of ruling over men who are equals.

Thus, Aristotle's analysis of the best regime focuses on the processes of education in moderation, the characteristic that he had previously ascribed to the good woman. The cities of Aristotle's time that catered to a concern with material wealth emphasized the virility that was necessary to pursue domination. The city of Aristotle's dreams exalts the feminine virtue of restraint. While the female herself appears only in her reproductive capacity in these last two books, the feminine, as opposed to the masculine, virtue provides the foundation for the city that offers human beings the truly happy life. The body of the female is not the same as the female soul; and just as those who attend exclusively to what is external are mistaken in their evaluations of the source of happiness, so are those who attend exclusively to the body of the female. Aristotle's books on the best city are incomplete, but in what remains, little is actually said about the public life of the citizen; the focus is on education in moderation. The female is part of that education, and thus part of the true life of the city.

Conclusion

Aristotle is well known in the literature today as the classic misogynist, and his words have often been used to support misogyny throughout the ages.[43] The accusation of misogyny today can condemn an author and relegate him to the scrap heap. In Aristotle's writing there is no hatred of women; rather, there is the attempt, from the perspective of the male, to understand the origins of the female and her role in the male city. The female is a defective male, but so are most of the males whom Aristotle sees around him. Seldom is the true man found, one who combines the physical, intellectual, and moral qualities of the individual who has reached the completion of his growing process.

Aristotle's understanding of the female in the political world leads to a vision of hierarchy, but not submission on all levels. The woman, he steadfastly maintains, is not a slave. Thus he must understand her distinct role in society, and he finds it in her capacity within the structure of the family—a realm in which she not only gives birth but also gives stability, preserves and educates the young of the city. It is a realm in which she can demonstrate her unique virtue.

The Socratic vision in the *Republic* had excluded the private realm. All virtue was public. Aristotle retains the private and encourages the pursuit of excellence and community there. Without that excellence on the part of both the male and the female, there can be excellence nowhere in the life of the city. Cities that ignore the female and her potential for excellence, such as Sparta or Socrates' city, Aristotle warns, are placing themselves in jeopardy of internal conflict, dissolution, and chaos. In no way can we pretend that the female is the central issue in Aristotle's writings, but she raises for him a variety of questions and alternative perspectives with which he must deal before he can complete his presentation of the full political life for the human being.

5

Rome: Women in the Political Life of an Empire

A Brief Introduction to the Roman Political Perspective

> Remember, O Roman, to rule nations with power [*imperium*]:
> These shall be your arts, to impose the habit of peace,
> to be sparing to those conquered, and to vanquish the proud.
>
> Vergil, *Aeneid* (VI. 851–53)

Thus Anchises speaks to his son Aeneas in Vergil's *Aeneid*. This epic poem celebrates the victory of Augustus over Mark Antony and Cleopatra, the founding in 27 B.C. of the Principate, with Augustus as prince, and the end of a century of domestic conflict. Aeneas, to whom the kings of Rome traced their lineage, visits the underworld on his travels from conquered Troy to the Italy that is to give birth to Rome, and hears these words from his father. Vergil, through Anchises' words, captures the Romans' self-image as a nation destined to rule over others and to exercise that rule nobly for the benefit not only of themselves but also of those they subjugated. Rome was founded, and the Romans were born, to lead an imperial state. While the polis in Greece was a small, homogeneous community in which all citizens participated in the exercise of power through discourse, the Roman political experience became one of a government dedicated to the acquisition and maintenance of empire. Anchises "foresaw" well the role that destiny had chosen for the Romans.

The sense that Rome was fated to rule over others, that her empire had almost been given to her because of the unique quality of her men, had parallels within the political life of the city. The political structure was based on the notion that some men were better able to rule than others. Some men had *auctoritas*, a certain wisdom, a natural force of character, or, more often, a certain family background[1] that indicated their suitability for leadership within the state. Others who lacked these traits were to be led. Unlike the Aristotelian citizen, who ruled and was ruled by his equals in turn, the Roman citizen was part of a political system based on assumptions of inequality among its citizens and on theories of leadership.

Participation apart from military service was not expected from each citizen, as it was in Athens, where the one tending only to his private affairs was regarded as an "idiot."[2] Rather, participation in governing the state was expected of those of noble background. Such service to the state went along with being a member of the upper classes in Rome. Cicero, the great orator and author who lived during the first century B.C. and who, despite his nonaristocratic background, attained the highest position in the Roman government, wrote an extended letter to his son, *De Officiis* (On Duties), that expresses this orientation. He argues throughout that the offices or duties of a young man such as his son, with an education such as his son had received, are encompassed in service to humanity through political leadership. "To be drawn away from participation in the affairs of the state by one's studies is in opposition to one's duties," Cicero admonishes his son.[3] "Our talents are to be used to bind together the society of man to man."[4] Our duties, Cicero claims, come from Nature herself, who demands such participation and service to humanity from those capable of leadership.

This perspective separates those who are to tend to public life as a duty demanded of them by Nature and those who, like the subject nations of the Roman empire, are to be led and molded by their leaders. The conflict that arose in the Roman political life, the "Struggle of the Orders," often involved the unwillingness of those "meant" to be led to be so led. The populace rose up and tried to wrest from the patricians some power or access to power in the state, but always it was limited power or limited access that was conceded to them. As the moralists of the later Roman Republic interpreted it, the increasing political power of the people brought on the decadence for which Rome became infamous. When the hierarchical order of born rulers and born subjects was questioned, the cohesion of republican government faltered. The populace, it was thought, should serve in the army when called upon, but then tend to its own affairs and leave the ruling to those who were capable, those who had the *auctoritas*.

In the Greek world the citizen had his private and public worlds competing for attention; being a member of the polis and of one's family led to the tragic tension discussed in Chapter 2 of this volume. The conflict between public and private takes on quite a different focus in Roman thought, where some men, but not all citizens, are to turn to public affairs, to sacrifice their private pleasures and attachments for the sake of the state. The political community of active participants did not equal the totality of the male citizen population and a new concept of citizenship emerged, one in which the tragic tension illustrated in Greek drama was avoided. The citizen was not necessarily the actor, the potential ruler, but one who possessed certain rights, whose individual person was protected from certain actions, such as whipping by a Roman magistrate. As Rome expanded, so did citizenship with its (or some of its) attendant rights, in part in an attempt to cement relationships with former enemies, but also to increase the size of the army.

Citizenship, while it may have meant fighting in Rome's wars, was no longer tied to participation in the political system. Granting of citizenship did not need to affect the internal governance of the city. Similarly, with citizenship expanding, the individual qualities of potential citizens became less important because participation was not expected.[5] The expansion of citizenship did not mean the involvement of more and more people in the political process. One could be a Roman citizen and never hold political office, never attend an assembly, and never have one's vote counted.[6] Thus there could be those who engaged in public activities, who saw that activity as the main focus of their lives, and alongside them could live citizens who were not active in the political leadership of the city but nevertheless enjoyed its benefits: cheap corn, trading rights, access to public lands, public games, and so forth.

The leader was, or should be, in the vision of the time (though he may seldom actually have been so), the one devoted to the service of his state, the one motivated by a sense of pious responsibility to the nation destined to rule over others. Cicero's letter to his son constantly reiterates this necessary dedication to service to the state. The goals of such an individual differ from those of the average citizen. The national heroes of the Romans were men selflessly devoted to the public good, men like Horatius Coecles, who stood at the bridge across the Tiber to hold off the attacking Etruscans while the Roman soldiers destroyed the bridge behind him. Despite desperate odds, he did not yield.[7] The heroes were men like Brutus, the first consul of the Roman Republic, who had his son executed when the son dared to revolt against the newly founded order. They were men like the Horatio triplet, who slew his sister when she wept for her slain fiance, killed as an enemy of Rome: "Let every Roman woman perish thus who mourns a foe."[8] Though the people recoiled at such a deed, the father argued that his daughter deserved her punishment and that his son should be exonerated. Such men, so staunchly defensive of their state, were the models for the Roman nobility. Men who valued the state above personal and private satisfactions were responsible for Rome's rise and grandeur.

Such models, though, demanded a self-sacrifice that not all men, not even all those of the patrician class, were willing to make. After the fall of the Republic and the rise of the Principate under Augustus, these models of personal devotion to the state were no longer adequate for a political system that discouraged political participation. Thus, we find in some authors from this period the development of courtly love poetry, of pastoral poems that emphasize a life away from the harsh demands of politics, a retreat from the austerity demanded by Cicero, a retreat that often led to the love of women. Women came to represent a certain frivolity, an escape from the demands placed on men by a political community that saw itself as fated to rule over others. The life dedicated to the love of women could become a pleasurable replacement for a life dedicated to the service of the state. Women did not enter the political sphere in this capacity, but joyfully brought men out of it.[9]

The treatment of women in Greek political thought, as varied as it might have been in the several authors whom we discussed in the preceding chapters, never focused on women who had particular personalities or histories of their own. The feminine stood in contrast with the masculine in the same way that philosophy stood in contrast with politics in Plato's thought. In the Greek world women symbolized the tragic tension between the whole and the particular, between death and life, and, as creatures of his philosophic artistry, they served in Plato's thought as an abstract way to attack prevalent political values. We do not know if Diotima ever existed or if Aspasia ever taught Socrates the art of rhetoric. In both cases skepticism is warranted.

In Roman thought, in contrast, women are not, for the most part, abstract creations. They are real women, be they the objects of love poetry, the recipients of letters on moral life, or characters in the histories of Rome. In the latter, women frequently influence the direction of Roman history, sometimes for the better, more often for the worse, but nevertheless they are there, playing individual roles that depend on particular personalities and moral traits. These Roman women not only existed in the poetic or philosophic imagination but participated in Rome's destiny, and their actions were acknowledged by the historians of Roman society.

When Roman authors, except Vergil, discussed women, they did not do so in the abstract fashion of the Greek authors. Only in the poems of Vergil do we find a "Platonic perspective" in which the female raises questions about the political endeavor and the "fate" of the Romans. Vergil's questioning of the Roman enterprise is not matched by his joyful love for a particular woman, as is found in the love poets of his age, but is part of his brooding over the choices that must be made as a political community grows and destroys the tenderer emotions for the sake of a pious devotion to a political ideal. For Vergil, women raise questions about the polity destined to rule the known world.

Any discussion of Roman thought encounters special problems because of the extensive time period that we consider to be Roman and the radical changes in political form and size as Rome grew from a small, rural republic to a massive empire under the control of princes and tyrants. The literature under discussion in this chapter comes from a period of only about 200 years, from 100 B.C. to A.D. 100.[10] This period encompassed a major transformation of Rome from the Republic—a Rome ruled by the senatorial aristocratic class—to the Principate under Augustus—a Rome ruled by a single man with the senatorial class in sycophantic subjection. These changes had implications for the role of women in political thought, particularly as direct participants in the destiny of Rome. We begin with Cicero, the most famous author of Republican times, and his virtual exclusion of women. The reasons for this exclusion become clearer if we consider how certain elements of his thought are transformed when incorporated into the Stoic philosophy written by Seneca during the Principate.

Because of the hold that Cicero has had on Western literary and rhetorical style, and because his writings so epitomized the "Roman Way," it is easy to see in Roman political thought only the dour devotion to duty and the whitewashing of political institutions that one finds in his political writings. Thus, we must look elsewhere for a more vibrant analysis of the fundamental tensions in political life and a questioning of a life devoted to a decadent political system. For such analysis we must move from Cicero to the historians and the poets, in whose works we do indeed find the female who is so absent in Cicero's political works. The depth of the analysis of the political world in these other writings adjoins an awareness of women's part in life of any community.

Cicero: A Political Theory Without Women

The place to find women in Roman political thought is not in the works of the most famous and influential Roman author, Marcus Tullius Cicero; yet in considering his thought we must try to understand why they are absent. Cicero is renowned for his orations, delivered as he moved, dexterously at first and then fatally, through the civil turmoil and wars in Rome during the first century B.C. But there are also volumes of letters, essays, and dialogues. Two of the dialogues concern us. They are the ones consciously modeled after Plato's *Republic* and *Laws*; Cicero even adopts the same titles for his works. "But as the most learned and serious philosopher of them all Plato had done, who first wrote about the republic and then separately about its laws, I believe it is necessary for me to do the same thing."[11] In his *Republic* and *Laws*, Cicero also discusses the best political society, but he adapts the discussion drawn from Plato to his own understandings of the political world, derived quite obviously from the Roman political experience. In neither of the two dialogues does he even allude to Socrates' or the Athenian Stranger's prescriptions concerning the role of women.[12]

In his *Republic*, Cicero sets up a conversation in which several intellectual and political leaders from an earlier period in Roman history, prior to the first century's age of troubles, discuss the nature of the best constitution and the role of the best man within that constitution. In order to engage in such a discussion, Cicero has his interlocutors agree on the meaning of *res publica*, the term the Romans used to describe their state. Literally, *res publica* means "public thing," and Cicero has his character Scipio, the military hero who saved Rome from the invasions of Hannibal, suggest that we must extend the notion of *res publica* to *res populi*, a thing that belongs to the people. As a "thing" that "belongs," it becomes objectified. To own does not mean that one necessarily participates in the upkeep or preservation of a thing. One can hire or expect others to take care of one's house or one's cat. The task of the Roman statesman or leader was to care for that which belonged to the people. The *res publica*, in contrast with the polis, was not a way of life. The Greeks, when referring to their own communities, did not speak of Athens or Sparta. Athens and Sparta were places. Athens as a city was "the Athenians." It did not exist apart from the citizens who participated in it.

While the tension between public and private was central to the Greek experience, the two were never separate. As Aristotle had emphasized, education within the *oikos* was crucial for the stability of the political community; Plato had built his best and second-best cities around the destruction or preservation of the family. In Rome the two realms were clearly demarcated. The family not only was private, but what went on in it was under the jurisdiction of the father, who had extraordinary powers of control.

In the one brief reference to women in the parts of Cicero's *Republic* that have survived the vagaries of manuscript preservation, all political concern with women is abdicated, as Cicero suggests: "Nor indeed should an overseer be put in charge of women as is customary among the Greeks, but let there be a censor to teach husbands to govern their wives."[13] Instead of bringing women into the public realm through public control over their activities or by making the internal direction of the family relevant for the polity, as had been the case in both of Plato's dialogues, Cicero leaves the women under the control of their husbands. The tension that marked the relationship between the community and the family is transcended here as the *res* of one realm is isolated from the *res* of the other.

In the *Republic*, Plato had had his Socrates search for the best city, based on justice; and Socrates found it in a community incorporating equality of the sexes and communism, a community that destroyed the family and thus what might draw individuals away from attention to the unity of the public sphere. In his *Republic*, Cicero searches for the best city but, in contrast with Socrates' abstract city founded in speech, looks for the best city in deed. He finds that city in Rome, albeit the Rome of an earlier period, of the second century B.C., before agrarian reforms and demands by the populace had limited the senatorial control and before those demands had spawned, as he saw it, the internal unrest that characterized the political world in his lifetime. Cicero's *Laws*, rather than explicating the laws appropriate for the second-best city, discusses the laws for the Rome he has described in the *Republic*. Certainly in the Rome of the past there had never been any equality of the sexes, any communism, or even any women participating in military messes with the men of the city, as they do in the regime of the Athenian Stranger.[14] Thus, the best city in deed, presented in Cicero's works, has no visible women.

Plato's *Republic* and *Laws* had been marked by a pseudo-historical focus in which Socrates and the Stranger compose historical backgrounds for their cities. Socrates focuses on the original diversity of natural talents and the consequent need for specialization and interdependence. The Stranger talks of floods and nomadic peoples. Cicero copies the Platonic model insofar as he feels compelled to revert to history in his *Republic*. But the history he includes is that of an actual city, Rome. As he recalls this history, in marked contrast with that of Livy (as we shall see below), he virtually excludes women. Lucretia, credited by many with precipitating the overthrow of the kings, is given a scant two lines in Cicero's history. The Sabine women, Verginia, and the brave Cloelia are ignored.

As suggested above in the discussion of *De Officiis*, the virtuous individual was the one who participated fully in the political life of Rome, with courage and with gusto. The one who failed to do so was, in Cicero's mind, effeminate, with "effeminate" meaning the lack of a great soul or spirit, that which adds an exalted quality to any noble actions. Only actions in the public realm, given as service to the state, could qualify as great. Women, removed from such a realm, were of no concern to the lawgiver. The dignity of the home was of a different order, outside the concern of the political community. Rome was not a regime, a way of life, but an imperial state.

Women had entered Plato's writings not only because of their role in the family but also as models of the withdrawn philosophical life. In his *Republic*, Cicero rejects both. We do not have its actual beginning lines, but the sections that remain introduce the work with exhortations to public life and to patriotism. Unlike the Platonic dialogues, which launch immediately into the dramatic action, Cicero's *Republic* begins with the author speaking. On the first page he obviously addresses someone who follows the Epicurean withdrawal from political life. The Epicureans represented a prominent intellectual style in Rome—rejecting the dominant focus on public service for a private world of pleasure. Cicero asks this Epicurean listener to reflect on all the heroes of Roman history who were motivated by a sense of public duty.

> Without it, the two Scipios would not have quenched with their own blood the rising fire of the Second Punic War; nor when fresh fuel had been added to the flames would Quintus Maximus have

stayed its violence. . . . Now take the case of Marcus Cato, who
serves as the model of an active and virtuous life for all of us
whose interests, like his, are political. Unknown and without an
inherited tradition of public service, he might surely have enjoyed
himself in quiet repose at Tusculum, a healthful and convenient
place. But he was a fool, as your philosophical friends believe, because he chose to ride the storms and tempests of public life until advanced age, rather than to live a life of ease amid the calm
and restfulness of Tusculum.[15]

Cicero continues this introduction to his work by saying that
Nature has given men the need to pursue noble actions, and that
these needs are so compelling "that they have overcome all the enticements of pleasure and of ease." The virtue that he encourages
men to pursue is one based on actions—and actions, as he understands them, must be performed in the service of the state. This
is why we were born, this we owe to the state. We cannot, however,
perform this function at a moment's notice, when the state happens to be threatened. We must train all our lives to protect and
to serve the state; this is the lifetime occupation of the true man.
It is to support these contentions that Cicero launches into his
presentation of the discussion that supposedly took place between
the heroes of an earlier century.

Their conversation at first focuses not on politics but on the
value of scientific speculation. It was reported that two suns had
appeared in the sky recently, and some had asked what set of circumstances allowed this unusual event. But others had argued
that such questions were meaningless until the issue of whether
there should be two Senates in the state had been resolved. The
argument leads to the dismissal of scientific questions that have
no direct bearing on the political events of the day. It is not that
Cicero's main interlocutors denigrate such questions; rather, they
encourage the pursuit of the necessary "military commands and
civil magistracies" as a public duty owed to the state by men such
as they.[16] The questions of whether there are or can be two suns
pales in significance for Cicero before the question of how to unify
the state, divided by hostilities between the people and the
senatorial class. In other words, attention to the political realm of
public duty excludes the philosophic perspective, which requires
leisure and withdrawal. The political world that is to take the place
of these philosophical speculations entails attention to the *res publica*, not the private realm. That was the world Cato, Quintus Maximus, and other Roman heroes had to yield when they devoted
themselves to their public duties.

Once this demarcation has been made, the discussion focuses on the best form of government. The traditional typology of regimes since Aristotle—monarchy, aristocracy, and democracy—is presented and then rejected before the interlocutors turn to the state that supposedly incorporates all three forms: Rome. Whereas in Plato's works, the philosopher had been drawn into the political world, perhaps to his detriment, here the philosopher remains the one left behind, sitting in his garden contemplating the existence of one or two suns, and helping no one—not answering Nature's call to serve the rest of mankind.

In Cicero's thought here, there is no union between philosophic speculations and politics. Despite his reliance on the *Republic* of Plato, he excludes such a union at the outset of his work on the best regime. And with that exclusion he also excludes the female, who had played such an important (albeit relatively important) role in Socrates' city. As Socrates drew women into his city along with philosophers, so Cicero exiles both. With his understanding of politics dependent on an imperial city of vast size, he conceives of the public as separate from, as demanding the abandonment of, the private. It is a separation that Cicero leaves as a heritage to be picked up later in the development of liberal political thought.[17]

Stoicism and Seneca's Consolations to Women

Cicero's emphasis on the importance of public service as the basis of the moral and good life must be understood in part as a reaction to the persistent conflict in Roman thought between the Epicureans and the Stoics. The Epicureans, concerned with the avoidance of pain in a world filled with many sources of pain, rejected political involvement for the sake of an isolated quietude. The poet Lucretius, writing in the first century B.C., around the time of Cicero, expresses the Epicurean view as he notes the delights of distance from the turmoil of civil life. He uses the imagery of one watching a shipwreck from shore:

> It's sweet, when winds blow wild on open seas,
> to watch from land your neighbor's vast travail,
> not that men's miseries bring us dear delight
> but that to see what ills we're spared is sweet;
> sweet, too, to watch the cruel contest of war
> ranging the field when you need share no danger.

> But nothing is sweeter than to dwell in peace
> high in the well-walled temples of the wise,
> whence looking down we may see other men
> ...contending, striving, straining night and day
> to rise to the top of the heap.[18]

The avoidance of pain went along with the avoidance of political ambitions. Cicero encouraged the endurance of the pain along with the pursuit of political power.

Stoicism responded to the Epicurean challenge by encouraging the political life as that which was demanded by a Nature invested with a divine quality. Nature, according to the Stoic thinkers, entails a divine *logos* or reason that governs the world. We each partake of this *logos*, which gives us a spark of its divinity. This divinity, what ties us to the universal *logos* or spirit, is our reason; and our reason perceives the duty we all have to serve the community of men rather than tend selfishly to our own interests and fears. All happens according to divine reason, and thus occurs for the best. We must learn to accept this divine plan even though it may appear to lead to individual pains and sorrows.

Stoicism went through many changes before it became part of Cicero's and other Romans' outlook.[19] The most significant change, for our purposes, was the narrowing of those who partook of the divine spark of reason from all members of the human species to a limited number of leaders in the Roman state. In its earliest manifestations Stoicism was a universal philosophy. All, and that included women, partook of divine reason. This suggested both an equality among humans and a unifying force in nature. The world may have been divided by political boundaries, but the unity of the human race transcended those boundaries.

With the decline of the polis after the conquests of Alexander, the political world had declined in importance for the individual. Government was a distant bureaucracy. Thus there was room for the unity of people bound together by a suprapolitical force.[20] Among the humans invested with this divine reason, according to the Stoics, there were some who were more attuned to its influence than others. These were the Stoic sages, men or women enduring all that Nature meted out, understanding the unity of all experiences, and representing in their acceptance and wisdom the best of human form.

The early Stoic equality and unity yielded to the Stoics of Rome, who, adopting the thought of the Stoic thinkers from the second century B.C., defined following divine reason as aiding the Roman state through public service. Moral virtue called for by that divine spark demanded an active life in the affairs of the city. This was the means to help one's fellow humans. Since the life in the Roman forum was not open to women, at least on an official level, the women were excluded from the realm of Stoic virtue. By collapsing virtue with political action, Cicero and those like him took virtue away from women.

This, however, was not true of all the Stoics in the Roman period. The post-Republican Stoic authors take us back to the original equality at the base of Stoic thought. Lucius Annaeus Seneca, living during the decadent years of the middle of the first century of the Christian era, years when Caligula and Nero were at the helm of Rome, did not always live the austere life of moral rectitude, but his writings give expression to the fundamental Stoic themes as they developed under the Principate. In letters of consolation written to women, he urges them to pursue the Stoic fortitude of men and argues that sex is no excuse for women to be weaker in their response to painful situations.

After he had been banished from Rome for having had an affair with the sister of Caligula, Seneca wrote a letter to his mother to relieve her anguish at his exile. He contrasts her with other women of her time who may use their sex as an excuse for immoderate tears, and he berates her husband and his father for being "so set on following the practice of his elders" by not allowing her "to acquire a thorough grounding in philosophical doctrine, instead of only a smattering." If she had access to such teachings, then "you would not have to shape your campaign against Fortune but merely set it going."[21] He concludes this letter with the recollection of the brave deeds of his aunt in the face of painful moments as but one example of women who have shown Stoic fortitude.

In another letter, addressed to a certain Marcia on the loss of her son, Seneca begins by asserting that he would not write to her if he did not know that she was far away from the weakness of a woman's spirit or soul (*anima*).[22] Indeed, the greatness of her *anima* "prevented me from attending to your sex."[23] At one point in the letter, he puts into Marcia's mouth the reproach, "forgetting that you offer consolation to a woman, you bring up models of men," to which Seneca responds in his own voice: "But who has said that nature has acted grudgingly with the temperament of women. . . . Believe me, there is for them equal strength, capacity, if you like, for great deeds."[24] And the deeds that he cites are Lucretia's suicide—"to Brutus we owe liberty, to Lucretia we owe

Brutus"—and those of the girl Cloelia, who led a party of young Roman girls in a daring escape across a raging river.

Seneca's examples of women's fortitude are ones of action, specifically actions that served the interests of the political community. However, in his letters of consolation he does not encourage action, as Cicero had; he encourages endurance. Some isolated women may stand out in the history of Roman heroes, but the women of his time must endure the hardships that Nature deals them.

Seneca's brand of Stoicism with its emphasis on endurance, so different from Cicero's with its emphasis on action, signifies a change in the political situation at Rome from the Republican days, when political participation could be the expected behavior of those in the privileged classes, to the Principate, when the task for the old senatorial class was survival and endurance. While women could not participate in the political life of the Republic, and thus disappear in Cicero's Stoicism of public service, women could be taught to endure their sufferings along with the men, at a time when endurance, and not participation, became the political virtue. Seneca was able to treat women as capable of the same virtues as the men because the struggle for a virtuous life came not from external actions in the public realm, but from an internal ordering of the soul. With the decline of political participation, virtue is internalized and the political regime retreats as a realm of interest. Women become the potential equals of men, as they had been in the early ages of Stoic thought.

The Historians' Women: Moral and Immoral Participants in the Rise and Fall of Rome

In the second chapter of this volume, as we looked at the comedies and the tragedies of the Greek playwrights, we saw that political thought need not be confined to the writings of those traditionally categorized as "philosophers." The plays of ancient Athens reveal a critical understanding of the role of political life in human existence and the role of the female in that life. The same is true in the writings of the historians, both Greek and Roman. The recording of how things were and how they changed is not simply the recalling of relevant historical data. Judgment must be used as to which "facts" are worthy of description; judgment must be used in placing details, in language describing those details, in the emphasis given to any of those details. All these judgments reflect a view of what is important as well as the vision of the good and the bad society that the historian wishes to offer to his readers. The historical "facts" with which the ancient historian dealt were no more limiting than the myths with which the ancient playwrights dealt in composing their tragedies.

History began as "investigations" in the fifth-century B.C. work of Herodotus, but came to be focused more directly on political developments in the writings of Thucydides, Herodotus' junior by one generation. Thucydides' history traced the conflict between Athens and Sparta and the effects of this conflict within the poleis of Greece and Sicily. Women appear in Thucydides' history only in the funeral oration, and then just to be told to endure the loss of their husbands and sons, to bear more children for the city, and to know that a woman is never to be spoken of—whether for good or for ill.

Though the Roman historians owed much to Thucydides, they differed profoundly from him in that they did not exclude women from their histories. Women were for the Roman historians, as they were not for Cicero, part of the public life, and they appeared precisely because the Romans did not separate public and private morality. Unlike the organization of the family, morality within the family was perceived as crucial for the moral life of the state. While Cicero and the Stoics of his time envisioned a world in which public affairs dominated private ones and devotion to the public realm was the appropriate moral stance, proper behavior was necessary in both realms.

If we look again at the funeral oration and Pericles' exhortation to the citizens of Athens, we see the sharp break between public and private morality: "It is right that manliness in war on behalf of their fatherland be more important than other weaknesses. For the good action makes the bad deed disappear and he benefits the community more with such action, than he does harm as a private individual."[25] If a man beat his wife, stole, was rude to his father, this meant nothing in Pericles' scheme if he was a valiant warrior in the defense of his city. All his personal failings were to be ignored before this one important virtue. The sharp distinction, so evident in this passage from Pericles' funeral oration, is not part of the Roman conception of politics, despite the demarcation between public service and the private realm. For the Roman authors, a man's moral virtue could not be ignored when one looked at his public deeds.

The moral stature of that private life often found itself reflected in the women with whom a man lived. At times the women reflected well on the men with whom they were associated and they appeared as models of virtue for all to emulate; at other times their ambitious pride was an incentive to the men in their lives to commit deeds they might never have dared alone. There are good men and there are evil men in the history of the Roman state; similarly there are good women and evil women. In the record of the political life of Rome, these women, good and evil, could not be ignored, and thus they entered into the political thought of the Roman historians.

The Roman historians were on one level concerned with bolstering political and social morality. They saw the foundation of stable political life in the individual virtue of a state's inhabitants. Often the women came to represent and offer models of the virtue necessary for such stability. When the virtue of the women wavered, so did the state. When they remained strong, the state prospered. On the other hand, there was the question—as among the Greeks—of *capax imperii*, who had the capacity to exercise power. We find in the historians that while women often demonstrate the requisite morality for the political system to survive, their forays into leadership positions or their meddling in power politics from behind the scenes usually has disastrous consequences. They are not capable of exercising power, however much the state might depend on their private virtues. In both cases, though, the thought of the Roman historians rested on political and personal morality. The period of political decline, as they understood it, was marked by declining moral standards, and the grandeur of the empire was threatened by the degradation of its citizens.[26]

Livy: Private Morality and Public Virtue

Titus Livy's massive tome, 142 books in all (not all survive), tells the story of Rome from its founding through the early years of Augustus' Principate, a total of 744 years. Livy explains in his preface to the history his motivation for embarking on such an endeavor:

> Here are the questions to which I would have every reader give his close attention—what life and morals were like; through what men and by what policies, in peace and war, empire was established and enlarged; then let him note how, with the gradual relaxation of discipline, morals first gave way, as it were, then

sank lower and lower, and finally brought us to the present time, when we can endure neither our vices nor their cure. What chiefly makes the study of history wholesome and profitable is this, that you behold the lessons of every kind of experience...from these you may choose for yourself and for your own state what to imitate, from these mark for avoidance what is shameful in the conception and shameful in the result.[27]

He is moved by the corruption, both public and private, in the Rome of his own time. In response to this corruption the historian's task is to provide models, *exempla*, of behavior worthy of emulation. He finds these *exempla* in the history of Rome as an emerging world power, and in recounting these deeds he expects to improve the moral life of his readers, his fellow citizens.

Though Livy's history covers over 700 years and traces the growth of the Roman state from a small, rural community to an imperial power with dominion over most of the known world, it is nevertheless filled with detailed stories that give expression to the main themes of moral probity and degeneracy. Many of these are famous tales from Roman legend, and several of them center on the role of women in the Roman state.

Perhaps the most famous of these is the story of Lucretia. This tale has all the charm and the force of a traditional legend. It begins as young men from the leading families of Rome, encamped outside the city, debate the virtues of their respective wives. Since they are not far from Rome, they decide to return to the city to observe, unannounced, the activities of their wives. All except Lucretia are entertaining themselves luxuriously at a dinner party. Lucretia, in contrast, is the truly virtuous wife: "Though it was late at night, [Lucretia] was busily engaged upon her wool, while her maidens toiled about her in the lamplight."[28] But this is only the beginning of the tale, for Lucretia's beauty sparks the lust of one of the young princes, the son of one who has become more tyrant than king. The young prince returns the next evening and, with the threat that he will kill her and place her naked body next to that of a slave if she resists, he rapes her. Her chastity violated, she calls her husband and some of his trusted friends back from their camp, and after imploring them to seek revenge for the rape, kills herself. The pleas of her husband and his friends that it was not her fault, that she yielded in body but not in mind, are met with Lucretia's renowned response: "Never shall unchaste women live through the example of Lucretia."[29] Her death provides the impetus for rebellion against the tyrannical ruler and thus, as Livy tells it, the Roman Republic is founded; never again will a king rule over the Roman people—all because of the chaste virtue of one woman.

We can see in this tale the blending of the private and the public spheres as Lucretia's chastity, her virtue as a wife, her dedication to "womanly virtue," not only proves to be the source of political actions but also lead to a major improvement in the character of Roman political life. The private virtue of a woman was the basis for the public virtue of the men. They were not ready to rid Rome of the tyrant on their own; they needed the impetus of Lucretia's noble act. The female here enters political life not as a public actor on her own, but as an inspiration for noble political deeds that match the virtue exhibited by the female on the level of private morality.

Many years later in Livy's history, chastity again provides the stimulus for political rebellion against tyrannical rule. The story this time is of a certain beautiful young girl named Verginia, the object of the lustful designs of one of the decemvirs, temporary tyrants appointed to deal with brief crises. Again the girl proves chaste, resists all the demands, entreaties, gifts. The decemvir then devises a legal ploy to get the girl as a household slave under his authority. This time it is the father who inserts the knife in his daughter's breast to protect her from debauchery. That act becomes the clarion call for the Roman people to rise up against the decemvir's extension of his tyrannical rule beyond the needs of the current emergency. He and his fellow decemvirs are overthrown, just as the kings had been for a similar breach of a woman's chastity. Livy himself comments on the commonalities. As he introduces the story of Verginia, he notes: "Its origin was lust, and in its consequences it was no less dreadful than the rape and suicide of Lucretia which led to the expulsion of the Tarquins."[30]

Historical causation and political transformation are understood as the result of private virtues or vices. The life of the ruler is not abstracted from his private passions, and often these passions are directed against the chastity of women. The chaste women of olden times, so unlike the women Livy sees in Rome at the end of the first century B.C., preserve public morality by attending to their private morality. Verginia's preserving her chaste nature has an effect on Roman political history that would have been impossible had she yielded to the lustful decemvir. As Livy presents it, the decline in the moral life of Roman women serves well to mark the decline in the moral life of the men who rule the state. Lucretia and Verginia are the *exempla*, "the fine things to take as models," for those, male or female, who care about the welfare of the political unit.

In contrast with these paragons of womanly virtue, Livy introduces aggressive women who are dissatisfied with their husbands' lowly status. Tanaquil provides the first example of this sort of woman; she urges her husband to leave his native Etruscan land to pursue greatness in the small but growing community of Rome. Her desires are met, and her husband becomes King Tarquin of Rome. His ascension to the throne marks the decline of Roman kingship. After he is murdered, Tanaquil hurries to an upper room of the palace and urges the people to remain calm, insisting that her husband has received only superficial wounds. She uses the time thus gained to arrange for her protégé to take over the kingship. Her self-confidence in the role of the political actor, her intrusion into public life through her ambition, make her unlike those women who influence public affairs through their private morality. Her impact on political life is a negative one. Although she ushers in the rule of Servius Tullius, one of the better kings, she sows the seeds for further intrigue and murders that undermine the legitimacy of the kingship and eventually help to bring about its downfall.

As aggressive and scheming as Tanaquil is, she is no match for her daughter-in-law, Tullia. Tullia finds herself married to a weakling, a son of Tarquin, resents his lack of ambition, and plots with another son of Tarquin to kill her husband and the king, who also happens to be her father. Tullia and her new husband, also named Tarquin, ascend the throne; and it is this Tarquin who will be the last king of Rome, for he is the one deposed by those avenging the rape and death of Lucretia.

We should note that both Tanaquil and Tullia, as Livy tells the stories, did not, and could not, act alone; in each case her ambition needed to be matched by the ambition of a male. The women themselves could not effect the evil they plotted, but neither were they alone responsible for the pursuit of power. In each case there was a willing male accomplice. We find in Livy two very different models of the female role in the politics of early Rome, one positive and one negative, as the private devotion to private virtue is played off against the desire for public power.

On a different level, there are stories in Livy's history of women displaying the public virtue of courage in times of crisis for the Roman state. In the Greek language it was linguistically impossible for a woman to be brave; the term for courage derived from the word meaning "to be a man." In Latin there are images of women displaying courage in the public realm as no woman in Athenian history did.[31] In one of Livy's stories a young woman named Cloelia, along with other girls, had been captured by the Etruscans. She was moved by the heroism of a certain Mucius Scaevola, the Roman who, as a prisoner, had thrust his hand into a fire to show his captors "how cheap they hold their bodies whose eyes are fixed upon renown."[32] Inspired by his courage, Cloelia led the group of captured girls in an escape across the Tiber, eluding a hail of missiles from the Etruscans. The Etruscans were so impressed with the courage of Cloelia that they ceased hostilities against Rome. The female's courage is as valued as that of the male, if not more so, and can, as it did in this instance, serve the city well.

A somewhat different sort of courage was displayed by the Sabine women. They had been captured during a festival by the Roman youths, whose recently founded city lacked sufficient women. Once captured, the Sabine women became Roman wives and then Roman mothers. Meanwhile, their fathers, angered by the rape of their daughters, came to take them back. A fight between the husbands and the fathers ensued: "The Sabine women, whose wrong had given rise to the war, with loosened hair and torn garments, their woman's timidity lost in a sense of their misfortune, dared to go amongst the flying missiles and, rushing from side to side, to part the hostile forces and disarm them of their anger."[33] Their courage, as Livy tells it, brought about peace between the Romans and the Sabines, just as the courage of Cloelia ended the conflict with the Etruscans. Though we, with a very different sense of causation, might have difficulty with Livy's ascription of such female courage as the cause of peace, for Livy, concerned with the presentation of moral *exempla*, this understanding of historical causation is central.

The portrait of the political life that Livy offers to his readers is not one of institutions or governmental organizations. The goodness and the badness of a political system depend on the moral qualities of the leaders and the people—both male and female. In Aristotle's vision, political life was the realm of reasoned discourse among like-minded men. With the assumption that women lacked the capacity for reasoned discourse, they could generally be excluded from the model of political life, confined to the private sphere on which the city was based. As noted above, citizenship for the Romans, in contrast, did not necessarily entail participation; the citizen was not just the one who debated in the assembly. The good citizen could be the one who demonstrated good citizenship through personal virtues, and the devotion to the public realm could be expressed by a concern with private morality. Though women did not participate in the military endeavors as the men did, and did not attend the assemblies, they could nevertheless show their devotion to Rome through the preservation of a private morality and unusual courage at critical moments. Private virtue was not the exclusive prerogative of the males. When that virtue disappeared among both the men and the women of Rome, the whole state was threatened.

It was to counter that threat to the survival of Rome that Livy wrote his history, telling his tales of deeds to be emulated and deeds to be avoided. Part of the charm of his work is the expectation that the stories of ancient Rome from its founding, in all their detail, will influence behavior of both men and women in both public and private life. Tacitus, whom we consider next, was not so sanguine either about the efficacy of history to bring about this transformation or about the potential positive role of the female, at least in Rome.

Tacitus: Women and the Regime of Tyrants

Tacitus wrote some 100 years after Augustus took control of the Roman state. While Augustus had ended the Civil Wars, the establishment of the Principate had meant the end of the republican life that Rome had enjoyed for some 500 years. At first, Tacitus claimed, the people welcomed the relief from civil strife, but the solidification of the rule of the prince led, as he interpreted it, to the degeneracy of the society on both the moral and the political level, despite Augustus' attempts to enforce morality through legislation. Tacitus comments at the beginning of his *Annals*, in reference to the death of Augustus after 13 years of rule: "How few were left who had seen the republic. The state had been revolutionized and there was not a vestige of the old sound morality."[34]

Tactitus' histories are attempts to explore the origins of this decline, to understand what it was about the particular political configuration in the Rome of the Principate that led to this decline. They thus become a profound analysis of the political regime of a hereditary dictatorship. Whereas in Livy's history of the Republic, the period up to the ascension of Augustus, women became at times models of just and honest behavior, *exempla* for both men and women, in Tacitus' work women are closer to those women scheming for political power for their husbands during the declining years of the Roman kingship. In Tacitus' analysis the participation of women in the political life of Rome is one of the diseases of the Principate.

Tacitus' writings include two extensive histories, one describing the period from the year of four emperors, A.D. 69, to the death of Domitian in A.D. 96, entitled the *Histories* and written sometime around the beginning of the second century, the other detailing the period from Augustus' death in 14 B.C. through the reign of Nero in A.D. 69, called the *Annals*. Tacitus also wrote several monographs; the most important for our purposes was the *Germania*, which describes the Germanic tribes whom the Romans met and tried to conquer at the borders of their empire. The *Germania* is something of an essay on comparative government and comparative anthropology, perhaps closest in spirit to Herodotus' histories, which offered the details of people's lives in lands other than Greece. While the *Histories* and the *Annals* trace a progressive deterioration of the political system founded by Augustus, the *Germania* offers a (perhaps utopian) vision of societies in which such corruption, both public and private, is absent. In both genres, though, the position of women serves as a parallel to the purity or the decadence of the society as a whole.

By looking first at the *Germania*, we are given a view of Tacitus' understanding of the proper place for women in the community, how they can help to preserve the community rather than work to destroy it, as they do in Rome. The Germans, as he describes them, are a "pure race" free from intermarriage with other peoples, free from the love of silver and gold. They fight bravely and show their virtue by never abandoning their shields. Kings are chosen by birth; generals, by merit. Their kings have neither unlimited nor arbitrary power, and the generals do more by example than by authority. All forms of punishment are exercised by priests, not by the kings or generals, but "what stimulates their courage the most" is that their battalions are not formed by chance, but are made up of families and clans, "so that they hear the shrieks of women, the cries of infants. They are to every man the most sacred witness of his bravery—they are his most generous applauders. The soldier brings his wounds to his mother and wife, who shrink not from counting or even demanding them and who administer both food and encouragement to the combatants."[35] The female relatives are thus responsible for rallying the armies of male fighters, for they entreat their men by vividly describing the horrors of captivity.

Rather than separating home and the battlefield, as was done in Rome, the Germans, according to Tacitus, made every effort to keep them close, to intermingle them so that the battlefield almost became the home. In terms of the Greek model described before, the reasons for fighting were kept constantly before them, not back in the city.

In contrast with this practice among the Germans, Tacitus records in his *Annals* a debate among the Romans concerning the advantages and disadvantages of having a man's wife join him when he went off to the colonies as a commander of a legion, even when administration, not war, was the purpose of the trip. One of the speakers, Severus Caecina, argues during the debate that "a train of women involves delays through luxury in peace times and panic during war, and converts a Roman army on the march to the likeness of a barbarian progress."[36] Caecina continues to chronicle the deleterious effects of women on the order of the legions, as when the women appear beside their husbands as a rival force of power capable of capturing the affections and attachments of the subordinate members. He urges a return to the austerity of the past, when women's luxurious instincts were restrained by sumptuary laws. In response, a certain Valerius Messalinus welcomes the softening of the ancient austerity and suggests that while war may require men to be unencumbered, "when they return, what worthier solace can they have after their hardships than a wife's society?"[37]

Though Caecina and Messalinus take opposite sides on the question of women, neither approaches the intensity of the unity between battlefield and family. Among the Germans the presence of wife, mother, and children was crucial; a dedication to their welfare encouraged the male warriors, who fought well and in turn benefited from the support of the women. The wives, uncorrupted by the declining morality characteristic of Rome, supported rather than hindered the actions of their men in wartime. Courage on the part of the male was not for individual glory accorded by the state, nor for gifts or honors or the rights to land, such as a Roman soldier might get for success in war; rather, he fought directly for the family. And it was the women, the wife and the moher, who honored the soldier's courage.

Tacitus' praise for the actions and customs of the German tribes must always be understood as the obverse of his condemnation of Roman society. In Rome neither wives nor mothers any longer encouraged virtue on the battlefield, and as much as they might have been solace to their husbands returning from battle, they were also the rapacious and voluptuous women whom Messalinus, even in his support for their presence on the outskirts of Rome, suggests need the vigilance of their husbands. By keeping them home in Rome, he argues, they can satisfy those less than useful passions. The question for the Romans was how to limit the harm that the women could do, not how they might positively help the community. In contrast, the female presence among the German warriors was a sign of a certain sanctity attributed to women and respect for their prescience. Women's counsel was taken seriously; the implication in Tacitus' report is that this recognition of women's abilities is well deserved. In the proper social order, women could be an asset to the community. In the Rome of the Principate, they were a problem.

The contrast is captured again in the discussion of the marriage code of the Germans, which Tacitus describes as "strict," adding that "no part of their manners is more praiseworthy. They mostly enjoy just one wife and the gifts they give one another suggest the avoidance of extravagance. The husband gives not jewelry or the like which yields to a woman's fancy and weakness, but oxen, a shield, lance, and sword, and the wife in her turn gives a set of arms."[38] The marriage is thus a community of work and protection, and avoids the frivolous relations Tacitus sees in Rome. There is among the Germans, bound by marriage, a sense of mutuality in the pursuit of virtue, of interdependence that makes each one stronger than he or she would be as an individual. In sharp contrast with his portrayal of German women, Tacitus' history of Rome is filled with stories of women pursuing their own advantage or the advantage of their offspring. These are tales of horror, vindictiveness, and disaster for the Roman people. Tacitus concludes his section on the women of the German tribes with the note that they venerate their men, "but not with servile flatteries or with sham deifications."[39] The servile flatteries and the sham deifications were reserved for the hypocritical Roman women and the men with whom they consorted.

Let us look at only some of the women in Tacitus' version of the Rome of the first century. The *Annals* begins with Augustus' death in A.D. 14. However, Augustus, having taken to himself all the functions of the Senate, the magistracies, and the laws, is in the position to choose his successor. As Tacitus tells the tale, all the young men Augustus views as potential successors die under mysterious circumstances, which always lead back with an accusing finger to Livia, his wife, until finally her son (Augustus' stepson, who was not well liked by his stepfather) is the only one left to inherit the title of prince. Tacitus goes so far as to suggest that Livia brought about Augustus' death once the succession of her son had been assured. It was not Tiberius' capacity to rule, his *capax imperii*, that brought him to power, but a women's manipulation.

Tiberius is portrayed by Tacitus as arrogant, cruel, venal, and hypocritical, the beginning of a line of rulers whose failings, particularly moral rather than political, defile the sanctity of the Roman state. Tacitus reports in his introduction to the personality of Tiberius that the gossip of the time was hostile to Tiberius and that while he ruled, the people whispered, "There was his mother too with woman's caprice. They must it seemed be subject to a woman."[40] In describing Tiberius' reign, Tacitus constantly plays up all the defects of his character. The ambitious female is thus accused of introducing into Rome, through Tiberius, the rulers who will make a sham of all virtue, public and private, in their political and personal lives.

The *Annals* offers several other examples of women like Livia. There is the elder Agrippina, the wife of Germanicus, a nephew of Tiberius. As Tacitus portrays him, Germanicus represents the chance for Rome to overthrow Tiberius and reestablish the Republic, but Tacitus' comments raise the question of whether Rome can indeed return, whether the return to the Republican government would not lead to chaos. As a result, Germanicus' appeals to republican freedoms are portrayed as directed toward acquiring power and popularity for himself. In the midst of all this stands Agrippina, currying favor with the people, wooing them to support her husband and, after his death (murder?), herself, while implicating Tiberius in the death of her husband and undercutting his authority. She stands as a constant irritation to Tiberius, but there is no suggestion by Tacitus that this role in which Agrippina delights will in any way benefit Rome; rather, it draws out the suspicious and harsh nature of Tiberius, and makes his despotism worse. Agrippina acts out of devotion not to Rome but to herself and the advancement of her own family.

Though Agrippina often stands as the suffering female threatened by the cruel power of the evil prince, Tacitus makes sure that the reader remembers the character of her offspring. She was the mother of Caligula and the grandmother of Nero. However strongly she may have rallied against Tiberius' tyranny, when her young became powerful in Rome, they made his rule look mild by comparison. As Tacitus tells of her fight against Tiberius, he makes frequent reference to her children to remind his audience of what is to come. In the obituary notice that he offers upon recording her death, Tacitus remarks: "But Agrippina who could not endure equality and loved to domineer, was with her masculine aspirations far removed from the frailties of a woman."[41] These comments are not words of praise; rather, her desire for domination meant her participation in the cruel and immoral political world of the Principate.

The portions of Tacitus' work that deal with Caligula have been lost. His record of the Roman decline resumes with the reign of Claudius, whose wife offers yet another model of the degenerate female in Roman political life of the first century. However, while Livia and Agrippina manipulate their men and the public because of a concern with the acquisition and preservation of power, Messalina uses the power that she has as the wife of Claudius to pursue her private debauchery. She lusts after gardens of one man—she gets them; she lusts after the husband of a noble-woman—she gets him. She gets whatever she wants until she goes too far, marrying her lover while she is still the wife of Claudius and while Claudius is still the prince. A forced suicide soon follows. Tacitus records this incident in considerable detail to illustrate how the Principate is totally out of control in both the public and the private realm on the highest governmental level. That the prince lacks control over his wife reflects his failure to rule the empire at large adequately.

After Messalina's death Claudius needed a new wife; Agrippina, the daughter of the elder Agrippina and Germanicus, was chosen, although, since she was Claudius' niece, they were technically guilty of incest. She had a son by a previous marriage, a young man named Nero. As evil as Livia was in her machinations to get Tiberius assured the succession to power, as debauched as Messalina was, and as eager for power as the elder Agrippina was, so—and more so—was the younger Agrippina. Even Claudius' selection of Agrippina as his wife is presented as the result of her manipulation. "On the pretext of her relationship, she paid frequent visits to her uncle, and so won his heart."[42] Once the marriage has taken place, Tacitus comments: "Then came a revolution in the state, and everything was under the control of a woman."[43] First she arranged for the death of Claudius' son-in-law so that her Nero could marry Claudius' daughter, and then she arranged for Claudius to adopt Nero in preference to his own son Britannicus. As Tacitus presents it, she moved to the worst cruelties until, poisoning Claudius, she ensured that Nero came to the throne after him. She arranged for a magnificent funeral for Claudius, but "his will was not publicly read, as preference of the stepson to the son might provoke a sense of wrong and angry feeling in the popular mind"[44]—that is, in the mind as well of those who are reading Tacitus' version of the events surrounding the ascension of Nero to power.

Thus, as the result of a mother's influence, the 17-year-old Nero became the prince of Rome, though over time "the mother's influence weakened, as Nero fell in love with a freedwoman, acting first without the mother's knowledge, and then in spite of her opposition."[45] Agrippina was unable to retain control over Nero even though she "offered the seclusion of her chamber for the concealment of indulgences youth and the highest rank might claim."[46] At the end, she completely lost her influence and the young prince decreed her death.

Tacitus' histories and the shorter pieces are concerned with the decline of the political community, the inefficacy of political participation, the deterioration of political morality, the depravity of the rulers of Rome, and the sycophancy of the Roman citizens. He offers a powerful portrait of a political regime in decline, suggesting the public and private manifestations of this decline. The women of Rome are not omitted; they are part, if not on occasion the cause, of the decline. They demonstrate and exacerbate the depravity of the regime. Tacitus highlights the inadequacy of the Principate by detailing the roles vicious women play, but it is clear that the political analysis he offers of the decline does not place the blame on the women. There they play a minor role. Rather, it is the institutional structure of a regime that limits political participation to a few and accords those few inordinate powers to control the lives, the deaths, the speech of others that accounts for this decline.

Women are part of that inadequate political system. An understanding of political life in the Principate is captured by an understanding of the role that is possible for women in such a regime. Whereas Livy had given us *exempla* of how virtuous women could serve the interests of the Republic, Tacitus can find none in a regime that destroys not only the men of the city, but the women as well. The purity of the German races stands as a model of what is possible for women elsewhere, how they can support the community. In Rome, Tacitus finds no support forthcoming from women, only self-serving ambition and immorality characteristic of both males and females in regimes ruled by tyrants.

Vergil's *Aeneid*: Women's Role in the Birth of a Nation

In the previous section we saw how two of the Roman historians used history to confront contemporary circumstances. The past is commentary on the present: Livy's noble Lucretia is commentary on the decadence of the women of his Rome; Tacitus' Livia similarly tells us about the threat of women in the Principate. Vergil was not a historian; he was a poet who wrote during the first years of Augustus' reign, under the patronage of the new prince, about the founding of Rome. As with the historians, Vergil's story is meant as commentary on the present. This story of Aeneas' departure from Troy, his travels, his affair with Dido, the queen of Carthage, and his arrival on Italian soil and alliance through marriage with the Italian people was written as the national epic and has been recognized as such. Aeneas was the national hero dedicated to future generations of the state and to the gods of the state, and pious in his devotion to do what is decreed by destiny. *Pietas* is the virtue that follows this founder of Rome from Troy to Italian soil; *pietas* is the devotion to something higher, more important than oneself; it is the devotion to one's parents, to one's gods, to one's state.

Vergil introduces women in a variety of roles as he explores their role in the founding of a great empire. It is only with the princess of the Latins, empty of all personality, that the nation can be founded. Throughout the poem other women engage our interest, but they must be rejected for the nation to be born. However, the fate of these women is no different from—indeed, highlights—the fate of the men, for Aeneas must be in the end as colorless, as lacking in personality as the bride he must take to begin the nation of the Romans. The women in this poem, particularly Dido, remind us of what must be sacrificed to found the nation that will rule the world.

The famous opening lines of the *Aeneid* set the theme for the poem: *Arma virumque cano* (I sing of arms and the man). It is a man's tale, which means that it is a tale of war. And yet throughout the epic poem, women remind us that there is more than arms and the man, that human life goes beyond the wars of men, the founding of cities, and the building of empires. The women of Vergil's poem bring out the other side of human existence; as in the Platonic works, they raise questions about political life, stand as opposites to that male experience, rather than adjusting to needs of the polity as they had, for instance, in Livy.

Aeneas follows the destiny determined for him by the gods, but, as many have noted, never does he smile or laugh as he engages in this divine mission. He is the austere man serving his nation, such a man as Cicero urged his son to become. What emotion he does express is weariness of the destiny that moves him constantly forward to Italian shores. The first picture of Aeneas offered by the poet is of a man frightened by a violent storm at sea. "At once the limbs of Aeneas are weak with fright; he groans stretching his two hands towards the stars and speaks these words: 'O, three and four times happy were those who chanced to fall before the eyes of their fathers beneath the tall walls of Troy!'"[47] Destiny weighs heavily on his shoulders.

It is this storm that brings Aeneas to the outskirts of Carthage, the land where Queen Dido rules. In contrast with the occasionally petulant Aeneas, driven by a destiny he resents, Dido is building the vibrant city of Carthage. She had fled the kingdom of Tyre, where her husband had been murdered by her brother, the king. A phantom of her dead husband appeared to her and urged her to flee. "Moved by these words she prepared the escape and her allies. They come together, those for whom there was a cruel hate for the tyrant or a sharp fear; ships, which happened to be ready, they take and load with gold...a woman accomplished all these deeds."[48] The woman here is a leader, a founder of a nation; she arranges for the escape from Tyre with the resources available to her.

As Aeneas looks down on the city from the high walls, "he marvels at the huge structure once huts, he marvels at the gate, and the noisy, paved roads." Vergil continues: "Eagerly the Tyrians press on, part raise the walls to build the citadel and turn over the stones by hand, part select a place for the home and surround it with a furrow. They choose laws and magistrates and a sacred assembly. Here some dig up a harbor, others a deep foundation for the theater...."[49] At the sight of all this Aeneas exclaims: "O, happy ones, whose walls already rise."[50]

The successful queen inspires envy in the man who must endure much before the walls of his city rise. The passive Aeneas, driven on by the gods, is no match for the energetic queen. In a sharp contrast, Aeneas "wonders and stands," "marvels at" a representation of the fall of Troy, and longs for what was, while the beautiful Dido, bearing a quiver on her shoulder, moves happily through the workmen, "pressing on the work of the rising nation."[51]

However, Dido's political skill, her energy, and her enthusiasm at the founding of the city are all undermined by her passionate nature, and the success of her reign falters as she yields to her love for Aeneas. All duty and responsibility leave her; all the political acumen disappears as her enemies, angered by her love for a foreigner, gather at the borders of Carthage. She sacrifices all for this man who will leave her. She who had once been seen pressing on the workers within her rising nation now "madly wanders through the whole city, just as a deer hit with an arrow,"[52] as her growing city ceases to grow. "No longer do the towers once begun rise up, nor do the youths practice with arms, nor prepare safe gates and ramparts for war. The works have stopped in the middle and remain idle."[53]

The passion that turns Dido away from her city also turns Aeneas away from Rome. Until fairly recently many have seen in Dido the evil queen, the Cleopatra of the past, who held Aeneas back from his destiny. She hindered progress; she was irrational, passionate, and dangerous. However, this view of Dido ignores the sympathy and admiration of the poetic depiction. Dido, the impediment to the growth of Rome, is also the individual who shows the tender, human emotions in her love for a specific man. As Rome grows, that specific man is subdued for the sake of the grander political unit. Thus the gods castigate Aeneas for being "a lover forgetful of a greater fame"[54] as he, now happy in the love of the queen, involves himself in building the towers of Carthage, not Rome.

He accepts with equanimity the gods' orders that he leave. His icy attitude toward Dido startlingly contrasts with her passion. The anguish he feels is not whether to sacrifice his love for the sake of his duty; his duty to destiny is clear. Rather, he agonizes over how to tell the queen; ultimately he avoids doing so until she, having learned of his prospective departure, confronts him. Even then he does not comfort her but explains the duty that drives him to Italy. Dido reviles him for his failure to pity her as she hisses her accusations of desertion. The passionate Dido evokes the readers', though not Aeneas', sympathy. But the state cannot be built on such passion, and the gods do not allow the man who must found the nation that is to rule the known world to be moved by love.

The story of Dido and Aeneas is told in the first half of the epic, and the contrast between the founders of the cities that will be at war in the second century B.C. is emphasized by the different responses to their love affair. Dido the queen rules well and builds a city; but when the most private of passions interferes with her public life, the city falters. Aeneas, not moved by private passions but responsive to the call of duty, founds the city of Rome and progresses to the second half of the poem, in which war and arms, political issues, dominate the love and pleasures he enjoyed in Carthage. In Vergil's vision, the female is not incapable of ruling well. He does not turn her into a vicious monster like Clytemnestra or Livia. Rather, she calls forth our admiration for her original perseverance in building her city against adversity, and our sympathy for what she suffers as Aeneas follows his destiny away from Carthage's shores.

The passionate love story of Aeneas and Dido is replaced by Aeneas' difficulties subduing the Latin tribes who already live on Italian soil and are not immediately willing to accept this stranger and his people into their midst. In Italy there is already a nation with its own king and queen, its own customs and traditions. The question that confronts the Trojans is how to conquer or to assimilate these peoples; the answer is union through marriage. This leads to the appearance of Lavinia, a mere name in the poem, a girl with no personality, no passion, no skills. The only relevant attribute is her status as daughter of the king of the Latins. In contrast with the passionate Dido, this cardboard figure of a princess illustrates what women must become if the city of Rome is to be founded.

Princess Lavinia, however, had been betrothed to a certain Turnus. He is the character who replaces Dido as the threat to Rome's founding. This time it is the anger of the male at losing his bride that leads to the difficulty, but, as with Dido, the rise of Rome depends on the crushing of the spirited individual, the one who demonstrates a certain valor and courage. The splendid individual, no matter whether male or female, must yield as destiny founds the nation that will rule over all others. The identity of Dido and Turnus, the female and the male, on this dimension illustrates the universality of the state's oppression of the outstanding personalities. Dido's anger is resolved by Aeneas' departure from Carthage, but Turnus can be conquered only by his death. Thus, the poem ends quite suddenly when Aeneas drives the sword into Turnus' breast and "his limbs loosen and become cold, and with a groan his angry soul flees to the shades below."[55] With Turnus dead, the bride will be Aeneas'; and with the last obstacle to the founding of Rome removed, the poem can end.

Through all this conflict, Lavinia remains virtually invisible. Her mother, Amata, however, does not. She, driven by a demon, passionately opposes the marriage of her daughter to the foreigner. She wants her daughter to marry Turnus, and urges the Latins and other tribes to resist the marriage to which her husband has agreed. She talks of maternal *ius*, right, which has been forgotten in the agreement to this alliance. The women of the Latins are against the alliance, for they (again like Dido) do not care for the pronouncements of the soothsayers, predicting a future greatness for Italy. They wish to preserve the nation as it exists, a pastoral haven with no pretensions to greatness. Thus, to found Rome, the women, with Amata as their leader, must be conquered as well. This happens through the death of Turnus, whom they had supported. Once he is dead, they will have to yield to the king's wish and allow Lavinia to wed the stranger, Aeneas.

Lavinia, the character in the poem with no character, parallels the pale Aeneas as he founds the nation. The forceful personalities of a Dido, an Amata, a Turnus must be overcome. The women must be pliant, easily manipulated to serve the needs of the community for alliance and for children. But, we must note, so too must the men yield and be pliant before the gods. Dido must die, and so must Turnus. Those unwilling to accept fate cannot become part of the rising nation of the Romans. The role of Lavinia seems empty to us as we read the poem, and we question the existence of such a woman as the mother of the nation; but empty too is the role of Aeneas. As Vergil writes his national epic of praise for Rome, he also indicates for his readers the cost in human terms of political greatness and the necessary subordination of resistance. For the sake of the greatness of the Roman nation, both men and women must become vacant figures. Vergil is capable of presenting strong, powerful personalities, both male and female, but these do not stand at the foundation of Rome. Those who do stand out, male and female, undermine the future greatness and must yield to the march of destiny. The brooding content of this poem, a poem intended to glorify Rome and the prince who rescued the state from civil war, finds a focus in the strong women and men who are rejected as the city grows.[56]

Conclusion

The Roman authors are not known for the sophistication of the philosophic perspectives that they offer. The comprehensive and complex visions offered by Plato or Aristotle are missing. Nevertheless, the Latin authors demonstrate a direct confrontation with the political life of a nation that sees itself as destined to rule, whether as a republic or as a principate. And in this direct confrontation with the political experience of empire, they do not, with the major exception of Cicero, ignore the existence of women. But women appear not only as representatives of the family, as we had seen in Greek thought, as symbols of the private *oikos*, but as individual participants in the political process. They become important when they can emerge from the limits of the household and influence political activity directly.

If one were to study the portrait sculptures of Roman matrons, and of Roman men, one would note the individuality of each face: the sternness of one, the tenderness of another. The women portrayed by these sculptors are individuals with their own personalities and identities. The political theorist of Rome focused on Rome, the particular nation, inhabited by particular individuals, and ruled by particular laws. Their understanding of the political world was bounded for the most part by those particulars, and failed to reach the broader perspective of their Greek predecessors. But their orientation turned the reader to the individual—and those individuals included both women and men. The *Aeneid* suggested the threat to individuality inherent in the Roman state. But, then, it is Vergil and not Cicero who is truly closest to being the Roman Plato.

6

Early Christianity and Medieval Political Thought: Virginity, Equality, and the Meaning of Community

Introduction

It was during the reign of Tiberius that Jesus Christ was crucified in what was then a distant part of the Roman Empire. Christ's disciples, expounding on his divinity and the meaning of his teachings and miracles, incorporated into the developing Christian theology many of the themes and traditions of the Jewish, Greek, and Roman heritage from which they came. However, in contrast with those traditions out of which Christianity grew, there was at first in this new religion an unusual acceptance of the female. From the very beginning, as reported in the stories of the apostles, Christ spoke to women as he spoke to men, acted for the sake of the welfare of women as he acted for the welfare of men. Among his followers were women as well as men, and at the crucial point of his resurrection, he revealed himself first to two women, his mother and Mary Magdelene. These were the ones to report the miracle of Christ's resurrection to his male disciples.

We learn from the apostles that during his life, Christ's miraculous healing powers worked on both men and women. After he heals a man of palsy, a woman who touches his cloak is healed of her untoward bleeding. In the Gospel of St. Luke especially, Christ's teachings appear as parables, but these parables are paired in such a way that one appeals to the experiences of a man while the other appeals to the experiences of a woman: the man understands the kingdom of God by reflecting on the mustard seed that becomes an enormous plant; the female, by reflecting on the leaven that makes her bread rise. To help one understand the joy of saving a sinner, Christ refers to a man's joy at finding the one sheep that has strayed from the flock and to a woman's joy at finding, as she sweeps, the one coin out of ten that she has lost.[1] The stories, the parables, the history from the gospels all indicate that the apostles, carrying forth the teachings of Christ, speak equally to men and to women, that the divinity of Christ is in no way diminished by his associations with and attention to the female.[2]

While appealing to both female and male, Christianity turned its adherents' attention away from the current world and focused their concern on the world to come, on what the early Christians saw as the imminent second coming of Christ, the *eschaton* (the end of history in this world). At that moment in time, those worthy of salvation would be rewarded for their virtue and devotion to God, while those unworthy of salvation would be sent to their eternal damnation. The final judgment at that moment and the life after death claimed priority over the political world and its petty affairs. One turned beyond all experienced in the day-to-day lives of families, of markets, of politics. Salvation no longer came, as it did to a man such as Cicero, from participation in the city, but from the devotion to God, who transcended the immediate realm of experience. Salvation depended on an internal love, private to the self (though often nurtured in a community of Christians), which others might never be able to perceive or understand. From the visible world of action and of bodies, of wars and of kings, Christianity turned to the invisible world of the soul and the afterlife.

For the Romans, what was real was Rome, the city itself. The political thought of the Romans centered on the value of that city. However much Tacitus might have criticized the regime of the Principate, he wrote his histories because he valued Rome and cared about its potential for improvement. For Cicero, Rome was the best regime, not a figment of his imagination (as Socrates' city had been for him) but one that truly existed. Christianity raised questions about the value of Rome or any city, about a world of constant change and multiplicity. By turning away from the city of experience, Christianity also turned away from the particularity of each city.

The Christian God, unlike the Jewish God or Roman and Greek gods, was a God for all peoples. The gods of the ancients identified with a particular unit—political or familial—and gave to that unit the cohesion and strength to ward off its enemies. The Christian was to give up those particular gods for the universal God. Religious life thus was not, at least at first, to be tied to the political life of the community. Instead, the political community, the Roman Empire, was to be endured, its rulers obeyed. The focus was not directed toward a particular regime, but toward that which bound together men and women as no political and social ties could ever do. Christianity thus threatened the viability of the political community to which the ancients had been devoted.

The impact of Christianity on the traditional institutions of Roman society is well captured by the activities of St. Jerome, who, in the fourth century, educated the wealthy women of the upper classes in Rome to a love of Christ and the Christian way of life. He drew them away from the vulgarity and immorality of the Rome in which they lived and toward a love of God, but in so doing he also drew them away from their families, from which had come the leaders for political administration at Rome. Some of the women he educated followed him to Bethlehem to participate in the establishment of some of the earliest monasteries and convents.

Among his writings one finds praise of women, such as the famous Paula: She "left behind her house, children, servants and property...[whose] infant son, Toxotius, stretches forth his hands and [whose] older daughter, Rufina, sobs silently on the pier, but 'overcoming her love for her children with her love for God,' and turning her eyes heavenward, she sails out to sea, with never a backwards glance."[3] The divinity that had been associated with the hearths of the city and of the family has ascended to a higher realm beyond the city and beyond the family. With the gods no longer part of the individual household, a religious woman turns away from her family in her devotion to the divine. Both male and female, then, left the old gods of city and family to find the new God offered them by the Christian missionaries.

The Greeks too had recognized a tension between a devotion to a particular city and to a transcendental reality. Plato's writings are filled with the conflict between the demands of the philosopher, who looks to universals beyond the city, and the demands of the city. Plato's philosophers recognized a truth that was higher than the city, at the same time that they recognized that the human needs the city to survive. Aristotle, even as he saw the *telos* of man in the city, knew that a better life existed in the life of contemplation. But for both Plato and Aristotle this life of contemplation was open to only a few. Plato's philosophers could never be the numerous masses.

Christianity, in contrast, opened that life to all. Anyone could love this universal God: slave or master, female or male. The city, which in Greek thought had been so necessary except for those very special individuals such as Socrates, declined in importance. It was no longer necessary, since humans could now find their salvation and a meaning for their lives outside the confines of the city. The city was to be endured like all the other trials and tribulations of this life. The city was not a good, or an institution that could be made better, but a necessary consequence of original sin. Thus, it could no longer be the center of the male's fulfillment of self-expression. Therefore, the separation of the male and the female demanded by the ancient city or the ancient empire was not required by the early Christian perspective, which transcended both city and family.

The dichotomization between the seen world and the realm beyond sight had definite roots in Platonic philosophy, roots carried forth in the early and late expressions of Stoicism as well. In both Platonism and Stoicism, the body is denigrated while reason and the soul, the unseen, are elevated. With this dichotomization between the world of perceived bodies and unseen souls, the female need not be tied to her body—that which is seen—but can transcend that merely physical aspect of herself. Among some followers of the Platonic or Stoic schools, the potential for sexual equality existed precisely because of the denigration of the body that separated the female from the male. In Plato's *Republic* the denigration of the body had allowed for women in the guardian class. In Seneca's Stoicism, denigration of the ephemeral world joined with the expectation of female virtue and stamina.

This perspective also permeated some of the early expressions of Christianity as the body came to be of lesser importance. Later in the Middle Ages, when the *eschaton* no longer appeared imminent, when history did not seem about to end, and when Aristotle was reintroduced into Western thought through the Arab authors, this denigration subsided. The realm experienced by our senses, and thereby the political realm, resurfaced as an important and valued part of the divine order with a worth that went beyond the simple endurance found in earlier Christian writers. With the reestablishment of the importance of the political realm, however, there returned the lowered status of the female, who was denied access to this public arena. As the political community increased in importance, the female found herself in a subordinate and inferior position.

The tension in Christianity's response to the physical world, as the realm that must have a certain worth since it was a divine creation or as that which is all bad because it moves one away from devotion to the divine, directly affected attitudes toward political life as well as toward women. As we shall see below, the denigration of the physical allowed the female to rise in her status as soul, while the acceptance of the value of the physical world led to a lowering of her stature as body. In the following sections we shall consider only three of the outstanding authors of this period who considered the issue of how the female could be a part of God's universe and the social system men endured or enjoyed as they passed their time on earth.

Early Christianity: St. Paul, St. Augustine, and the Retreat from Politics

In the fourth century Christianity became the official religion of Rome, endorsed and adopted by the Roman emperor Constantine. The spread of the religion from a minor, illegal mystery cult at the beginning of the first century to the official religion some 300 years later was marked by early struggles to define its doctrines and to establish the organization of its church. The apostles and the Church Fathers were those active in the early period of self-definition; among them were men as different as Tertullian, who declared women to be the "gateway to hell," and St. Jerome, who seriously engaged in the education of women and wrote extensive, detailed letters on the education necessary for a young girl. The aim of these writers was to clarify what it meant to live the life of a Christian during the first four centuries of the religion's existence. They wrote at a time when the new religion was struggling to assert itself emotionally among the inhabitants of the vast Roman Empire and politically against the competing sources of authority, be they the institutional structure of the Roman state or other religious sects.

At the same time, and continuing for some centuries, there arose two new phenomena: single-sex communities based on Christian principles and the female leader whose strength and influence depended on her devotion to the divine. We shall consider below some of the political implications of these developments that run counter to previous political and social experience. We shall then consider two of the major authors from this period: St. Paul, from the first century, whose letters in the New Testament helped to establish the guidelines for the Christian community, and St. Augustine, writing at the beginning of the fifth century, when Christianity, already well established, was under attack for its failure to protect the Romans against invasions from the north. Paul's letters contain some of the more famous misogynist statements of the early Christians that need to be reevaluated in terms of their context. Augustine presents the most comprehensive perspective of all the early writings on the questions that arise from Christianity's approach to theological, moral, and political questions, an approach to be challenged in certain selective ways only some eight centuries later, in the writings of St. Thomas Aquinas. St. Paul and St. Augustine, each in his own way, reflect the radical transformation of political thought that accompanied the rise of Christianity and the place of women in the changing political perspectives.

St. Paul: A New Freedom and a New Equality

It is in the speeches and the writings of Christ's disciples during the century after his crucifixion that Christianity acquired its distinctive characteristics and ecclesiastical organization; the writings of St. Paul had the most significant impact on the political role of this new religion, for Paul, concerned that the new Christian communities not alienate the officials capable of destroying them, told the followers of Christ to accept the authority of those who were set to rule over them: "Let every person be subject to the governing authorities. For there is no authority except from God, and those that exist have been instituted by God."[4]

However, while obedience to the political authorities and their laws is necessary, such obedience is separated by Paul from justice, the traditional political virtue. Justice for him is no longer part of the political community; rather, justice and the true law are external to the political world. Obedience to the law is not defined by political powers. Instead, "he who loves his neighbor has fulfilled the law . . . love does no wrong to a neighbor; therefore love is the fulfilling of the law."[5] The highest virtues do not come from political life, nor are they defined by the political authorities. No longer does the classical question of who should rule, who is *capax imperii*, control political thought. Such a question is beyond consideration for human beings, because it is God who decides who should rule, not we mortals. God's choices may not always be comprehensible to those of limited vision, but they need not be.

The denigration of the political world as a realm only of

authority and not of virtue relates to the place of women in Paul's thought. St. Paul is notorious among some for what appears to be blatant misogyny. We find him, for example, telling the Corinthians that women must be silent in church and that they must cover their heads, lest they offend God, since "the head of every man is Christ, the head of a woman is her husband."[6] He also belittles the married state: "It is good for a man not to touch a woman....For I would that all men were even as myself."[7] Though he then admonishes that it is better to marry than to burn, marrying is appropriate only for those who are weak. However, we must consider the context of these quotes concerning women and the place of marriage, and unravel their implications for the relationship of this new religion to the political world that surrounded its followers.

The admonition to women to keep silent in church suggests that among the Corinthians to whom Paul spoke these words, women were not silent—they participated in the activities of the church as they could not have done in the other religions of the time, especially in the Jewish religion, in which women were kept physically apart from the men during religious services and in which St. Paul was raised. But more important, their silence was necessary, not because women lacked the intelligence or spirituality to speak well in the house of God, but because their speech would distract the men in church from devotion to God. The speech of females aroused in men sexual desires inappropriate when they were supposed to be worshipping and concentrating on their love of God. Paul recognized the power of sexuality to draw men away from the world that really mattered, and thus the female speaking in church threatened the salvation of the men worshipping there. Paul's writings also include the admonitions to women to cover themselves in church, lest vision of their flesh blot out the vision of the divine. Not because of their inferiority, but because of their power, were women to be silent in church.[8]

In a similar fashion we must understand Paul's invocations against marriage. Marriage is to be accepted in order to escape the greater immorality of promiscuity, but it is best to be able to escape any desire for sexual relations. Again, this is not because of the denigration of the woman to whom a man binds himself through sexual ties, but because marriage ties one to the realm of worldly troubles instead of allowing undivided dedication to God:

> The unmarried man is anxious about the affairs of the Lord, how to please the Lord; but the married man is anxious about worldly affairs, how to please his wife, and his interests are divided. And

> the unmarried woman or girl is anxious about the affairs of the
> Lord, how to be holy in body and spirit; but the married woman
> is anxious about worldly affairs, how to please her husband.[9]

The married man and the married female were both bound by the
decadent world of the flesh. Only through a life of chastity could
they both be free and show a singleness of purpose in their love
and worship of the divine. Only through such chastity could the
female legitimately escape the family, which had defined her existence until this time.[10]

We saw in our discussion of the Greek authors the tension between the family and the polis, the latter, demanding the willingness to sacrifice oneself, opposed the life-giving family; this did not
mean that the polis was to be rejected, but neither could the family
be transcended. Each was necessary for the continued existence
and completion of the human species. However, the Greeks
throughout maintained the priority of the city. Neither among the
Greeks nor among the Christians was marriage totally to be
avoided, but it was recognized that marriage, and the family that
comes from marriage, opposes in some ways what is truly important in human life. In one case it is God and the world of the divine; in the other, the political world and the public realm. The
family, the community of man, woman, and children, though
necessary for many in Christianity, considering our bodily existence, and necessary in the polis to provide new citizens, is
nevertheless an inferior community.

While Paul sees marriage as the life open to those who can do
no better, much as Aristotle sees the polity as the realm open to
those who cannot be philosophers, Paul encourages within marriage mutual obligations between partners that had not been
characteristic of the earlier understandings of the marriage relationship. Though the husband retains authority over his wife, there
is a new emphasis on his responsibility to her. The relationship between man and woman in marriage replaces in certain ways the
reciprocal political relationship that had characterized some of the
earlier authors we have considered. "The husband should give to
his wife her conjugal rights, and likewise the wife to her husband.
For the wife does not rule over her own body, but the husband
does; likewise the husband does not rule over his own body, but
the wife does."[11] Involvement in the marriage is one of cooperation and fidelity. The male is no less bound to preserve his chastity
than is the female.

The mutuality of the obligations reflects the general equality at the basis of Paul's thought. In Galatians he reminds his audience: "There is neither Jew nor Greek, there is neither slave nor free, there is neither male nor female; for you are all one in Christ Jesus."[12] The wife's expectations from the marriage relationship need not be less than those of the male. Yet, with all this new emphasis on mutual obligation and fidelity within marriage, the relationship between man and woman is still inferior to the potential one that men and women might have with God, if they could abstain from their sexual passions. Thus, while marriage serves as a bulwark against promiscuity, virginity remains the most highly praised state for both male and female.

While the family in a certain sense replaces the city as the realm of mutual obligations, there develops in Paul's writings a new concept of community that replaces both family and city. It is not a political community, as had been known in the classical period, but a community in which each member is formed in the body of Christ.

> For as the body is one, and hath many members of that one body, being many, are one body, so also is Christ. . . . And those members of the body which we think to be less honorable, upon these we bestow more abundant honor; and our uncomely parts have more abundant comeliness. . . . That there should be no schism in the body; but that the members should have the same care one for another. . . . Now ye are the body of Christ, and members in particular.[13]

There is an interdependence expressed between the male and the female in this new conception of community, an interdependence that transcends the physical realm. No longer is it necessary, as it was in Greece and Rome, for one to be a member of a family, an *oikos* or *familia*, to be part of the community. The celibate or childless couple whom Augustus fined for their lack of support for Rome become the most worthy members of the new community.

The community incorporated in the body of Christ is not a physical one, and thus external criteria for participation in that community are no longer relevant. Membership in the Jewish community had been dependent in part on circumcision. In the new Christian community circumcision is no longer required; it is even scorned, since physical traits are no longer relevant for membership in this community. Similarly, the female or the male bodies are irrelevant, since the sex of the individual does not determine membership in a community dependent on a common worship rather than on any common physical or intellectual traits. There is thus the replacement of the concept of community from the world of daily experience by the world of the spirit, and with that replacement, politics and its discrimination of the roles of the male and the female declines in importance.[14]

With this change in the concept of community, women become potential participants in the community in a fashion denied to them when participation had been based on strength in battle or on the ability to speak well among men. This potential participation, however, could best be realized by the abstention from other forms of community that had dominated the classical world.[15] For women, as for men, this meant the abstention from marriage, from the carnal relationship that led to the birth of children. What had previously been seen as the only function for the female now was rejected and another option, virginity, was available for women, no longer limited by the physical characteristics of their bodies.

Women could deny their sexuality and become part of the community in the body of Christ on an equal basis with the males who similarly preserved the sexual innocence of their bodies. By remaining virgins, both sexes freed themselves for devotion to the divine as they avoided the distractions of a worldly existence. Equal in their abstention, male and female were equal in their relation to the divine. Thus they reached a "celestial mentality."[16] By so striving to be joined with God and preserving her virginity, the female could avoid the pain and hardship women suffered in childbirth, woman's punishment for her part in original sin.[17]

Central to the new understanding of community and to the emphasis on the virginity of those who were to be part of the body of Christ was the expectation of the imminent *eschaton*, the second coming of Christ. In the midst of his discussion of virginity and its exalted state, Paul comments: "For the fashion of this world passeth away."[18] Within their lifetime, Paul promises the Christians to whom he speaks, the world as they know it will cease. Even stronger are the words of Tertullian, writing a century later than Paul: "The world is full . . . the elements scarcely suffice our needs. Our needs press. . . . Pestilence, famine, wars, and the swallowing of cities are intended, indeed as remedies, as prunings against the human race."[19]

Since this world is to pass soon, since Christ is about to appear again and mark the final day of judgment, one need not be concerned with the creation of children. The world does not need to be populated with new souls; the old rationale for the family and the female's role within the family—the propagation of the next generation in order to keep the city in existence—disappears. Pericles, speaking to the Athenians in his funeral oration, had said to the parents of the soldiers who died in battle: "Bear more sons as a security to the city."[20] The community of the spirit does not require sons to defend it, and thus the female need not enter into the marital relationship for the sake of the community. A life devoted to a love of God, and not to the birth and nurturing of new citizens, becomes a viable option.

The equality inherent in Paul's vision of Christianity is not a social equality, but a new form of equality that admits the soul, but not the body. Since the body is no longer needed to reproduce itself, this new form of equality becomes a meaningful alternative to the ancient hierarchical relations between male and female. Paul's radical proposals for the place of women in this new religion and their implications for the transformation of political thought were not always readily accepted by the developing institutions of the Church, which structured itself according to the modes of organization found in the society around it. Some of Paul's comments came to serve conservative purposes within this context, instead of working to carry forth the transformations implicit in them. This does not mean, however, that Christianity lacked the capacity to envision a genuinely new perspective on the female as a member of a newly conceived community.

St. Augustine: Women in the City of God

Some 300 years after Paul and 100 years after Christianity became the official religion associated with the institutional structures at Rome, St. Augustine became bishop of Hippo in northern Africa. Before and during his tenure as bishop, he produced a massive number of books, 117 in all.[21] These writings and sermons gave Christian theology its shape and orientation for centuries to come. In the most important work for those interested in the development of political theory, *The City of God*, Augustine divides humans into two communities, one focusing on man and the other on God. Augustine adopts the political vocabulary of Rome for his analysis and accepts Cicero's definition of a *civitas* as a group of men joined in their agreement about the meaning of *ius*, right. For Cicero, the expression of this *ius* is captured by the *res publica* of Rome. For Augustine, what unifies each community is either a love of God, for the *civitas dei*, or the love of self, for the *civitas hominum*.

Using an explicitly political vocabulary, Augustine writes of these two *civitates*, inhabited by citizens (*cives*); at the same time, he removes any political connotations from these terms. There are no political boundaries, no institutions, no membership criteria such as birth, or wealth, or military service—or sex. Rather, the differences between the two cities depend on the orientation of the souls of the citizens, whether toward a love of God (which entitles one to citizenship in the City of God) or toward avarice and greed (which indicates citizenship in the City of Men). The language used previously to describe a political unit and the members thereof becomes in Augustine's works the language of spiritual relations.

With this transformation of political terms, Augustine establishes the priority of the nonpolitical world. The political realm, as we know it, is the result of man's fall from grace; it is an unfortunate necessity required by man's inclination to dominate others. The political institutions created to restrain men from harming one another will always be part of the defective conditions of this life, of a world in which we have lost control of our physical being. Even in the best circumstances, the political realm as we know it can be only a weak reflection of the realm of true virtue and true justice. For instance, no matter how honest a judge may be, justice can be found only with God. The City of Men, that community of individuals concerned only with this world, is one of deceit, ambition, and vice, one of slavery, hierarchy, and repression. The aim for mankind, thus, is to recognize the weakness of the body, which can lead only to false pleasures such as those that come from our sexuality, and to turn to that which is divine.

In the City of God, the universal community where all citizens overcome the control their bodies exercise over them, humans are unified in their love of God as they strive for a complete happiness in the knowledge of God through the soul. No political institutions are necessary to create and preserve this community; no inequality dominates human relations; no hierarchy determines an individual's place in this city. The political implications of this perspective are obvious. Traditional political life can lead only to a false and incomplete happiness; it is not a pursuit worthy in itself.

In the City of Man, where the body rather than the spirit is dominant, the female is inferior because of her inferior body and her weakness. In the City of God she transcends the limitations of her body to become part of the new conception of the *civitas* as the unity of those who love God. Since the directly political implications of the terms *cives* and *civitas* have been removed, the female can be part of a community that had been denied her by the definitions of citizenship in the Roman state. Augustine's analysis here is related to his interpretations of the two stories of the creation of women in Genesis. In the first version, at Genesis 1:27, the Bible says: "And God created man in His own image, in the image of God He created him; male and female created He them."[22] The second version portrays Adam in a deep sleep as God

> . . . took one of his ribs, and closed up the place with flesh instead thereof. And the rib, which the Lord God had taken from the man, made He a woman, and brought her unto the man. And the man said: This is now bone of my bones, and flesh of my flesh: she shall be called Woman, because she was taken out of Man. And therefore shall a man leave his father and mother, and shall cleave unto his wife and they shall be one flesh.[23]

In the first version the Bible describes an instantaneous creation; there, Augustine argues, the souls of the male and the female are identical. Eve's soul comes from God and is not derived from that of Adam.[24] She comes into being at the same time as Adam. In the spiritual relationship Eve need not be an inferior to Adam, nor woman to man. In the City of God all are equal. Temporality gives precedence to neither sex. Their equality derives from their direct relationship to God. Here Eve is *homo*, a human being. The second version, in contrast, focuses on the body, on Eve's creation from the body, the bones of Adam. Here she is *femina*, woman, created to serve the needs of man, as well as a constant reminder of sin.

The duality characteristic of all human experience determines the ambiguous position of woman as both equal and inferior. The woman who is defined by her body reflects carnality, and thus sin. On the other hand, the journey to God by the human goes beyond what is carnal and ties one to the world of masters and slaves, superiors and inferiors. When the female's soul is oriented toward God, then she can be equal to the male. When she is a member of the City of God, she is a *civis*, as is the male.[25] At the time of the Last Judgment, when salvation is at hand, the female will rise along with the male. Indeed, the female body will rise with the male body; at that point the body will no longer be bound by the remembrance of sin, for lust ceases when the Kingdom of God has come.[26] Then even the body of the female will not lead to inequality.

Augustine's exhortations to recognize the inferiority of the political world as it searches for an unattainable peace and offers false happiness was matched by his exhortations to rise above the world of sexuality, marriage, and the children who emerge from these expressions of sexual pleasures. Augustine's views elaborate the themes developed in Paul's writings, but are given a sharper focus because his writings are in part a response to the Manichaeans. Between the time of Paul and that of Augustine, there had arisen a variety of Christian sects. Among these were the Manichaeans, who divided the world into good and evil, viewing the soul as good and the body as evil. The world was a realm of conflict between these two forces, and the body needed to be subdued in the battle to bring about the final victory of God against the devil. Augustine, confounded by the problem of the cause of evil, turned for a time to the Manichaeans for an answer. They assuaged his guilt at his lustful desires by asserting the ultimate separation of the body from the soul,[27] and thus the freedom from the evil part of himself once the body could be sloughed off.

Augustine came to reject Manichaean theology partly on the grounds of oversimplification, but also because of his ultimate acceptance of the physical world as the creation of God and not of the devil. The physical world, therefore, could not be dismissed as wholly evil. Rather, evil came from human sin and man's consequent failure to control his physical being. Sexuality in particular reveals the limits of our powers. "The lust that excites the indecent parts of the body . . . assumes power not only over the whole body, and not only from the outside, but also internally; it disturbs the whole man, when the mental emotion comes and mingles with the physical craving."[28] The mind cannot function when so affected by lust, nor can the mind control the expressions of this lust. The language used to describe the nature of the punishment for original sin is explicit: "Sometimes the impulse is an unwanted intruder, sometimes it abandons the eager lover, and desire cools off in the body while it is at boiling heat in the mind."[29] The Manichaean separation of body and soul was inadequate to deal with these tensions so vividly suggested by sexuality. Nor did the Manichaeans deal adequately with "the almost total extinction of mental alertness" during the sexual act.[30]

Augustine's response to the powerful force of sexual desire was to encourage virginity and chastity. Virginity was the highest condition of life; widows should not remarry, for when married, one is always subject to distractions from the love of God and to the weaknesses of the soul and mind. In the Old Testament, Jews had been exhorted to be fruitful and to multiply; this was a divine blessing. But for Augustine this exhortation was necessary so that the Messiah could be born. Now, after the birth of Christ, such fruitfulness was no longer necessary; thus marriage no longer held an exalted position. It was demoted to an inferior state where humans satisfy lustful desires, those signs of their sinfulness and inability to control their will. Christianity, instead of leading to a physical fruitfulness of bodies, was to lead to a spiritual fruitfulness.[31]

This change in attitude toward marriage was reflected in the political situation as well. Whereas the Old Testament had focused on political regimes, on kings and on rulers for the Jewish people, now, since the birth of Christ, the world no longer needed the political realm to prepare for his birth. The political world, so important as the world looked forward to the birth of Christ, could now yield to the spiritual world of the City of God. Now that fruitfulness was no longer a physical term, marriage was to be like the City of God, a spiritual relationship in which the sex of the partners in marriage did not matter, rather than the physical relationship in which the sex did matter very much. Thus, Augustine emphasizes the importance of continence in marriage.[32] The love of one spouse for another is not as a husband for a wife or a wife for a husband, but as a creature of God. As the City of God replaced the traditional political community mired in the physical realm, so did a new conception of a spiritual marriage replace the relationship that previously had been concerned with the creation of the child.[33]

The consequences of thus abstracting from sexuality are similar to those noted in reference to Paul. Marriage, the formal relationship between the husband and the wife, lost its fundamental ties to the political world. Whereas previously marriage had been the concern of the political community because in the family the future citizens of the state were to be born, now the asexual marriage from which no children would issue had no direct links with the political structure. In Greece membership in the city depended on membership in the *oikos*; in Rome men who failed to marry were fined and bonuses were given when children were born. Both Greece and Rome acknowledged the transience of the community of men. Thus, they relied on generation to turn the mortal city into an immortal community. The state could not survive without a steady stream of new bodies. With the decline in the value of the state, new bodies were no longer needed. The marriage relationship could ignore the relationship to the physical state. The City of God, as a spiritual orientation of the soul, did not depend on the production of bodies, on the physical conjoining of male and female. The City of God took away the need for the female to perform within the context of the family, and thus the marriage relationship lost its earlier meaning for the political world.

Leadership and the New Community of Women: The Theoretical Significance of the Rise of Convents and Female Saints

In the world of ancient Greece, tales had been told of the Amazons, women who lived without men. On the temples at Athens, on the pottery were scenes of these warrior women in battle with the male forces of civilization, Heracles and Theseus. The women, riding horses, carried bows and quivers of arrows; their right breasts were cut off so that they might use their weapons more easily. Thus their name, *a-mazon*, without a breast. The existence somewhere on the Asian continent of a community of women who consciously and forcefully excluded men represented for the Greeks an anti-polis. The Amazons not only fought on the battlefield but they organized themselves, had their own leaders and warrior heroines, and even, in some versions, enslaved other cities. The single-sex community of the Amazons was the Greek world turned upside down, for the Greeks depended on women not as warriors but as bearers of children, as the means by which the wealth of the family and the existence of the community continued over time.

The historicity of the Amazons is questionable at best. The isolated community of women warriors was part of the Greek world's series of myths of self-definition through a consideration of what is opposite. In the early centuries of the Christian era, the idea of single-sex communities no longer represented a myth or fantasy world of the "real world" turned upside down; in their actual institution they became a confirmation that the political world, among those who accepted Christianity, *had* been turned upside down. Their creation and their survival depended on the complete rejection of the political apparatus of Greece and Rome, which had required the existence of the family for their preservation and definition of legitimacy. The emerging monasteries and convents were not theoretical anti-communities, but new forms of social relations in their own right, based on principles antithetical to previous political structures.

The asceticism of early Christianity, with its focus on the *eschaton*, was behind the attempts to "segregate the sexes [so as] to improve the circumstances for prayer and contemplation."[34] This concentration on the other world meant the disregard not only of sexual reproduction but also of the political and organizational models of Rome and Athens, which had in their time emphasized action—of the warrior or of the speaker—rather than contemplation.[35] The new single-sex communities of nuns and monks consciously eschewed both sexuality and politics. They were replenished by recruits drawn to them by the pull of asceticism and its specific withdrawal from political life. For them membership was not defined by strict lines of legitimacy, nor was it a reward for successes in military campaigns, as had become the case in Rome.

The history of the rise of convents is difficult to trace precisely,[36] though it appears that "by the fourth century monastic life was attracting increasing numbers of women and men who strove for moral perfection through asceticism."[37] Although salvation is an individual event in Christian theology, from its earliest expressions the individual is aided by the support of others in his or her devotion. Thus, the community of ascetics devoted to the individual salvation of each member grew up alongside the ascetic hermits isolating themselves from all human affairs through a retreat to the most inhospitable areas of the world. Among the most famous establishments for nuns was that of the abbess Macrina, sister of St. Basil, who founded her convent in the latter years of the fourth century.[38]

At about the same time Paula left Rome with her daughter and other Roman matrons to follow St. Jerome, an enthusiastic defender of monastic life, first to Palestine and then to Bethlehem. There she founded four monasteries, three for nuns, headed by herself, and one for monks, to be headed by Jerome. Jerome had been an emphatic defender of the perpetual chastity of Mary against those who argued that she had borne children with Joseph after the birth of Christ. He transmitted to the Roman women who became his followers the emphasis on celibacy that became a crucial factor in their retreat to their convents. It appears that several of the early religious communities were founded as double monasteries, as was the case with Jerome and Paula; one section was for nuns and the other for monks. The level of interaction between the two and the locus of final authority in the abbess or the abbot varied with time and place, but at least in the early period it was possible for "abbesses [to] rule establishments that some-times included thousands of men and women and vast amounts of territory."[39]

As Paula and the circle of women from Rome who followed St. Jerome demonstrated, in the early years of the rise of monasteries and convents, asceticism, the total rejection of worldly goods, and religiosity were not limited to males. Women could show the same level of self-denial and devotion to God as men. There was no priority attributed to being a male rather than a female ascetic; both denied the demands of the body, the luxuries they had previously enjoyed, and both denied their sexuality. While the political hero in the ancient world had often been defined by heroic efforts in battle or in the assemblies, the new notion of virtue that turned men away from political participation allowed for new models of virtue—models that, because they depended on the denial of body rather than on the exploitation of the activities of those bodies, allowed for the inclusion of women. Early on, the lions had not attended to the differences between the sexes; later, when the lions were no longer a threat, the depth of devotion remained unrelated to sex. Thus, by depoliticizing virtue, virtue was no longer sex-specific; no longer was the "heroine" one to be imitated only by women. The female saint who had shown the extremes of devotion through self-denial and the nurturing of others was a model worthy of imitation by both sexes. Virtue was not only depoliticized; it was desexed.

Along with this new vision of virtue went a new vision of power and a new answer to the traditional question of who is fit to rule. Again the political model of power accorded to military victors or fine speakers such as Cicero was replaced; power belonged to those having the greatest devotion to the divine and the deepest knowledge of religious questions. Some were repaid for that devotion and learning by visions and direct contact with divine figures such as Christ and the Virgin Mary. While this could be the basis for authority in the monasteries, it worked in the secular world as well.[40] The hagiographies of the Middle Ages describe notable women who had transcended the traditional limits that sex might have placed on them in pre-Christian society, women whose devotion, asceticism, and learning led to a power over others unexperienced by women before them.

There was, for example, Lioba in the eighth century, whose "erudition gave her an almost magical authority, and in addition afforded practical power in the vast administrative task of bringing order to the new church of Germany."[41] Or there was

Christine of Markyate in the twelfth century, who defied family and a corrupt Church to seek a spiritual ascetic life. Such a defiance of secular pressures indicated a profound holiness that in turn led to power for her as "a director of souls."[42] With a redefinition of the source of power, women could become legitimate possessors of a power that was in no way tied to their sexual attributes.[43]

Christianity in many ways removed the self-identification of the individual from the political community of which he or she had been a part. It took political terms such as "justice" and "community," and radically transformed their meanings. In doing so, it also took the traditional dependence of the ancient political unit on the separation of sexual roles and their relation to reproduction and war, and replaced that dependence with a new form of potential equality based on the denial of body and of sexual differentiation. This potential equality opened possibilities for females, but not primarily as participants in the political structure of the time.[44] Instead, they could become leaders, could found communities—even several communities—and live apart from men, organizing their own lives without being perceived as a threat along the lines of the horseback-riding, bow-carrying women warriors of antiquity. Rather, males could turn to the saints and to the abbesses for advice and guidance, since these women supported rather than threatened the aims of the males.

Indeed, in the twelfth and thirteenth centuries, one even sees the questioning of traditional male values of leadership in the monasteries as their leaders eschew images of traditional authority as too domineering and assimilate feminine imagery; the male leaders envision themselves as mothers to their monks and talk of the nurturing qualities of the divine.[45] Thus Christ appears with life-giving breasts, a potent image to counter the masculine orientation toward domination that would undermine the Christian emphasis on the importance of submission to the divine.

Christianity's early focus on asceticism meant a changing attitude toward the physical world. In such a world the reproductive qualities of the bodies of males and females were not relevant. The female was not to be understood with respect to her eroticism; she was to abstract from the erotic aspect of her body. Thus the male could appropriate the female sexuality while the convent provided for the female the realm within which she could deny the physical sexuality of her body,[46] without denying the notion of community. Previously, community was possible only insofar as the female was a member of the family. Though there may have been a variety of reasons for women to enter convents throughout the

Middle Ages, the association of women in their own communal structure no longer represented the threat that the Amazon warriors had. The single-sex community was instead an affirmation of the necessity for a new conception of social life that could abstract from the physical facts of human existence, both male and female.

Those who write on the place of women in medieval history trace an increasing control over women in the later years of the Middle Ages as they came more and more under the social control of male leaders and as Christianity came to be more and more tied to the political forms of a feudalistic society.[47] Our task here is not to repeat what the historians have told us, but to recognize the theoretical significance of a religion that, by rejecting the political relationships of the past—and, indeed, the whole realm of existence in which politics played itself out—had opened up possibilities of sexual equality that the previous world had denied. Single-sex communities—even of women—could be seen as full expressions of the aims of this new religion and not as signs of a world turned upside down.

St. Thomas Aquinas: The Misbegotten Male and the Christianizing of Aristotle's Teleology

St. Thomas Aquinas, writing in the latter part of the medieval period, during the middle years of the thirteenth century, represents the acme of the Scholastic tradition. Originating in the monastic schools of the ninth century, Scholasticism attempted to integrate contradictory sayings found in Scripture and in the writings of the Church Fathers. After the twelfth century, through contact with the Moors in Spain and with the Arabs during the Crusades, the Western world once again had access to the writings of the Greek philosophers. While Aristotle's works on logic continued to be consulted in the West during the earlier years of the Middle Ages, his writings on ethics and on politics were not. Instead, they were preserved by the Islamic philosophers in Arabic translations.

In the thirteenth century, Latin translations of Aristotle's *Politics* and *Ethics* appeared and became part of the curriculum at the universities, especially at the University of Paris. Thomas, who had studied under Albertus Magnus in Paris, not only attempts a Scholastic integration of the sayings in Scripture and Christian authors, but aims at a synthesis of pagan philosophy, particularly that of Aristotle ("The Philosopher," as he is called in Thomas' works), and faith. Unlike Tertullian, who in the age of the Church

Fathers had said, "I believe because it is absurd," Thomas' work was dedicated to the unity of faith and reason, of Christianity and Aristotle.

Since, in Thomas' view, God gave reason to the human being, there could be no contradiction between the conclusions to which reason led and the precepts of faith. Aristotle, living before the birth of Christ, lacked only revelation, which tells us about the world to come and the nature of man's relationship to the divine. Though he offers no insights into truths revealed by Christ, his writings, the products of sustained logical endeavor, are of value because they discuss the nature of our life on earth, of the role of the political community in that life, and even of the role of the female in human existence. Through Scripture, Christianity reveals the telos, the final aim, of the human being in the full knowledge of God in the world to come; Aristotle explains the telos of that human being in this world and the relationship of that telos to the political community.

While Aristotle cannot tell us about the highest things, he can help us with the present world of politics and of the family. These relationships are no longer seen as a weak reflection of the City of God, as they were in Augustine's writings. Now, in part under the influence of Aristotelian ethics and politics, the world of action becomes not a brief stay, but a positive expression of our divine creation. Thomas' Aristotelianism replaces Augustine's Platonism as an optimism about the possibilities of political life replaces the pessimism found in Augustine. The question for us will be what effect, if any, this change has on an understanding of the role of the female in the political life of the community.

Aristotle's teleology entailed a view of the world as a realm of growth, of order, and of purpose. Thomas recaptures this view in a Christianized teleology with each being moving toward an end defined by God. Each creature has a share of the eternal reason, whereby "it has a natural inclination to its proper act and end: and this participation of the eternal law in the rational creature is called the natural law."[48] God thus directs our growth to an end proper to each being. It is an end we understand through reason. In addition, divine law, Scripture, reveals our spiritual end; this law is not accessible through reason. Natural law, though, as "a dictate of practical reason," gives rise to the human laws of the political community.

> Just as, in the speculative reason, from naturally known indemonstrable principles we draw conclusions of the various

sciences, the knowledge of which is not imparted to us by nature, but acquired by the efforts of reason; so, too, it is from the precepts of natural law, as from general indemonstrable principles, that the human reason needs to proceed to the more particular determination of certain matters.[49]

The laws of the polity arise as men apply their reason, which can discover the natural law, to the particulars of day-to-day existence. Laws are not, as they had been for Augustine, restraints on men intent on harming their neighbors. Rather, human laws, through human reason, reflect and participate in eternal law. Laws within the political community are elevated through their association with the eternal reason and, thus, with justice.

When Augustine wrote about the justice of a community, he was describing the City of God; when Thomas refers to the value of the community, he includes the polity. It is indeed "natural" for the human being to live in a political community.[50] Different skills, different abilities make us interdependent and draw us into society with one another. The community, with its attendant authority and structure, is not the result of sin, but a positive expression of interdependence within the human species. The hierarchy that one finds within the political community, such as the position of the king, is a reflection of the order of the universe; it does not illustrate the defects of a material world that resorts to hierarchy because of the lost perfection of an equality present before the Fall. Augustine had emphasized the inadequacy of this life, of the hierarchy of men ruling over other men because of sin. Such a perspective, joined with a concern for the life to come and a vision of the soul as implanted in the corruptible body, rose above bodily differences between the sexes and saw in both sexes the potential equality that would characterize life after the resurrection of the dead. The realm of inequality for Augustine was life on earth; the female was subordinate before the Last Judgment. Beyond life on earth, at the end of history, was the transcendence of hierarchy and inequality.

The adaptation of Aristotle to Christianity by Thomas did not allow for the denigration of the political that was characteristic of Augustine's thought, nor for the dismissal of bodily reproduction necessary for the preservation of the city. As a consequence, Thomas accepted hierarchy as part of the eternal order among humans. Kingship, he argued, was the best form of government. Similarly, the subordination of the female was part of the order of nature. While Thomas agreed with Augustine concerning the equality of the sexes *after* the Last Judgment, the resuscitation of the political world and its hierarchical structure meant an acceptance of a system that placed women in a subordinate role. In Augustine's thought, that was part of the inadequacy of a corrupt world. In Thomas, it is part of the natural world.

In adapting Aristotle's biology, Thomas reasserts Aristotle's presentation of the biological inferiority of the female with certain important limitations that derive from Christian theology. Aristotle's biology, based on his teleology, emphasized the process of growth: the animal grows toward its telos, the complete expression of its potential. Creatures that fail to reach their telos are defective. Among the defective creatures are the females of any species, conceived at the wrong time and formed in the absence of adequate heat. Thomas explicitly recalls Aristotle's biology: "The generation of a woman is not occasioned either by a defect of the active force or by inept matter...but sometimes by an extrinsic accidental cause; thus the Philosopher says.... The northern wind favors the generation of males, and the southern wind that of females."[51]

At the center of Thomas' understanding of women is Aristotle's theory: the female is "a misbegotten male, as being a product outside the purpose of nature considered in the individual case."[52] In Thomas' thought, the body and the soul are not separated, as they are in Augustine's. The soul acts as form to the body and is described as being proportionate to the body's sense organs.[53] Since the rational soul is proportionate to the body, the misbegotten body of the female has a soul that is proportionate to it and, therefore, inferior. Thomas concludes that she must be subordinate to the male for her own interest, since, as Aristotle had taught, the inferior must accept the rule of the superior. Like her children, woman benefits when she performs the role in marriage to which her lower capacities are suited.[54]

However, for Thomas, the female was not simply a defective being, for she was also part of the divine plan, created by God in his rule over the universe. Thus, Thomas appends to his comments that describe women as "outside the purpose of nature considered in the individual case," the additional note "but not against the purpose of universal nature." Aristotle's biology had focused on the individual and the completion or incompletion of each individual case. For the human being, completion was possible only in the activity of a citizen in a polis—a world from which women were excluded. The impact of Christianity on Aristotle's teleology is to suggest that any consideration of the telos for the human being must be extended on at least two levels: as a creature who is a part of the divine plan and order, preserving that order through his or her biology, and as an individual with an end that goes beyond his or her biology, an end related to the soul's final knowledge of God after the Day of Judgment.

With regard to the first point, Thomas contends: "But as regards human nature in general, woman is not misbegotten, but is intended by nature, and ordered for the work of generation. Now the intention of nature depends on God, Who is the universal Author of nature. Therefore, in producing nature, God formed not only the male but also the female."[55] Inferior as an individual being, defective in her reason, [56] she is nevertheless elevated because she is part of God's plan. However, precisely because she was created for the sake of procreation, the female's subordinate status is ensured. Her role in the reproductive process, as in Aristotle's biology, is that of matter, to be impressed with the form (soul) of the male. She is auxiliary, not an equal participant, in this process that carries forth God's plan on earth.

With regard to the second level, according to Thomas, the human being is not understood only in terms of his or her biology and its relationship to the community of men. The soul has its own end. The soul of the female, created, as was the male's, in the image of God, can reach that end, just as the male's soul can. Aristotle had suggested a permanent hierarchical relation of superior authority over the inferior. The failure to conform to this hierarchy opposed nature. Thomas' theology, moving beyond the perfection of the being on earth, posited an order in which the female could equal the male: no longer limited by her misbegotten body, she could be part of the "order of salvation."[57]

Even though elevated through the Christian transformation of Aristotle's teleology, the female remains subordinate in social relations with the male. The argument for this subordination rests in part on her defective reason (Aristotelian biology), but also on arguments drawn from Scripture, specifically, the story of the Creation in Genesis. Thomas focuses on the creation of the woman from the side of man. She is brought forth for the sake of procreation, not merely as man's helpmate (for that, another man would have been more useful). However, that Eve came from the side of Adam has special significance for Thomas. He argues that this creation distinguishes the human race from other species: "That man might love woman all the more and cleave to her more closely, knowing her to be fashioned from himself."[58] This brings about unity in domestic life. Furthermore, she cannot be utterly debased before him, as she would be had she been created from his feet. If she had been drawn forth from his head, she would have been his equal; that she is not, but neither is she merely his slave. The understanding of women in this world derives, for Thomas, from a mixture of scriptural evidence concerning creation and Aristotelian biology and teleology.

Aristotle's political philosophy had raised the question of who is to be a citizen, why some should be included and others excluded. Sex had been a criterion, assumed and accepted, though reliance on such an external standard could lead, in unusual cases, to the rule of the worse over the better. The role of the female in political life was not normally understood in terms of direct participation; rather, Aristotle had been concerned with the education of the female, whose support for the regime might lead to stability or conflict. Thomas' political world also has no place for woman as direct participant. She exists for the sake of procreation, and her intellectual capacity, her participation in natural reason, is limited by the individual defects of her body. As for Aristotle, she remains within the context of the family structure. However, whereas the family in Aristotle worked to support the political community through its own unity and its inculcation in the young of the values of the city, in Thomas the family goes beyond, and in fact is abstracted from, the needs and the ends of political life.

For Thomas marriage is instituted for the preservation of the species; it is an obligation ordered by nature, by God. It exists as a remedy to passionate sexual desires, offering the legitimate outlet for these passions. It is also a sacrament representing the union of Christ and the Church. Thus, it demands of the partners a mutual and equal commitment to fidelity.[59] Thomas explicitly adopts Aristotle's discussion of justice within the family and sees that the husband-wife relationship is closer to political justice than either the father-child or master-slave relationship,[60] and he acknowledges the centrality of the family for education. In part, he argues, marriage is indissoluble because of the long process of educating the child, but this "long process" is not concerned with political stability. The interest lies beyond politics. Since man's telos goes beyond the polity (in contrast with the vision offered by Aristotle), the family too has the final end in view.

Classical political philosophy for the most part presented women within the context of the family. Their role within the family was important precisely because of the family's relationship to the political community—it created sons to fight the community's wars and citizens to debate and carry out its policies. It could offer a form of stability, a model of unity, and an arena in which to train the young in the values of the society. With early Christianity—its denigration of the political sphere, its focus on the world to come, its exaltation of the chaste life—production of young men for the sake of the state lost its significance; true justice and peace were not possible on earth. Thus the direct relation of the family and the women within it to the political structure disappeared.

Thomas, returning to Aristotle's politics and ethics, adapts Aristotle's analysis of the structure of the family in terms of its hierarchical relationships and its associations in justice, but he does not proceed, as Aristotle had, to suggest how the family works to support the political community. Thus, the female's role in the preservation of the life of the city disappears, however subsidiary that role may have been in the past. Rather, for Thomas the family is a sacrament and a realm for the expression of a virtue that is independent of the values of the city. The family and the female within the family have a stature that does not rely on the political. In moving us away from the classical world, Christianity opens the door for the separation of public and private lives, public and private virtues that had previously been intertwined. In this development the female is taken further and further from the realm of political life.

Conclusion

The effect of Christianity on the development of political thought lies at the heart of modern liberalism. On the one hand, Christianity offered an argument for equality that transcended the physical attributes of sex. This equality might never be part of the "order of nature" or the City of Men or the life on earth, but for many the perfection of the world to come allowed for an equality of souls never before anticipated. On the other hand, Christianity offered a world away from political life, a world far more important than the political world that had dominated the classical models. Thus, relationships between men and between men and women need not be considered *only* with regard for their implications for the polity. Relationships between people could be defined in terms of their meaning for an entirely different order of existence. When the centrality of religion fell with the rise of modern liberalism, it nevertheless left open a realm in which social relationships, families, associations between men and women, could also be understood as separate from the political world and not existing only in terms of their relation to the political, as they had until then.

7

Niccolo Machiavelli: Women as Men, Men as Women, and the Ambiguity of Sex

The Female and the Transformation of Values in *The Prince* and *The Discourses*

Readers of Machiavelli's writings always face both the ambiguities and the outrageousness of his words. Machiavelli intends to startle, to shock his readers into questioning their values, their beliefs, and especially the certainties on which they have based their lives. What had been accepted as true is now to be questioned. Natural hierarchies, clear lines of authority are undermined as Machiavelli confronts his readers with a chaotic world subject only to an order imposed by the extraordinary efforts of individuals capable of employing extraordinary means to achieve their ends. He had been a Florentine civil servant until his exile during the reign of the Medici at the end of the fifteenth and the beginning of the sixteenth centuries.

During his exile Machiavelli turned to writing what were to become his most famous (or notorious) works, *The Prince* and *The Discourses on the First Ten Books of Titus Livius*. In these works he attempts in a variety of ways to overthrow and transform the certainties on which political thought of the previous two millennia had been based. In the process of breaking down the old hierarchies, he reassesses the sources of political order and turns good into bad, bad into good, virtue into vice, men into women, and women into men—or, more precisely, he makes the differences between what had been opposites so ambiguous that we can no longer tell good from bad or women from men.

To effect this series of transformations of certainties into un-

151

certainties, Machiavelli employs a variety of shocking techniques. One is to use old forms to suggest radically new perspectives. The "mirror of princes" pamphlets, common in Renaissance Italy, which Machiavelli's *The Prince* imitates, had exhorted princes to act according to Christian principles; Machiavelli uses his pamphlet to exhort princes to deceive, to kill their enemies, and to eschew reliance on God. While previous authors had urged the prince to be Christlike, to imitate the man-God, as he ruled the city, Machiavelli says that the prince must imitate the man-beast, the centaur, if he is to be successful in his rule.[1]

Key to his task of teaching men to lower their aims, in effect to learn to be "bad," is the rejection of classical utopian thought. Thus he encourages us, in his oft-quoted phrase, to look at how men act rather than how they ought to act.[2] We must yield our vision of the perfect society, whether it be Plato's city in the *Republic*, Augustine's City of God, or Cicero's Rome, and instead attend to what it is men can do. With powerful rhetoric he calls for a focus on the "effectual truth," that which matters in this life. That "truth" tells us that men act out of self-interest and it underlies the claim, intended to shock all good Christians of his time, that "a man who wishes to make a profession of goodness must come to grief among so many who are not good."

Beginning with chaos, with men as they are, Machiavelli gives his readers the opportunity to create, to found new political regimes, new orders and modes of relationships. There are no preexisting models into which everyone and every regime must fit; there are no ideals, no perfection of form, no ends. Along with the terror with which he confronts his readers as he condones the fratricide, the cruelty, the deceit that must accompany the creation of political order, there is also the opening up of possibilities, of new ways of defining old terms, of changing roles for men and for women, for princes and for subjects released from the world of precise hierarchies characteristic of the medieval period.

Among the certainties that Machiavelli is willing to question creatively is the perspective on the female, which had been captured and crystallized during the Middle Ages by the opposition between Mary and Eve, between good and evil, and, with particular significance for Machiavelli, between submission and action. This dichotomous view of women needs, in Machiavelli's vision, to be reassessed because of its stark opposition between good and evil and because of its failure to recognize the limits of submission and the advantages of domination.

Mary and Eve in Medieval Thought: A Preface to the Transformation of Values in Machiavelli

The medieval mind had thrived on analogy and symbolism to explain the relationship between the human being and the divine, between the individual and the universe. Throughout the Middle Ages, Eve and Mary participated in symbolic representations as opposing female forces. Eve, the temptress, was, in Tertullian's famous phrase, "the gateway to hell." She was sexually provocative, arousing the male's carnal passions and thus preventing his total devotion to the divine spiritual world. The sexuality of Eve and the female in general gave her a power that threatened the male, that caused the original Fall, and that continued to make men act as they should not. Popular among the medieval legends, for example, was that of Aristotle and Phyllis, the mistress of Alexander. So taken with Phyllis' charms was Aristotle that he agreed to get down on all fours and allow her, whip in hand, to ride upon his back. This story, often depicted in the art of the period through the sixteenth century, illustrated how even The Philosopher, as Aquinas called him, could be controlled by female sexuality.[3] The response to this threat was subjection and denigration of women in the art and the literature of the time.[4] The female was to be restrained lest she drag men to their downfall, as Eve and Phyllis had.

Yet, Eve also plays a different role, for she reappears for some as a new Eve in the person of the Virgin Mary,[5] just as Christ in some interpretations had become the new Adam. Mary replaces the woman who originally led to the Fall; now, as the mother of Christ, precisely through her passivity and submission, she becomes the source of redemption, she *through* whom God acts, *through* whom the Son of God is born. Though in the early Christian era the focus on Mary was more common in the East, after the twelfth century there was in the West an intensification of the adoration of Mary as the gentle reminder of the potential for salvation.[6] As the bride of God, Mary was analogically associated in Christian theology and iconography with the Church, the bride of Christ. As Mary offered redemption to man through her marriage with God, so the Church offered redemption through its marriage with Christ. The bride analogy, as it related to the Church, carried with it meekness and submission. In the writings of Paul, the Church in its subservience to Christ parallels the wife in her submission to her husband:

Wives submit yourself unto your own husbands as unto the Lord. For the husband is the head of the family, as Christ is the head of the church: and he is the saviour of the body. Therefore as the church is subject unto Christ, so let the wives be to their own husbands in everything. Husbands love your wives, even as Christ also loved the church and gave himself for it.[7]

Mary's grace, purity, and redemptive power conform to her submissive role, a role expected of the wife in the family and of the Church before Christ.[8] Her virginity and grace set her up as an ideal of human perfection to counter the image of Eve.

Although these characterizations of Eve and Mary hardly capture the multiplicity of themes surrounding the two female forces in the Christian West at the end of the Middle Ages and into the Renaissance, they do suggest the contrast between action and domination (the evil Eve) and passive submission (the holy Mary). Machiavelli was to take these two portraits of women, transfer them to the men about and for whom he wrote, and transform them by turning the model of the active Eve, exploiting all of her capacity to control others through their passions, sexual or otherwise, into a positive portrait while the passive Mary, subordinate to others, is the symbolic cause of the enslavement of Italy. Throughout Machiavelli's writings, domination, submission, and liberty emerge as central themes. Liberty depends on the capacity to act—indeed, to dominate others, a trait embodied by the seductive Eve, who manipulates others not by her physical power but by sexual means. Slavery is the result of inactive, manipulable men, trained only in the art of submission, of men who in their submission to the Church and to God have become similar to Mary, the Bride of God.

Machiavelli's transformation of the two models of womanhood inherited from medieval thought and iconography underscores the fundamental transvaluation going on in his political philosophy in general. He is an author who can turn pity into cruelty, stinginess into magnanimity, deceit into a virtue, and submission—whether to a husband, Church, God, or the enemy—into a vice.[9] His writings revolutionized political thought by calling into question the traditional virtues, and the virtues and vices of women needed to be as thoroughly transformed as those of the men. Previous certainties for both sexes are made ambiguous. The certainty of the good Mary no longer plays against the evil Eve. The submissive female may not be better than the active, seductive Phyllis who can control The Philosopher who talks of ends and perfection. Indeed, as will be suggested below, men must, in Machiavelli's vision of the world, imitate Eve's capacity to dominate (as captured by his portrayal of Fortuna), and they must avoid Mary's submissiveness (as captured by his portrayal of effeminate Christians).

The images of women loom large in Machiavelli's explicitly political works, but women themselves play a relatively minor role. In the following sections we shall consider women's primary role as metaphor or image and their occasional brief appearance in the myriad historical examples that sprinkle Machiavelli's political writings. Here we shall see as well the ambiguity of sex and Machiavelli's own assimilation to the manipulative style of the female. In the second half of this chapter we shall look at Machiavelli's comedies, in which women and men enact roles not prescribed for them by standard social morality, but that show that along with the questioning of good and bad goes the questioning of what it means to be male or female. The disappearance of the old distinctions between virtue and vice parallels the disappearance of the old distinctions between male and female.[10]

Fortuna: The Female as Dominant

In the title of Chapter 25 of *The Prince*, Machiavelli asks: "How much is Fortuna able to do in human affairs and in what ways may it be opposed?" He begins to answer his own question noting that some hold that worldly affairs are governed by Fortuna and by God. Already there is a tinge of blasphemy, since Machiavelli thus separates God and Fortuna. In medieval theology, Fortuna is an expression of divine will. She appears capricious because mortals are unable to comprehend the plan behind the apparent chaos of everyday events,[11] but that does not mean the plan is not there. Machiavelli, instead of collapsing God and Fortuna into one force, removes God from the equation: "So that our free will not be eliminated, I judge that it may be true that Fortuna controls half our actions, but that she leaves the other half, or so, to us." Thus man and Fortuna (not God) face each other and determine the movement of history.

After offering advice on how men must be able to adapt to changing circumstances in order to control, rather than be controlled by, Fortuna, Machiavelli explicitly introduces the metaphor of Fortuna as a woman. The metaphor is not unusual; from Roman times Fortuna had appeared as the fickle female. Machiavelli, though, is to see in this feminine Fortuna the exhortation to action, rather than submission to whatever she may bring. Earlier in this chapter, Machiavelli had compared Fortuna to violent rivers "that when aroused, inundate the plains, tear down trees and buildings...everyone flees before them and everyone yields to their force, without being able in any fashion to stand against them." This Fortuna, like Tertullian's woman, is the gateway to hell. She destroys those who have not built dikes against her. Princes (or men), according to Machiavelli, must be prepared to meet this threat; they must build floodgates and embankments so that when the river rages (when the female threatens with her sexuality), her power is confined within prebuilt channels. But when Machiavelli clarifies how we are to contain Fortuna, he urges us to become like her. Key to limiting the effects of Fortuna is the capacity to change—just as Fortuna herself does. The vision of virility that has the soldier standing firm, the warrior never yielding, is in Machiavelli's world a recipe for disaster. Men must instead become women in their capacity to be fickle. They must learn from the female Fortuna.

However, after suggesting that most men find it difficult to imitate women, to "deviate from that to which nature inclines them," he proposes a more traditional masculine confrontation with the feminine force of mutability when he uses the language of forcible rape. "For Fortuna is a woman, and it is necessary for one wishing to hold her down to beat her (*batterla*) and knock against her." The alternative to learning from her is violence. Machiavelli adds that Fortuna yields more readily to those who act boldly than to those who are "cold," those who can match her passion with their own passion, her actions with their own actions. Indeed, this feminine Fortuna defines how men must act to assert their masculinity. The male depends on the female and must assimilate himself to her, whether it be by learning to be fickle or to be bold.

In answer to the question he had asked in his chapter heading, Machiavelli insists that Fortuna the woman can control us completely, if we do not learn from her how to act. Human affairs can be ruined for those who meekly submit, and neither adapt nor protect themselves through action. Man conquers Fortuna only by acknowledging her power and foreseeing that the stream may turn into a raging torrent. We must, Machiavelli tells us, deal directly with that passion rather than deny it; indeed, we must appropriate that passion to ourselves, if we are to survive the torrent.

As Machiavelli engages in his transformation of value terms, he takes the most fundamental moral term, "virtue," and gives it a new meaning, playing on the ambiguity in its etymological origins. The word derives from the Latin *virtus*, which has as its root the Latin *vir*, "male." *Virtus* is manly excellence, demonstrated by service to the state, whether in war or in political leadership. In the Christian appropriation of the term, virtue became the moral goodness of the Christian individual, the one who loves (submits to) God and practices the moral precepts of humility and universal love preached by Christ, the one active in the city of God, not of men. Machiavelli takes this value-laden term and focuses on its masculine origins; virtue is the attribute of those who act in a virile manner, who practice not humility but self-assertion. The female imagery in the latter part of Chapter 25 of *The Prince*, where Machiavelli establishes the opposition between virtue and Fortuna, draws out the masculine roots of virtue in opposition to what he sees as the feminization of virtue by Christian dogma extolling submissiveness.[12]

The sexual image in the confrontation of Chapter 25 is violent. The man must "beat" and hold down the female. It is the young, Machiavelli tells us, who have the physical, and particularly the psychic, strength to attack Fortuna in this way. He continues: "Therefore, as a woman, she is the friend of the young, for they are less cautious, more fierce, and command her with more boldness." There is a peculiar shift: from conquest we find the emergence of friendship. Being "held down" does not mean submission here. Eve does not become Mary as the result of this encounter. The acceptance and acknowledgment of her power, yet the willingness to resist and to subdue her, leads to a partnership not possible for those who either deny her or passively submit to her. Interaction between male and female creates an order otherwise unattainable. Her force here is tamed, but it must also be employed. For this to happen, she must be made friendly. The sexual confrontation as an analogue of the political confrontation suggests that the task of the prince is not only to dominate but also to create, to give life to a new being. In contrast with the Christian authors we discussed earlier, Machiavelli sees in sexuality an act of positive creation, not the sign of man's frailty.

In an earlier chapter of *The Prince*, Machiavelli discusses princes who have conquered without relying on Fortuna. These are men who acquired new principalities "with their own arms and by *virtu*." Fortuna gave them nothing but "occasions." She was not their friend; there was no sexual encounter. "And in examining their actions and life we see that they got nothing else from Fortuna than the occasion which gave them the material which they were able to put into whatever form pleased them; and without such occasion the virtue of their spirit would have been spent and without such virtue the occasion would have come in vain."[13] Such princes include Moses, Cyrus, Romulus, and Theseus, heroes from the realm of myth. These men function without the friendship of Fortuna, without her as a sexual counterpart to their manliness. They can give birth to the new principality parthenogenetically, ignoring the role of the female.[14] In contrast with these mythical heroes are the humans who must rely, as Machiavelli tells us in Chapter 25, on Fortuna for half their affairs, who must make her their friend through adaptation, audacity, and action. They must respond to sexuality and transform that power into a source of order. For the young, bold men of Chapter 25, Machiavelli has eliminated God, but he has not taken away the female. Humans must acknowledge and accommodate the feminine forces—indeed, utilize those forces—as the almost divine heroes of the earlier chapter did not have to.

Christianity and the Effeminate Male

In contrast with the vibrant female force Fortuna, it is the male who has become the complacent female, meekly submitting to those who dominate, who threatens the meaningful survival of the Italians of Machiavelli's day. In the final chapter of *The Prince*, immediately following the one in which Fortuna is compared to a woman, Machiavelli offers his "exhortation to liberate Italy from the barbarians [the French]."[15] The image of the female again appears vividly. This time, in marked contrast with the previous chapter, it is the passive female, awaiting her savior. She has been beaten (*battura*) and ravaged. Her weakness called forth violence. Machiavelli's response is to encourage the Italians and their potential leaders to act, to transform their passivity into action (to change from Mary to Eve). He urges the princes to see "how she [Italy] prays to God that He command someone to redeem her from this barbarian cruelty and insolence." Having in the previous chapter replaced God with Fortuna, Machiavelli now tells the Italian princes that God is with them, sending the manna, opening the seas.

The final chapter is filled with references to God, precisely because the Italians, unable to meet the challenge Machiavelli sees facing them, have become dependent on another (God) to save them. Religion and God, both systematically eliminated from political life in the earlier chapters, are brought back into this exhortation to the Italians because, in their submissiveness, they must rely on others, as Fortuna the female and the men who are willing to confront her do not. Having become slaves to others, even or especially to God, these Italians are now unable to free Italy. She waits in vain for her knight, who will not come; the men and princes of Italy, as submissive females, accept divine providence. *The Prince* is filled with admonitions to defend oneself and not rely on others; the "female," be she the meek wife, the submissive Mary, or the effeminate Christian princes and armies of Italy, cannot do so. The weak depend on others for protection. The men who confront Fortuna and acknowledge her power act on their own.

The question of the dependence on others is often captured in Machiavelli's writings with the example of fortresses. Chapter 20 of *The Prince* has the heading "Whether fortresses and many other things which are frequently done by princes may be useful or not useful." The answer he provides with regard to fortresses is ambiguous; the answer depends on the particular circumstances of a prince—whether he can expect the support of his people. There is, however, one example of a fortress being especially useful: "Nor in our time do we see any profit to any prince which comes from fortresses, except in the case of the Countess of Forli when the count Girolamo her consort died." A women ruler needs a fortress because she relies on others. Similarly, if the men of Machiavelli's world are women—if, losing the capacity to fight, they have become feminine—then fortresses are necessary.

In *The Discourses*, the book dealing with republics, Machiavelli answers in the title of another chapter the question he had raised in Chapter 20 of *The Prince*: "Fortresses are generally more harmful than useful."[16] In this chapter he reports the quip of a Spartan, whose city looked to "the virtue of her men and no other defense to protect her." When asked by an Athenian whether he did not think the walls of Athens beautiful, he responded, "Yes, if the city were inhabited by women." As with the example of the Countess of Forli, it is women—be they male or female—who need fortresses.

Throughout Machiavelli's work there are not only the physical walls that release men from relying on their own valor; there are also the religious walls on which humans depend to avoid direct confrontation with the disorder of the world in which they live. Effeminate men, like the princes of Italy appealed to in Chapter 26 of *The Prince*, rely on the fortress of religion. They turn to God, and thus do not act for themselves. Religion, fortresses, and effeminacy are all intermingled in Machiavelli's attack on the failure of his contemporaries to pursue freedom. When men exhibit true virtue, they rely on themselves, needing neither fortresses nor religion.

Then they become men. In a world in which order must be imposed by human endeavor, actions and self-reliance are the virtues that receive praise and encouragement. Such men's virtue does not always conform to the virtue of Christianity as it has come to be practiced. Instead, throughout *The Discourses* Christianity is associated with indolence rather than action.

The Discourses is a complex compendium of maxims, history from both ancient and modern times, and reflections on the possibilities of reintroducing ancient virtue such as found in the Roman Republic to the modern world, a world that changed radically with the introduction of Christianity. Machiavelli introduces the first of the three books of *The Discourses* with an attack on the indolence (*ozio*) that "prevails in most Christian states."[17] In the Second Book he reflects on "why it happened in ancient times that the peoples were more enamored of liberty than in this time." He concludes: "I believe it comes from the same cause that men were stronger, namely the difference between our education and that of the ancients, which is based on the difference between our religion and that of the ancients." He continues: "Our religion has glorified men who are humble and contemplative rather than active." But, he complains, "This mode of living has made men weak, easily controlled by evil ones who act, allowing themselves to be beaten down (*battitura*) rather than seeking vengeance."[18] Machiavelli describes this situation as the worlds having become "effeminate and Heaven unarmed," and blames this not on Christianity but on those who have interpreted it as a religion that encourages *ozio* rather than virtue as he understands it. The problem is with those who have turned from a world of affairs to a world we can neither see nor know.

In Book III Machiavelli discusses the failure of contemporary princes and republics to take charge of their armies, "so as to avoid themselves the cares and dangers of attending it," and castigates those "indolent princes or effeminate republics, who send generals to battle with orders to avoid action."[19] Weakness and the avoidance of any engagement in the affairs of the world are associated throughout Machiavelli's political writings with effeminacy—and that in turn with Christianity.[20]

With effeminacy perceived as the inability and/or unwillingness to engage in battle or to assert physical and social domination, the escape from effeminacy depends on making men soldiers who defend their states, making them participate in the world of action. In the First Book of *The Discourses*, Machiavelli turns to an example from fourth-century Greece. After Pelopidas and

Epaminondas liberated Thebes from Spartan rule, "they found a city accustomed to servitude, and themselves in the midst of an effeminate population.... Such however was their virtue" that they put the Thebans under arms, took them out to battle, and demonstrated that "not only in Lacedaemonia were men of war born, but they were born in any other place where one might find someone to teach them military techniques."[21] The effeminate, indolent inhabitants were remade into men through an education in war.

Two chapters earlier, Machiavelli felicitates Rome for her fortune in having kings who complemented each other; while Numa was peace-loving, his successor was eager to train the Romans in "the *virtù* of Romulus...else this city would have become effeminate and a prey to her neighbors."[22] Near the end of *The Discourses*, Machiavelli reflects on what makes men more harsh or more effeminate, differences that, he notes, characterize families as well as cities. These differences cannot be genetically passed on, "by blood," because marriage brings so much diversity into a family.[23] The reason is the difference of education in each family. Thus, effeminacy is the product of education, as is manliness. The task for leaders of cities is to understand how impressionable the very young are and to avoid anything that might educate toward effeminacy. For Machiavelli this can be done. His writings are his attempt to make the effeminate Italians masculine. The power of his language and of his images, and his shocking examples are to move the Italians out of the feminine passivity so that they can act to shake off the barbarians, rather than wait whimpering for God to send manna, to open the seas, to send his messenger.

The importance of discipline and training in overcoming effeminacy is emphasized when Machiavelli titles a chapter "The reason why the French have been and still are judged at the beginning of a fight more than men, but following a fight less than women."[24] He accepts the notion that the early fury of the French could be part of their "nature," but then insists that proper discipline could preserve their fury to the end of the fight. Again, he believes that those who have become women because they have been improperly educated in the art of war can be trained to exchange their effeminacy for masculinity. Thus, they *could* end the battle as men. On the other hand, he castigates the Italians, who lack the nature and the discipline. These armies are completely useless. They begin as women and end as women. Machiavelli seems to leave us a question: Is there any hope? Yet the fact that he writes—and does so in Italian—suggests an affirmative response. His is a battle of Eve against Mary that he, overturning Christianity, suspects he can win. Man is caught between the two models of womanhood. Machiavelli works to reinstate Eve over Mary.

Women and History in The Discourses: Models for Machiavelli?

Machiavelli's writings are filled with historical examples. One learns not from the Bible nor from moral philosophers of old, but from past deeds; not from thoughts, but from actions. Machiavelli relies in part on the ancient historians Livy and, to some degree, Tacitus, and thus revives the stories we encountered in our discussion of women in Roman political thought. We find Lucretia, Verginia, Tullia, and Dido. However, apart from Dido, who appears in *The Prince* as a model of a new prince in a new state, Machiavelli has very little to say about the women to whom he briefly refers.

For example, Lucretia, fabled in Livy's story of the downfall of the Roman kings, is virtually ignored in Machiavelli's version. Tarquinius lost his kingdom "not because his son Sextus had raped Lucretia, but because he [Tarquinius] had broken the laws of the kingdom and governed as a tyrant." Machiavelli adds that even "if the incident of Lucretia had not taken place, there would have been some other incident to produce the same effect."[25] Similarly, while Livy devoted several pages to the role of the Verginia incident as the impetus to the uprising against the Decemviri, Machiavelli barely touches on the incident in his description of the faults of the Decemviri and the cause of their downfall.[26]

Although Machiavelli largely ignores women in the history he records, he urges the princes and potential leaders of republics to whom he addresses his works to recognize the importance of women. Their importance, however, derives not from their erotic qualities, but from their being part of a man's definition of himself. Therefore Machiavelli encourages rulers to be particularly careful about interfering with the women in a man's life, for should the ruler so threaten a man, the offended husband or father will pose a potential danger to the ruler. In *The Prince*, in a chapter entitled "On fleeing contempt and hatred," he advises his prince that hatred and contempt will follow if he is rapacious and usurps the "belongings and the women of his subjects."[27] On the other hand, chastity is a "virtue" of the prince, not because it is good in itself, but because others care about it.[28]

In the longest chapter of *The Discourses*, Machiavelli warns that of the actions that incite revenge, and thus conspiracy, the most serious are attacks on men's honor, particularly those directed against their wives.[29] The two stories that he uses to support this general maxim, though, hardly support it. The first story alludes to an incident described in an earlier chapter, the homosexual rape of Pausanias by a minister of Philip of Macedon.[30] Philip did not avenge the rape, as he promised, and eventually Pausanias assassinated him. The second story at least has a woman in it: the tyrant of Siena gave his daughter as wife to a certain Giovanni Bonromei, then took her back. For this insult Bonromei conspired against the Sienese tyrant, and almost killed him. Clearly, sexual passion does not motivate these conspiratorial men. The females are almost incidental—if they are even present. Rather, the argument is that the ruler must understand the human psyche and his subjects' desire for self-respect; if that self-respect is violated, the ruler must be prepared for the revenge that will follow. Instead of revolution to defend the chastity of Lucretia, it is the violation of the male that calls forth conspirators.

Chapter 26 of the last book of *The Discourses* has women in its title: "How because of women a state is ruined." It is clear, though, in reading the primary example of this maxim, that women do not ruin the state; internal divisions do. A young woman of wealth in the city of Ardea is sought in marriage by a plebeian and an aristocrat. Since her deceased father had not chosen a husband for her, a conflict arises between the mother, who favors the aristocrat, and the girl's guardians, who favor the plebeian. This becomes a class conflict in which each side seeks outside aid; the conflict is resolved only when the state becomes subject to outsiders and thus loses its independence.

Machiavelli concludes: "There are in this text several things to note: First, one sees how women are the cause of much ruin to states and that they cause great damage to whomever it is who governs the city."[31] He then goes back to the cases of Lucretia and Verginia, whom he had previously dismissed as not being the causes of "much ruin and great damage" to their respective regimes. Why does he here blatantly contradict himself, within the same chapter? Forgetfulness might be one answer, but another is to be suspicious of his blaming women here after exonerating them earlier. In the cases of both Lucretia and Verginia the regimes fell because of their inadequacies: tyrannical rule and a blatant rejection of ancestral customs. The women who have been cited by others as the causes of downfalls of states were merely indications of a more general misrule by the political leaders. The causes of ruin were more profound. Similarly in the case of Ardea. That city's subjection to its neighbors is caused not by the "woman" but by the divisions between the plebeians and the nobles.

Women are the cause of the ruin of states, not because of any peculiar characteristic but because they indicate the divisions that exist among the human beings who comprise the state. On one level there are male and female. They must be joined to continue the city. The city of Ardea is divided, like the human species, in two. It must be joined in order to preserve itself. The unmitigated opposition of the two factions means the death of the city, just as unresolved conflict between male and female would mean the death of the species. As Machiavelli concludes his long work about foundations and the preservation of republics built up out of diverse elements, he acknowledges the instability of any regime that must reconcile opposites, be those opposites male and female or nobles and plebeians, as was the case in Rome. Thus, women do not "ruin" cities, but they do underscore diversity within the state, a diversity that will always be a source of danger for any community.

A few specific women do stand out in Machiavelli's historical examples, particularly in the chapter on conspiracies in *The Discourses* (III.6). In each case, though, the women act more like men than women, thus succeeding because of the male's failure to foresee that women under the yoke of necessity or revenge can act like men. Most dramatic is the story of Madonna Caterina. She appears when Machiavelli comments that there only remains to speak of the dangers that follow the execution of conspiracies: One must kill all who might seek vengeance. There may be sons or brothers, but the particular story that he tells is of a wife whose husband, the king, was killed by conspirators. When the people of the city held out against the conspirators, Caterina, a prisoner along with her children, offered to go into the city to win the people over to the conspirators, leaving her children behind as hostages. Once in the city she mockingly spoke from its walls to the conspirators; uncovering her genitals, she rebuked her enemies for not realizing that she still had the means to have more children. Thus, she kept the conspirators from the city. Machiavelli does not use this story to show the "unnatural" female who could so crassly yield her children for the sake of revenge; rather, he uses it to comment on the conspirators, who showed little wisdom and much negligence in ignoring the powerful passion of revenge. Even a woman can become a man in such circumstances.

Two other cases stand out in the same chapter. Epicarus, the mistress of Nero, was accused of participating in a plot to over-throw the emperor. Though guilty, she steadfastly denied her in-volvement and thus assuaged Nero's suspicions. Then there was Marcia, concubine to Emperor Commodus. He foolishly left a list of those to be executed where she might find it. When she discov-ered her name on the list, "necessity forced her to be brave." Showing herself to be feminine in the manner of Fortuna, she be-came manly (changed with changing circumstances) and success-fully conspired to kill him. There are no longer divisions between male and female. For Machiavelli a world in flux allows men to be-come women and women to become men.

In the last chapter of Machiavelli's long work on Livy, women reappear, this time in a conspiracy to kill their husbands. Though the title of the chapter focuses on the "providence" necessary to take daily precautions to prevent republics from losing their liber-ties, it recalls the plot by Roman wives to poison their husbands. Many succeeded before the plan was discovered. Machiavelli uses this incident and other large-scale crimes to discourse on the difficulties of punishing large numbers of malefactors and to praise the Romans for introducing the practice of decimation, whereby every tenth individual (or military unit) suffers death. All cannot be punished. Thus, decimation has the benefit of inducing fear without destroying all. To punish all the women of Rome for the crime of poisoning or planning to poison their husbands would mean the end of Rome.

However, the incident of the mass poisonings at the end of Machiavelli's book may not tell us only about the Roman style of punishment; indeed, it seems to tell us little about the "daily precautions" in the title of the chapter. Rather, these women poisoners at the end of *The Discourses* give us a portrait of women to whom Machiavelli must assimilate himself, just as those men who are to conquer Fortuna must be like the fickle female. When he wrote both *The Prince* and *The Discourses*, Machiavelli was in exile, a state of enforced leisure (*ozio*) that he says throughout his works turns men into women. He was also old, no longer enjoying the youthful audacity of those men who conquer Fortuna by vio-lence. Thus he was cast, in a sense, into the role of the woman. He was not active politically, nor did he have the passion of youth. But, learning a lesson from these female poisoners of Rome, eager to change the regime that exalts the passive Mary, eager to under-mine the world view of sixteenth-century Italy and the Christianity on which it was founded, Machiavelli must apply his own poison in secret and corrupt from within rather than from without.

Machiavelli's writings are similar to the poison of the Roman matrons because, in his particular condition and at his particular age, he cannot do otherwise. His chapter on conspiracies had told us that within a state there will always be those who are prepared to conspire and to resist. His chapter on women as the cause of much ruin to states had suggested the internal divisions that plague all communities, divisions waiting to be exacerbated by skillful manipulators. The Romans least expected their wives to conspire to poison them; they did not see in them the source of internal corruption of the regime, and thus did not take daily precautions against them. Machiavelli, living in political exile, a weak man lacking an army and youth, hardly seems a political threat to the princes of Italy and especially the Medici of Florence; but precisely because men least expect the apparently submissive female to be a subversive force, they are least prepared when she is. The women of Rome rely on secretly administered poison. Thus, the weak can cause the downfall of those who are presumed to be strong. And thus Machiavelli, presumed to be weak, can become surprisingly strong, adapting to the Fortuna who may mock his age and his political position, and who may have chosen to discard the old man.

The last paragraph of the last chapter of *The Discourses* praises Fabius Maximus, who restructured the citizen rolls of ancient Rome to limit the effects of the indiscriminate introduction of new citizens into the city. The leaders of Rome must carefully monitor those who can participate in the political regime. Fabius' great success, the reason he was called "the greatest [*maximus*]," was that he prevented subversive forces from participating in the city. Machiavelli's work (and the women of this last chapter) illustrate how even those excluded from direct participation within the regime can control it. Machiavelli, who in *The Prince* had praised the young able to beat and hold down the feminized Fortuna, now seems to learn his lessons from the weak women who can subvert because their strength is unexpected. He himself transcends the model of both Eve and Mary to find a mode of participation more compatible with his aims and his particular status.

Machiavelli's Comedies

Though the feminine forces of Eve and Mary permeate Machiavelli's explicitly political works, women as individuals appear infrequently. However, Machiavelli also wrote plays treating domestic relations in which women are active participants in the struggles for authority and security. Analogically, the family appears as a little principality, supposedly exhibiting the rule of the father over the other participants in the household. However, as in the principality, the lines of authority are not so simply drawn, conspiracies develop, rulers deteriorate and must be replaced, external and internal threats develop, orderly households are undermined and (since this is comedy) refounded. We will look at two of Machiavelli's comedies to see how his analysis of familial relations and women's roles therein illuminate his political thought, for by studying relationships on the personal level, Machiavelli crystallizes some of his political teachings.[32]

In both of the comedies discussed below, the motivating force is lust. In both a beautiful young woman is desired by one who should not have access to her. The enamored male tries to manipulate a variety of others so as to have the chance to sleep with her. In the *Clizia* the girl so desired is never seen on stage. However, her foster mother controls the situation; she is the true prince—or, rather (as Machiavelli perhaps envisions himself), the one who begins as adviser but then takes over the rule.[33] In *The Mandragola* the beautiful young woman and her mother appear actively on stage, but this time the daughter ultimately controls the situation. She accomplishes this by exemplifying Machiavelli's insistence on the transformation of the meaning of virtue. By choosing adultery over fidelity, she ensures the stability and continuation of her little principality. Had she remained chaste according to the dictates of traditional virtue, destruction would have descended on all. A character in the play describes her as "fit to rule a kingdom."[34] Her willingness to assert a new understanding of virtue demonstrates this capacity.

The Mandragola

In *The Mandragola* a young Florentine named Callimaco falls in love with Lucrezia, the wife of a profoundly stupid old man named Nicia, who "allows himself to be governed by her."[35] Lucrezia's name is intentional. The entire story recalls Rome's original Lucretia, the chaste maiden discussed so proudly in Livy's history and dismissed so hastily in *The Discourses*. Callimaco has been living in Paris, avoiding the wars that plague his native Italy. (The son of Tarquinius had been, before the rape of Lucretia, away from Rome in a military camp.) A Florentine visits Callimaco in Paris; a discussion about women ensues and they debate the relative beauty of the women of France and Florence. (In Livy's story, the debate precipitating the trip back to Rome was about their wive's virtue.)

So much is said about the beauty of the Florentine Lucrezia that Callimaco returns to see for himself—and he is immediately struck "aflame with so much desire to be with her."[36] (Tarquinius' son is seized "with an evil passion to violate Lucretia with force; since her beauty and acknowledged chastity excited him."[37]) Callimaco does not "violate" Lucrezia with force, though the familiar image of love as war is recalled in the song that ends the first act of the play. Rather, he employs the aid of a certain Ligurio to devise a plan that will give him access to his desired one. There is in this gentle story none of the violence of Tarquin's son. Instead, Ligurio and Callimaco play on Nicia's desire for children by offering him a drug for his wife, a vial of mandragola, which they claim will ensure fertility, knowing full well the falsity of their claims. However, they add that after Lucrezia drinks the drug, the first man to sleep with her will die.

For the sake of children, for the sake of her husband, for the sake of God (as explained to her by a corrupt friar), for the sake of her mother, Lucrezia agrees to take the drug and sleep with some-one other than her husband. Her chastity is to be "cured." Of course, this other man used to draw off the "poison" is Callimaco, who, once in bed with her, declares his love and promises to marry her when Nicia dies. Lucrezia, as Callimaco reports it, "tasting the differences between my thrusts and those of Nicia, and the kisses of a young man and those of an old husband," and citing the stupidity, the simplicity, the sadness of those around her, accepts him (Callimaco) "as Lord, master, and guide."[38] The two will enjoy each other in the home of her husband. The family, subverted by the intrusion of an outsider (though invited by the ruler himself), is reconstituted by Lucrezia's acceptance of Callimaco; it functions well according to a new principle in which chastity is replaced by adultery. This brings happiness for all: Lucrezia now has a young, strong lover instead of an impotent one; Callimaco has access to his love; Nicia will have the children he desires (thinking they are his own); and Ligurio can sponge off both Nicia and Callimaco. The happiness with which the play concludes depends on the corruption of the traditional female virtue.

Livy's Lucretia, once violated, commits suicide as she calls upon her husband and father to seek vengeance for her rape. In Livy's Rome, violation of a female could lead to the downfall of a regime. Machiavelli's vision is of the greater happiness that will ensue when the violation is accepted and, indeed, embraced. According to Machiavelli's presentation in *The Mandragola*, one need only accept what has previously been considered sin, and an intolerable state of affairs can become perfectly tolerable. Lucrezia learns that she cannot be good and preserve her chastity in a world in which most others are not good. The rule of *The Prince*, Chapter 15, changes her from an ancient Lucretia to a modern Lucrezia. The mandragola is a medication that supposedly gives life by killing. Though in the play its potency is a sham, Lucrezia's transformation mimics this death and birth. The old chastity dies for the sake of the new life of happiness. The cure does not come from the bottle, but from a transformation of the values of the main female character.

As Machiavelli develops the theme of rebirth in this play in a rather new context, he also works with the notion of age and youth. The old man, the fool, must give way to the young, inventive conspirators. In Chapter 25 of *The Prince*, Machiavelli had indicated that the young have more success conquering Fortuna than those who are old and less daring. In *The Mandragola*, Callimaco is the young man, the modern man who gains control over the woman, outmaneuvering the impotent Nicia. Lucrezia enjoys his strong embraces and chooses to support him in his corruption of the family. But Callimaco takes Fortuna as his friend not by violence, not by rape, but by trickery. Nicia is tricked by a story about the mandragola's powers. Callimaco, despite his amorous ardor, is something of a fop, avoiding the battles of his country and staying far from military adventures. He shows none of the virtue of the true prince or the citizen of the Roman Republic. Ancient virtue does not conquer Fortuna in today's world of lesser men. The method must be trickery, deceit, camouflage rather than simple boldness—and in the end must depend on the will of a woman.

As the play develops, we are always aware of the strength of Lucrezia, one "fit to rule a kingdom," for she sees through the foolishness of those around her and resists, at least at first, the attempts to corrupt her. She is the one who must decide whether to reveal the ruse to her husband or to assist in the subversion of his authority. Like the powerful Fortuna, she supports the young and thus allows the play to end on a happy note. She is the one who makes the final choice; Nicia, who thinks he controls her completely, is controlled by her. She decides what is to happen in this Florentine family. In the kingdom of the home, she is not only fit to rule, she does rule. But she does so in the end only because she accepts a change in the meaning of virtue and agrees to become an accomplice to the tricks being played on her husband. In the *Clizia* we meet another type of woman, one who rules through her simple good sense when all others around her lose theirs.

The Clizia

The *Mandragola* is an original play; the *Clizia* is Machiavelli's adaptation of a comedy, *Casina*, by the Roman playwright Plautus. Machiavelli has altered the plot in several significant ways, giving a more sympathetic role to the wife and mother. The general plot is the same as in Plautus' play. A young girl of unknown origins is raised in the home of an aristocratic Florentine family. In the several years she has lived with the family, she has matured; both the father, Nicomaco, and the son, Cleandro, have fallen in love with her. Neither, however, can legitimately marry her. Each tries instead to arrange for the girl to marry his servant; Nicomaco so that he can share the girl with his servant, Cleandro to keep her away from his father and his father's vulgar slave.[39] Amid the comic conflicts, the wife proposes that the two servants draw lots to decide which one will marry Clizia. Fortuna enters the play directly and favors the servant of Nicomaco. All is prepared for the wedding night, when Nicomaco will take the place of the groom.

Behind the whole story stands Sofronia, the mother and wife, who is distressed not at the infidelity of her husband but at his transformation from an upstanding citizen and father into a slobbering old fool. She devises a trick to foil his plans and cause him the shame that will bring him back to his old ways. She has Cleandro's servant disguise himself as Clizia and surprise the expectant Nicomaco in the nuptial bed. Nicomaco is thoroughly shamed after this incident, accepts that he must mend his ways, and leaves all things to the stewardship of Sofronia. She does not allow Cleandro to marry Clizia either, until—as happens in plays of this sort—Clizia's father appears and, revealing his noble ancestry, opens the way for the wedding of Cleandro and Clizia. The fortunate arrival of Clizia's father contributes to the happy ending, but the joyous conclusion depends far more on the wisdom and self-assurance of Sofronia, her insight into human nature, and her concern with the welfare of the family as a harmonious community.[40] She was able to overcome the Fortuna that went against her when the lots were drawn, while her son had to wait for Fortuna to bring Clizia's father to Florence.

Machiavelli says in the Prologue that this play is to be "instructive to the young," those eager to have Fortuna as their friend. But the young learn at least two things from this play: youth is not all they need to enjoy Fortuna's smiles, nor is masculine authority enough. Sofronia demonstrates the wiles and craftiness necessary to manipulate others in order to make things turn out as one wishes. The young may think that success is defined by the assertion of power in war or love, and thus conflate the two in their songs, but Sofronia shows that the female, no longer young, can bring order within the principality of the family, can acquire rule for herself and build a strong, viable community while all the males, both old and young, produce only chaos.

Sofronia, according to her name, is the one who suffers or endures; at the beginning of the play she endures an aged and incompetent[41] ruler. As in *The Mandragola*, the aged ruler is a fool, but in this play he becomes the fool because he allows the love of a girl to interfere with his duties as a citizen of Florence. In a speech absent from the *Casina* of Plautus, Sofronia describes the former Nicomaco: "He used to be a man serious, resolute and careful. He spent his time honorably. He rose early in the morning, went to mass...he attended to his affairs in the piazza, in the market place, with the magistrates...he dined and then discussed with his son, advised him, taught him to know men, with examples both ancient and modern."[42] Nicomaco, not recognizing the nature of the change in his behavior, complains to his son about Sofronia: "Your mother is crazy. She's ruling the house."[43] He insists that he wants to be master in his own house, he wants to have the wedding of Clizia as he has planned it. If there is no other solution, he will burn down the house. Shortly thereafter he says to his wife: "But isn't it reasonable that you act according to my rule, instead of me according to you?"[44]

As Machiavelli presents the interaction between the two, it is not at all "reasonable" that Sofronia submit to the rule of Nicomaco. Nicomaco's decline supports the overthrow of what traditionally was reasonable; there is no natural order that determines the rule of male over the female. Since there is no natural order, humans must impose the order whereby they live. Nicomaco, rather than imposing that order, now contributes to the disorder; thus it must be left to the female to structure the world around her and bring it back to its original principles. Sofronia is the adviser to the prince who takes the kingdom away from the prince.

At the end of the play, Nicomaco is completely overwhelmed by Sofronia's trick and transfers all his power to her: "My Sofronia, do what you will...govern as you wish."[45] When her son arrives, she recalls Nicomaco's words: "He wishes that I govern him according to my own wisdom." Nicomaco fails as a ruler; his authority is usurped by a woman who knows how to rule the family and how to use tricks to become the ruler. She says to Nicomaco, "I confess to have managed all sorts of tricks that have been played on you to make you change and reform. There was no other way than to make you ashamed."[46] Tricks indeed work against Fortuna. Fortuna did not favor Sofronia; the lot drawing went against her by giving Clizia to the one who would share the maid with her husband, but her skill and commitment to the family overcame her bad fortune.

Once again we must relate Machiavelli to the female; like Sofronia he suffers, endures the rule of foolish men, but lacks the stature and strength to overturn their authority. He must find other means to assert his control: trickery. As the successful female who does not meekly submit to a foolish ruler, to one who no longer properly educates his young, to one who pursues a shadow we never see, Sofronia is a potent model for a weak Machiavelli. She offers a model of action the males in the play do not provide. Among the others, Cleandro in particular relies on Fortuna. After the lots are drawn, the youth laments: "O Fortuna: being a woman you are a friend of the young, but this time you have been the friend of the old."[47] Later he rails against Fortuna for not favoring him: "When I believe to have finished sailing, Fortuna throws me back into the middle of the sea, among the most turbulent and stormy waves . . . I grieve my bad luck, for I was born never to have anything good."[48] He builds no dikes; he is tossed about on the waves of fortune and does not conquer it. He fails to act as Sofronia does.

The *Clizia* portrays the victory of the woman who gains power. It thus represents an inversion: those who traditionally rule do not; those who traditionally are submissive are not. Because of the disruptive impact of the passions, the old guidelines for human action do not lead to order. Sofronia understands and manipulates those passions. She knows how to shame her husband and make him a proper Florentine gentleman again. The weakness of the female sex does not mean that she lacks efficacy. While in *The Mandragola* the inversion is one of vice becoming virtue, fornication replacing chastity, in the *Clizia* it is of a woman "governing all things." In both cases the inversion indicates the inadequacy of the traditional expectations. It may be good that the father not know whether the child is his, as will happen when Lucrezia's child is born, and it may be good that the female rules within the family, as is the case in Nicomaco's household. Machiavelli's world sets up no precise guides. Thus, in his comedies adultery and the rule of a woman can become the new virtues.

Conclusion

Machiavelli is never completely open about his intentions. Some have seen him as an advocate of tyranny; others, as the spokesman for republican virtues; others, as the prince of evils; others, as simply trying to manipulate his way back into power in Florence. Through its ambiguity Machiavelli's work reveals the uncertainty at the foundation of modern political thought. The forms of Plato, the hierarchy of Aristotle, the political service of the Stoics, the God of Christianity all offered certainty. Machiavelli retreats from such precision, a retreat captured by the ambiguity of his political teachings. Within that ambiguity women play various roles. None of them, though, is definitive. Fortuna is a woman, but so is the weak man trained in the art of submission by Christian dogma. Men can become women and become fickle, changing with the changing times, as Machiavelli does; or men can become women and become submissive, yielding to whatever happens as they allow others—be they males or females—to dominate. While the images of women are central to Machiavelli's presentation of his political thought, women are unimportant in political life; they are easily dismissed by Machiavelli from the traditional tales that had emphasized their influence. Women in historical situations may have been the source of conflict among men, but here they are little different from property or the male's sense of self-respect.

Fluidity dominates Machiavelli's vision of world affairs. The task of the prince or of the rulers of a republic is to impose an order on that fluidity; in the process such leaders will specify the role of women in society. In the *Clizia*, in particular, we see a woman capable of ruling; in the case of Madonna Caterina we see another woman capable of the greatest deceit. The flux of nature does not determine who or what women will be. Unlike previous authors with whom we have dealt, Machiavelli leaves the status of women uncertain because all is uncertain, subject to manipulation. Thus, Machiavelli leaves open the movement to liberalism. The earlier models of women in society, as varied as they may have been, limited their role. These are cast down by Machiavelli as he destroys all hierarchical relationships. Men can become—indeed, often must become—beasts, private citizens can become rulers, men can become women, and women, as he has a character in *The Mandragola* say, can be "fit to govern a nation."

8

Conclusion: The Transcendence Of Difference

In Aristophanes' *Ecclesiazusae*, the women of Athens dress up as men. They don beards, they stay out in the sun so that their skin may darken as a man's does, they wear cloaks to cover their feminine features, and they borrow (steal?) their husbands' walking sticks to lean on as they make their way to the assembly. In sum, they try to obliterate the physical differences between women and men, and by doing so, they give women power over the affairs of the city. Mimicking the rhetoric of the males who normally attend and speak at the assembly, they convince those present to transfer public authority to women, and thus to change the nature of personal and public relations within the city. Aristophanes' comedy is an elaborate minuet in which the question of difference becomes the focal point. As Aristophanes presents it, in this comedy women can *appear* to be men, dressing as men do and talking (albeit in a voice reminiscent of a youth approaching manhood) as they do; thus, they fool the senses of the men of the city. However, once they have acquired power for themselves, they shed the appearance of males and act as women, at least according to the traditional images held by the Greeks and by Aristophanes in particular. They turn the city into an *oikos*, a household, and assure their position of authority by blurring the distinctions between what is public and what is private, in effect ignoring what is public.

In Aristophanes' work, then, we find ourselves back at the origins of philosophy and the questions raised in the sixth century B.C. by the so-called nature philosophers. These early thinkers had doubted the validity of our senses and had questioned the significance of the differences that we observe but that in fact may be

175

the result of our faulty vision. After all, we don't know whether the stick half immersed in water is bent or straight. Relying only on our vision, we know nothing with certainty; the observed diversity in our world may only be the result of our failure to recognize the underlying unity of it all. In Aristophanes' comedy, sight is deceived by the women's attempts to appear as men. Sight, as Aristophanes understands it, sees unity where in fact there is diversity, for, as the comedy continues to detail, the women are different from the men. The importance of these differences, which are not recognized when the women appear in their disguises, is underscored as Aristophanes introduces the ugly scenes in which the vile, old hags are made by the females' legislation to appear, in opposition to nature, to be no different from the sexually appealing and beautiful young maiden who awaits her lover.

In this play Aristophanes is not concerned with the potential of women actually getting power in the Athenian assembly—hardly a likely prospect in fifth- or fourth-century B.C. Athens; rather, he uses this comedy to criticize Athenian democracy, which had made equal those whom he saw as not equal, which had pretended that visual differences between people could be ignored for the sake of an underlying unity achieved by free birth to Athenian parents. To express this criticism through his comic art, he employs the differences between the sexes (cloaks and false beards were to hide fundamental differences) and between the ages (legislation was employed to transform the old into young). Neither attempt is any more successful than Athens' attempt to make the rich equal the poor or the good equal the bad. For Aristophanes, those differences are not just the result of men's faulty vision or of inadequate legislation; they are as fundamental as the differences between the sexes.

In Aristophanes' play the question of the differences between the sexes is introduced most graphically and with a good deal of bawdy humor, but it is the problem that confronted all the authors whom we have considered in this book when they introduced women into their analyses of the political world. And it is a problem that has resurfaced repeatedly in different guises: What makes women different from men? Are those differences superficial, differences that arise simply because of faulty vision, of a failure to see beyond our senses to an underlying unity? Or is the natural world as we observe it as fundamentally diverse as Aristophanes thinks? If differences do exist by nature and are not the result of our failure to recognize a basic unity in the natural world (or in human nature), how does or can a political regime—in its institutions and social organization—take into account those differences, sexual or otherwise, between people? To mock the Athenians' failure to take into account what he saw as natural differences between people, Aristophanes carried the theme to what he saw as its ultimate—and absurd—extension: women in the assembly and, at the extreme, women legislating the abolition of difference.

Nevertheless, apart from Aristophanes' comic introduction of women into public life in the city and Socrates' questionable proposals in the *Republic*, all of the authors we have considered see women as different enough from men to exclude them from direct involvement in the activities of public affairs; however, because of the differences that they see as natural and not as the result of a failure of the senses, differences that are based on a natural order of things, women are to complement the life of the city in various ways—or, as in the Greek tragedies, to set limits on its aims. While they do not direct it, they participate in it in their own way. The Roman maid and matron preserve traditional morality, and thus preserve the "public thing" as much as the Roman hero defending the bridge. The Aristotelian female engaged in the life of the household, walking to the temple so as to exercise the child growing within her, nourishing the young after their birth, preserves the regime; the Spartan female, in Aristotle's contrasting vision, who ignores the domestic world within the community, could—and did—bring ruin to that regime. The role of the female within the life of the city is central, but for these authors of the ancient world it is different from the role of the male, for, in their understanding, the female is fundamentally, by nature, different from the male.

In contrast, both Christianity and Machiavelli worked in their very diverse ways to undermine this focus on difference and to pave the way for a political theory that would abstract from individuals to an extent even Aristophanes with all his comic imagination could not envision. Though the Christian authors and Machiavelli would be loath to be associated with one another, with regard to the question of sexual differences both radically changed the terms of discourse. In the Christian authors we have considered, the ambiguity of the status of the physical world is reflected in the ambiguity of the status of sexual differences. The body and its passions are to be endured, reminders of the fall from grace yet also part of the creation of an omnipotent and omniscient God. In this world of physical being, of sight and sound, sexual differentiation matters. The bodies of the male and female are different; they were created at different moments in time, and temporal priority has given authority to the male body. Relations within the family derive from those differences. However, body, subject to the senses, does not define the totality of the human being.

The world beyond, the world of divine order, the *eschaton* or the end of history, transcends the body with its physical, sexual identity as well as the political regime and the family, which incorporate the differences between the sexes into their modes of organization. The world of differentiation between individuals, and especially between the sexes, is of lesser importance than that world where differentiation between bodies matters not at all—the world of the soul or the spirit. The creation of the soul, both male and female, was instantaneous; neither had temporal priority. Without bodies visible to the senses, the female could equal the male. The political community of this world, which incorporated the differences between male and female, was a hierarchical community that remained fundamentally inferior to that community of souls joined equally in their devotion to God and in the body of Christ.

The family as an institution of procreation and education had traditionally focused on the differences between the male and female roles. Incorporating such differences had been central to the earlier thinkers' conception of the structure of the polity and the female's relationship to the community. It is now replaced by the ennobling vision of abstinence from sexual relations, from activities of the body that produce new bodies precisely because of their differences. Replacing the physical family as a community in support of particular political regimes is the spiritual, which exists above and beyond such regimes. Even St. Thomas Aquinas, who saw in this physical world far more of value and the expression of divine omnipotence than either of the other two Christian authors we considered in detail, saw the superior way of life in abstinence, equally for the male and the female.

The Christian authors we considered in detail thus try to decontextualize both male and female, take them out of their bodies, out of their families, and out of the polity, to put them instead into a relationship with the divine where bodies—and differences between them—do not matter. The equality of souls, however, did not in any way lead to an equality of bodies. The two always remained distinct. It was part of the inadequacies of the political world that it could not capture the equality of the souls of the male and the female, the rich and the poor, before God. Thus, difference remained important in Christian thought, but only in the inferior realm of the political world and physical bodies that reveal themselves to our inadequate senses.

Machiavelli destroyed, as Christianity could never do, the importance of difference, for he dealt not with the ambiguous relation of body and soul, but with the ambiguity of nature. His was a natural world in which the senses saw and felt all, in which there was no underlying, unperceived unity that bound all diversity together. His was a nature marked by its own ambiguity, for the world we observe reveals no precise guidelines, no clear standards of evaluation against which we can make judgments; there are no well-articulated boundaries that mark the differences between one sex and the other, one class or political station and another. The nature that Machiavelli observes is one of flux. With his powerful portrait of a disordered nature he fractured the famous Chain of Being, a vision of political, social, and psychic hierarchy, an order that since Plato had defined who stood in which place in society, who had authority and who had precedence over whom, a model on which Filmer would hang his patriarchal theory.

For Machiavelli, the ambiguity of nature led to an uncertainty about this hierarchy, about how to define the boundaries between ruler and subject, between prince and counselor, between father and son, between male and female. A nature no longer so carefully structured opened doors and meant that what one could do or become was no longer defined by specified natural limits.

In a world where differences are clearly articulated, one can use them to establish lines of authority, to define places for each individual in the Chain of Being, to view the world as a realm of inequalities. One could, and many did, say that these inequalities were to be socially and politically institutionalized, that the rich should rule over the poor, the wise over the foolish, the virtuous over the evil, the male over the female. There was an answer to the question of *capax imperii*, though one might argue about that answer. But when differences were no longer obvious, when the foolish might indeed be wise, when the weak might indeed be strong, the hierarchical order no longer set forth a model of organization.

When the male has become effeminate under the influence of Christianity and the female can be as strong and distant from maternal care as Madonna Caterina, the old standards of difference no longer give guidance, no longer define one's place in the chain of authority. The prince may fall subject to the influence and power of his advisers, the husband (as in the case of Nicomaco) may fall subject to his wife. With no definitive answer to the question of *capax imperii*, different traits may be important at different moments in time. As Machiavelli had indicated in his discussion of early Rome, it was important for the growth and development of that city that there be rulers who differed from each other: first a Romulus to make the Romans warlike, a Numa to teach them religion and the arts of peace, and then a Tullus to revive their military fervor.[1] Machiavelli replaced the traditional order based on difference with a political structure tenuously preserved by a ruler who could understand and foresee the fickle turns of a disordered natural world. The liberal authors would not need to turn to such a hero, a Romulus or a Moses. They would see in the contract all men's (and, eventually, all women's as well) ability to transform the disorderly into the orderly.

Like Machiavelli, the liberal authors did not find the foundation for community in differences between individuals. Rather, community, as a human construct, was an act against nature; the liberals took Machiavelli's prince and generalized him to become all contractors. Community, thus, is no longer based on the hierarchy of differences, but derives from an equal assertion of the self against a disorganized world of flux. This perspective of the community as against nature, rather than deriving from nature, undermines the cohesion of a regime composed of interdependent units. The external imposition of order characteristic of liberal authors denies the notion of a natural social order that had permeated the writings of most of the authors discussed above.

Machiavelli insisted upon this imposition of order, for as he broke down the old barriers, he revealed to himself and to his readers that this is a world of flux. There is no permanent place or structure for any one human being in a universal hierarchy of things, no place where one belongs because of individual characteristics, for these traits not only change but are subject to dissembling, so that the wise may appear foolish,[2] the faithless may appear faithful, and the bad may appear good. Machiavelli's world is explicitly the world of appearances, in which there is no firm line between what is and what appears to be. Machiavelli, though a private citizen, could rule in Florence. The wives in Machiavelli's comedies can rule in their households. Assigned roles, dependent on ascriptive features such as birth, sex, or wealth, are to be questioned. They need not, in Machiavelli's understanding, be permanent, for over time they may change—or, indeed, may not be what they appear to be. Under Machiavelli's guidance, change became the coin of political discourse, change that allowed for political orders and public structures never before envisioned. It was the openness of his vision that allowed for a transcendence of difference.

As we saw in Chapter 4, Aristotle also recognized problems with observable differences that had been crystallized by custom but told little about the soul. It could be that the master was not a master by nature, that appearance, strength, and convention had given him authority that did not belong to him by nature. But for Aristotle, in contrast with Machiavelli, there was an order, whether the world of Athens met that order or not. According to that natural order, the male was superior to, and should have authority over, the female. If he was not superior and did not exercise his authority well, this was a perversion of nature similar to the oak tree that grew crooked instead of straight. The authority granted to the inferior male or the inferior master resulted from the limits of human observation, but did not mean that an order according to nature did not exist. The expectation and movement of nature in Aristotle's world was in one direction—toward that which was best. One might not always achieve that end, but it was there to define the Good.

In Machiavelli's world, nature moved not according to any criterion of good, but as a raging river that might at any moment overflow its banks. The flux of nature, the uncertainty of any natural lines of authority, a refusal to opt for the unseen over the seen, opened innumerable possibilities for Machiavelli and tore down the criterion of difference that had dominated political thought before him. There was no true ruler whom our deficient sight failed to discover. For Machiavelli, that ruler might change with the circumstances; for liberalism, the ruler was created by the subjects, and the specific traits of the ruler became less important than the way a ruler might be chosen.

In their very distinct ways, then, Christianity with its treatment of the ambiguous relationship between body and soul, and Machiavelli with his insistence on flux and the absence of precise boundaries, helped to set the stage for the liberalism of the seventeenth century. Liberalism as first presented by Hobbes with his articulation of natural rights, argues against considerations of difference.[3] All are equal; nature has made no distinction between individuals. The weak can kill (if only by subterfuge) as well as the strong. The female can claim obedience from the child whose life she preserves with her milk as much as does the male who may keep the child alive through physical protection. Authority cannot derive from natural difference, for notions of difference are suspect. Liberalism is for the most part an abstract theory. It is ahistorical and removed from the particular characteristics of the individual who is a member of that liberal society. Thus, it should (though, as noted in Chapter 1, it does not always) be able to abstract from differences between the sexes, to consider sex as irrelevant a feature as the color of one's skin or the width of one's hand for an assessment of one's role in the political community.

In this book we have seen the movement toward this abstraction. Earlier, the individual could be conceived of only within a particular context—often, in the case of sex, with respect to the particular role within the family and within a historical setting. The earlier authors considered above were not concerned with the transcendence of difference, with how the individual could emerge from the totality of his or her relationships to become independent beings capable of contracting to create the political structures of authority. Rather, those authors were concerned with how differences set individuals into particular associations and how those associations based on difference undermined or supported the nature of the political world.

On U.S. coins the Latin words *e pluribus unum*, one out of many, reflect the central political problem. In the particular case of the United States, the phrase refers to the original 13 colonies. But the issue is broader: how does a community become one? Liberalism gives one answer: we become one by ignoring whatever differences may exist in the body of individuals in terms of their relation to the public sphere. The private realm, where differences may matter, has been isolated from the political realm as the ancient authors never could do. They were not so ready to abstract from difference, to compartmentalize human existence so sharply into public and private as liberalism does. For them the relation of the female to the polity raised the questions of difference and of context.

Christianity and Machiavelli questioned, from their very diverse perspectives, the validity of those differences. While helping to remove the barriers between the sexes, though, they also made it more difficult for us to recover the place of women in the history of political thought. Whereas once women presented the political thinkers with the task of understanding community by incorporating difference and recognizing a world apart from the political, within liberalism that role for the female disappears. We move instead toward a vision of political life that, at least theoretically, tries to transcend differences and to limit politics not by a focus on what is other, but by diminishing its importance in the lives of its citizens.

Notes

References to standard texts are made according to the accepted methods of citation, since, in many cases, several modern editions exist. The page citation included when standard references are not sufficiently precise refers to the edition cited in the Bibliography. Where no reference to the translator appears, the translations are my own.

Chapter 1

1. Though liberalism has taken on a variety of forms in the last 300-plus years, there are certain common elements that underlie the varied expressions of liberal thought. What follows in this chapter is an attempt to draw forth certain of the central themes of liberalism, with no claim that all liberal authors uncritically ascribe to each one.

2. *The Political Works of James I*, Charles Howard McIlwain, ed. (Cambridge, Mass.: Harvard University Press, 1918), p. 12.

3. Robert Filmer, *Patriarcha or the Natural Power of Kings* (1680), I.4 (p. 255).

4. Thomas Hobbes, *Leviathan* (1651), I.13 (p. 183). The spelling has been modernized.

5. Ibid., II.20 (p. 253).

6. John Locke, *Two Treatises of Civil Government* (1689), II.4 (p. 122). That Locke does not carry these arguments forth to sexual equality is evident in II.82, where he notes that rule in the relation between husband and wife belongs to the man "as the abler and stronger"; but at the same time he sets careful limits on that rule—leaving open the possibility that the female can withdraw from the marital relation (as can the citizen from a tyrannical regime).

7. Again, not all those we consider to be liberal authors retain this perspective. See, for example, David Hume and Adam Smith.

8. M. I. Finley, *Democracy Ancient and Modern* (New Brunswick, N.J.: Rutgers University Press, 1973), can be helpful for clarifying some of the differences.

9. John Locke, *A Letter Concerning Toleration* (p. 30).

10. Aristotle, *Politics*, III.3 (1277b24-25).

11. John Stuart Mill, *On Liberty*, Ch. IV (p. 93).

Chapter 2

1. We find a similar theme in one of the fragments from the Sophist authors at the end of the fifth century B.C.: "The Macedonians think it fine for girls to have lovers and sleep with them before they are married, but a disgrace after marriage; the Greeks think both disgraceful. In Thrace, tattooing is an adornment for women; everywhere else it is punishment for wrongdoing." The text is in Hermann Diels and Walther Kranz, *Die Fragmente der Vorsokratiker* (Berlin: Weidman, 1951-52) II, p. 405.

2. For family law, which gives us the best insight into the actual relations within the family and its relationship to the city, see W. K. Lacey, *The Family in Classical Greece* (Ithaca, N.Y.: Cornell University Press, 1968); A. W. R. Harrison, *The Law of Athens: The Family and Property* (Oxford: Clarendon Press, 1968): and David Schapps, *Economic Rights of Women in Ancient Greece* (Edinburgh: Edinburgh University Press, 1979).

3. We must attend here to the differences between modern and ancient notions of citizenship. In contemporary society one is a U.S. citizen if one is born within the boundaries of the United States, is born of a citizen parent, or goes through the process of naturalization. The emphasis is on the rights that one acquires as the result of citizenship, rights to be protected equally under the laws and protected from harm from others. For the Athenians, citizenship entailed participation in the assemblies, in the juries, and in the armies. Pericles, for 20 years the leader of the Athenians, supposedly said of one who attended only to his private affairs rather than actively involving himself in the affairs of the polis, that he was to be dismissed as "useless" (Thucydides, *History*, II.40).

4. The degree to which the family actually supported the city or created tensions within the structure of the city is a matter of debate among the analysts of ancient society. For contrasting interpretations, see Gustave Glotz, *The Greek City and Its Institutions*, trans. N. Malinson (New York: Alfred A. Knopf, 1930); and Numa Denis Fustel de Coulanges, *The Ancient City* (Baltimore and London: Johns Hopkins University Press, 1980). Both authors discuss the rise of the polis, but Glotz puts a far greater emphasis on the individual needing to break out of the family in order to become a member of the polis, while Fustel de Coulanges emphasizes the dependence of the city on the family and their parallel development.

5. The following interpretation of the *Iliad* owes much to James Redfield's analysis in *Nature and Culture in the Iliad: The Tragedy of Hector* (Chicago and London: University of Chicago Press, 1975). See also Marylin B. Arthur, "The Divided World of *Iliad* VI" in *Reflections of Women in Antiquity*, ed. Helene P. Foley (New York, London, and Paris: Gordon and Breach, 1981), pp. 19-44.

6. *Iliad*, VI.490–92.

7. See Werner Jaeger, *Five Essays*, trans. Adele M. Fiske (Montreal: Mario Casalini, 1966), pp. 121-23.

8. Thucydides, *History*, II.44.

9. Ibid., II.42.

10. See A. W. Gomme, "The Position of Women in the Fifth and Fourth Century B.C.," in *Essays in Greek History and Literature*, ed. A. W. Gomme (Oxford: Basil Blackwell, 1937), pp. 89-115; H. D. F. Kitto, *The Greeks* (Baltimore: Penguin Books, 1951), pp. 219-34; Sarah B. Pomeroy, *Goddesses, Whores, Wives and Slaves* (New York: Schocken Books, 1975), pp. 58-60; Lacey, *The Family in Classical Greece*, Ch. VII. Pomeroy has a good discussion of the literature.

11. In using this language I do not mean to suggest that *all* women attend to the particular or *all* men focus on the general, only that the Greeks used female and male in this way. Helene P. Foley, "The Conception of Women in Athenian Drama," in *Reflections of Women in Antiquity*, ed. Helene P. Foley (New York, London, and Paris: Gordon and Breach, 1981), pp. 127-68, deals with some of these issues. For a contemporary philosophical treatment of this, see Sara Ruddick, "Maternal Thinking," *Feminist Studies* 6 (1980):343-67, which introduces contemporary literary expressions of similar themes.

12. Aeschylus, *Oresteia, Eumenides*, lines 658-60.

13. Ibid., lines 736-38.

14. Aeschylus, *Agamemnon*, lines 1415-19.

15. Sophocles, *Antigone*, lines 60-67.

16. Euripides, *The Trojan Women*, lines 728-31.

17. Ibid., lines 698-700.

18. Ibid., lines 563-66.

19. Ibid., lines 394-97.

Chapter 3

1. We shall see later that in the *Laws*, Plato's last dialogue where an Athenian stranger describes the laws of the second-best city, the processes of reproduction are central to determining the position of women in that society.

2. See Arlene W. Saxonhouse, "Comedy in Callipolis: Animal Imagery in the *Republic*," *American Political Science Review* 72 (1978): 888-901.

3. *Republic*, 451c.

4. Ibid., 451d.

5. Ibid., 452b.

6. Ibid., 454d.

7. Ibid., 456b–c.

8. Ibid., 452d.

9. Ibid., 455c–d.

10. Ibid., 457b.

11. Ibid., 460d.

12. See the discussion of Apollo's argument in Aeschylus' *Eumenides* in Chapter 2 of this volume.

13. E.g., *Republic*, 457c and *Ecclesiazusae*, 617; *Republic*, 496e and *Ecclesiazusae*, 673; *Republic*, 417a and *Ecclesiazusae*, 598; *Republic*, 465a–b and *Ecclesiazusae*, 640–42.

14. *Republic*, 462a–b.

15. The discussion in the *Republic* here should aid in understanding the much misinterpreted conversation with the laws at the end of the *Crito*. Socrates encourages in Crito a love of Athens because the city is Crito's own, not because the city is right in its condemnation of Socrates.

16. *Republic*, 496b–c.

17. Ibid., 514a–521c.

18. Ibid., 490a–b.

19. E.g., *Theaetetus*, 150b–151c, 157c, 161e, 210c.

20. Ibid., 156a, 160c, 210b.

21. *Republic*, 519d.

22. Ibid., 495c.

23. Ibid., 496a.

24. Ibid., 487d.

25. Thucydides, *History*, II.40.

26. One needs to consider here also the *Gorgias*, the dialogue on rhetoric.

27. *Menexenus*, 236c.

28. Ibid., 237e.

29. In Plato's dialogue the *Statesman*, the Eleatic Stranger describes the age of Cronos, when men sprang from the earth and possessed no wives, since women were not necessary for sexual reproduction.

30. *Laws*, 781a. With regard to the disparaging attitude toward women in the *Laws*, see, e.g., 944d, where the cowardly man who throws away his shield is a male changed into a female.

31. Thomas L. Pangle, *The Laws of Plato* (New York: Basic Books, 1979), p. 473.

32. *Laws*, 805a.

33. Ibid., 806a.

34. See the discussion of the *Lysistrata* in Chapter 2 of this volume.

35. *Laws*, 781c–d.

36. Ibid., 792c.

37. Ibid., 947c–d.

38. Ibid., 833c.

39. *Republic*, 454c.

40. Ibid., 459d.

41. *Laws*, 773b.

42. Ibid., 785b.

43. Ibid., 784e.

Chapter 4

1. Apparently Aristotle began by writing dialogues in the form used by his teacher, but abandoned that mode of discourse. What remains are most likely notes for his lectures edited posthumously by his son and his students.

2. My comments concerning Aristotle often will not conform to the standard view of the misogynist philosopher responsible for the inferior position of women throughout the history of the Western world. There are indeed certain misogynist presumptions underlying his thought, but they do not control the entirety of it. Aristotle develops his thought by seriously considering, but not always accepting, the ideas of others. Thus, his works are filled with ideas that come from the times in which he lived and that he heard others repeat. But not all these ideas are his own. His task as a reporter is often confused with his role as a philosopher. Thus, for example, when he is considering the virtues and their applicability to all or to specific individuals, he mentions the accepted view that "It seems to be [to many] that a man is cowardly if he is only as brave as a woman." These are not Aristotle's words, but the views of the society in which he lives. I try in this chapter to keep apart the speech reported and the speech of Aristotle. My thoughts in this chapter have been greatly influenced by the writings of Mary P. Nichols, Steven G. Salkever, and Catherine Zuckert on Aristotle.

3. Thomas Hobbes, *Leviathan*, I.11 (p. 160).

4. *Generation of Animals*, 731b30-33.

5. Ibid., 767b8ff.

6. Ibid., 732a6-7.

7. Ibid., 765b10ff., 766a30ff., and passim.

8. *Aristotle's Generation of Animals*, A. L. Peck, ed. and trans. (Cambridge, Mass.: Harvard University Press, 1943), p. xiv.

9. *Politics*, VII.16 (1335a11-13, 1335a39-1335b2).

10. Ibid., I.1 (1252a2-3).

11. Ibid., III.17 (1288a26-29); see also I.5 (1254b33-1255a2), quoted in full at the beginning of Subsection "Freedom for Women: The Case of Sparta."

12. Aristotle describes the institution of ostracism in his *Constitution of Athens*, XXII.

13. *Politics*, I.5 (1254a36-37).

14. Ibid., I.6 (1255b1-4).

15. Ibid., (1255b12-15).

16. Ibid., I.12 (1259b4-6).

17. Ibid. (1259b7-8).

18. Ibid., I.13 (1260a30).

19. Susan Moller Okin, *Women in Western Political Thought* (Prince-

ton: Princeton University Press, 1979), Chapter 4, argues from this perspective.

20. *Politics*, I.5 (1254b27-1255a1).

21. Ibid., II.2 (1261b9).

22. In the *Nicomachean Ethics*, V.6 (1134b8-18). Aristotle distinguishes paternal and despotic relationships from the marital relationship with regard to justice. There can be no injustice to things that are one's own possessions (slaves) or to children (up to a certain age), since no one can wish to harm oneself. "Wherefore there is more justice towards a wife than towards children and possessions." This he calls household justice in the *Ethics*. Justice is not part of one's relationship with slaves.

23. *Politics*, II.9 (1269b12-22).

24. J. Peter Euben, "Political Equality and the Greek Polis," in *Liberalism and the Modern Polity*, ed. Michael J. Gargas McGrath (New York and Basel: Marcel Dekker, 1978), p. 210.

25. However, see the discussion in Book VII of the *Politics*, where Aristotle explicitly rejects a focus on military achievements as the aim of his best regime, esp. Chapter 2.

26. *Rhetoric*, I.5 (1361a9-11).

27. *Politics*, II.3 (1262a14-16).

28. Ibid. (1262a21-24). Aristotle may be alluding here to Socrates' references to the breeding of dogs and birds in the *Republic* (459a–b), which, rather than supporting Socrates' eugenics scheme, show the inherent contradictions in the idea of a community of children.

29. Ibid., II.5 (1263a41-1263b1).

30. In the *Nicomachean Ethics*, IX.7 (1168a24-26), Aristotle comments: "On account of these things mothers love their off-spring more [than fathers do]. They suffer in childbirth and know with greater certainty that they [the children] are their own."

31. *Politics*, II.3 (1261b36).

32. *Rhetoric*, I.5 (1361a2-7).

33. *Nicomachean Ethics*, VIII.12 (1162a16-29).

34. Ibid., VIII.10 (1160b35-36).

35. *Politics*, V.1 (1301b26-27).

36. Ibid. (1301b35-39).

37. Ibid., II.5 (1264b2).

38. Ibid. (1264b4-6).

39. We might, nevertheless, see in Aristotle's framework a greater potential for an egalitarian, nonhierarchical relationship between males and females than emerges from Plato's thought. If the female could be shown to be the intellectual equal, if her reason could be shown to have authority, and if leisure were hers, participation in the political community could follow. Plato, in contrast, in his works sees the potential for such intellectual capacity, but because of the female's ties to the processes of reproduction, she cannot participate fully. Plato's equality depends on advances in reproductive technology, while the Aristotelian model could incorporate

women once their capacity was acknowledged and women were not denied the leisure to engage in the deliberative life.

40. Questions have been raised about the order of these books. For the most recent assessment that would place them after Book III, see Carnes Lord, "The Character and Composition of Aristotle's *Politics*," *Political Theory* 9 (Nov. 1981): 459-78.

41. *Politics*, VII.16 (1335a7-10).

42. Ibid. (1334b19).

43. See Maryanne Cline Horowitz, "Aristotle and Woman," *Journal of the History of Biology* 9 (Fall 1976): 183-213; she traces some of the uses to which Aristotelian quotes about women were put in the Middle Ages.

Chapter 5

1. F. E. Adcock, *Roman Political Ideas* (Ann Arbor: University of Michigan Press, 1959), p. 14.

2. See Chapter 2 of this volume.

3. *De officiis*, I.6.

4. Ibid., I.7.

5. Obviously, though the Romans admitted non-Romans to citizenship, they did not take the next step—or the one after that—and allow women to be citizens. The advantages for Rome offered by potential citizen-soldiers were not anticipated should women become citizens.

6. An example to note here is that before full citizenship rights were granted to the conquered Italians, citizens were not allowed to move from the outlying areas into the city; but if they chanced to be in Rome when the public assemblies were being held, they had the right to vote. F. R. Cowell, *Cicero and the Roman Republic* (Baltimore: Penguin Books, 1948), p. 24.

7. Livy notes that the story may be legendary, but nevertheless was destined to be celebrated in future times. *Ab Urbe Condita (From the Founding of the City)*, II.10.

8. Ibid., I.26.

9. The Roman love poets, such as Catullus during the Republic and Propertius, Ovid, and Tibullus during the Empire, use romantic attachments to replace attachments to the political life such as Cicero urged. The "amatory elegist . . . display[ed] a certain cynicism about politics; Propertius, for example, actually appears to question whether he or *any* individual can influence the governmental processes. . . . Instead, they invested their hopes and energies into maintaining romantic attachments, replacing the loyalty they were expected to pledge their *patria* with undying allegiance to their *puellae*." Judith P. Hallett, "The Role of Women in Roman Elegy," *Arethusa* 6 (Spring 1973): 109. See also David Ross, *Style and Tradition in Catullus* (Cambridge, Mass.: Harvard University

Press, 1969), esp. pp. 85-95. Ross describes Catullus' use of political metaphor in his love elegies.

10. This means I am omitting a lot, most significantly a discussion of Roman law that would take us from the Twelve Tables in 450 B.C. to the codification of Roman law in the Code of Justinian, compiled during the first half of the sixth century of the Christian era. The issue to consider here would be the nature of the law of persons and the degree to which women were legal persons.

11. *Laws*, II.vi.14. Of course, Cicero is incorrect here, since Plato's *Laws* does not offer the laws intended for Socrates' city.

12. One can find comments that denigrate women in Cicero's writings elsewhere—e.g., *Tusculum Disputations*, III.17, where he asks "What is worse or more base than an effeminate man?" and IV.28, where fear is the quality of an effeminate mind, to be avoided at all costs by a nobleman. But such comments are not lacking in Plato's works, and thus we cannot account for his exclusion of women from his political work simply by referring to his misogyny.

13. *Republic*, IV.6.

14. Plato, *Laws*, 781. See Chapter 3 of this volume for context.

15. *Republic*, I.1.

16. Ibid., I.17.

17. See here the discussion of "regime" in Chapter 1 of this volume.

18. Lucretius, *De Rerum Natura*, II.1-13. Translation by Frank O. Copley in Lucretius, *The Nature of Things* (New York: W. W. Norton, 1977) p. 29.

19. There are reasonable questions about the adequacy of describing Cicero as a Stoic rather than as an Academic skeptic—that is, one who followed Socrates' suspicions about the accessibility of the ultimate truth. Cicero never adequately refuted for himself the arguments of the skeptics emphasizing the uncertainty of all opinions; but the language he uses throughout, despite indications of a world of uncertainty, is that of the Stoics, with an emphasis on actions and good deeds rather than the political paralysis that might characterize an Academic skeptic or the conscious withdrawal of the Epicureans. See Frederick Copleston, *A History of Philosophy*, I, Part II (Garden City, N.Y.: Image Books, 1962), p. 163: "Realizing the danger of Skepticism for morality, he sought to place the moral judgment beyond its corroding influence and speaks of *notiones innatae*. These moral concepts proceed from our nature and they are confirmed by general agreement."

20. In breaking down the barriers between nations and peoples, Stoicism introduced an equality that was to become part of the Christian perspective on the possession by each individual of an immortal soul.

21. Seneca, *On Consolation (To His Mother Helvia)*, XVII.3-4. Translation by Moses Hadas, *The Stoic Philosophy of Seneca* (Garden City, N.Y.: Doubleday Anchor Books, 1958), p. 131.

22. *On Consolation (To Marcia)*, I.1.

23. Ibid., I.5.

24. Ibid., XVI.1.

25. Thucydides, *History*, II.42.

26. The historians' works are so extensive that only a brief consideration is possible here. Thus, much is omitted where a comprehensive picture is needed. However, I hope to give a flavor of the ways women enter the flow of political history. Since the historians' perspectives on politics do not come from arguments, but from their presentation of specific events, the consideration offered below is limited to a selected number of incidents.

27. Preface, 9-10. Translation by B. O. Foster, *Livy with an English Translation* (Cambridge, Mass.: Harvard University Press, 1919).

28. *Livy*, I.57 (Foster translation).

29. Ibid., I.58. Although contemporary feminists might find in this emphasis on chastity evidence of the repression of women in Roman society, the significance of these stories for our purposes is that this virtue was given political implications and suggests the female mode of participation in the morality—or immorality—of the regime.

30. Ibid., III.44.

31. Those courageous women who do appear in Greek literature are non-Greeks, such as Artemesia, who fought for the Persians during the Persian Wars (Herodotus, *Histories*, VIII.89) or the Amazons, the mythical female warriors who lived outside of Greece.

32. *Livy*, II.12 (Foster translation).

33. Ibid., I.13.

34. Tacitus, *Annals*, I.4. Translation by Alfred John Church and William Jackson Brodribb, *The Complete Works of Tacitus* (New York: Modern Library/Random House, 1942), p. 5. All subsequent translations of Tacitus will come from this edition.

35. *Germania*, 7.

36. *Annals*, III.33. We should note here that they are only talking about military leaders, since the soldiers were not allowed to marry while on duty.

37. Ibid., III.34.

38. *Germania*, 18.

39. Ibid., 8.

40. *Annals*, I.6.

41. Ibid., VI.25.

42. Ibid., XII.3.

43. Ibid., XII.7.

44. Ibid., XII.69.

45. Ibid., XIII.12.

46. Ibid., XIII.13.

47. Vergil, *Aeneid*, I.92-96.

48. Ibid., I.360-64.

49. Ibid., I.421-27.

50. Ibid., I.437.

51. Ibid., I.494.

52. Ibid., IV.68-69.

53. Ibid., IV.86-89.

54. Ibid., IV.221.

55. Ibid. XII.951-52.

56. The questioning of the political realm that in the *Aeneid* is expressed in reference to women is present also in Vergil's pastoral poems. These are poems touched by a sensitivity to the problems of the individual and society; in their focus on the individual and the delights of a pastoral life untarnished by the ambitions of the political realm, they offer the same questioning of the political ideal expressed in the tension in the *Aeneid* between duty to the state and individuality. See further Charles Segal, *Poetry and Myth in Ancient Pastoral: Essays on Theocritus and Virgil* (Princeton: Princeton University Press, 1981), esp. the Introduction.

Chapter 6

1. Luke 13:18-21, 15:4-10; also 7:36-50 and 13:11-13, for example, For this point see especially Constance F. Parvey, "The Theology and Leadership of Women in the New Testament," in *Religion and Sexism: Images of Woman in the Jewish and Christian Traditions*, ed. Rosemary Radford Ruether (New York: Simon and Schuster, 1974), pp. 138-42.

2. Elisabeth Schüssler-Fiorenza, *In Memory of Her: A Feminist Theological Reconstruction of Christian Origins* (New York: Crossroads, 1983), Chapter 5, argues for the active participation of women in the early Christian missionary movement. This fascinating book had an important influence on the first two sections of this chapter.

3. Cited in Rosemary Radford Ruether, "Virginal Feminism in the Fathers of the Church," in *Religion and Sexism: Images of Woman in the Jewish and Christian Traditions*, p. 176. In another article Ruether discusses Thecla, the legendary disciple of Paul who gave up family and fiance to follow him in his travels. For the women of this time, "Her life clearly demonstrates that obedience to Christ can sanction sweeping disobedience to the established order of family and state. Rosemary Ruether, "Mothers of the Church: Ascetic Women in the Late Patristic Age," in *Women of Spirit: Female Leadership in the Jewish and Christian Traditions*, ed. Rosemary Ruether and Eleanor McLaughlin (New York: Simon and Schuster, 1979), p. 75. In her discussion of the reaction of the Roman family to increasing influence of Christianity, Ann Yarbrough notes: "Familial opposition sheds some light on the aristocratic family of the fourth century: two of the primary duties of children to families, it seems, were the transmission of familial wealth to the next generation and the continuation of the lineage itself. Conversions to asceticism were inimical to the fulfillment of these responsibilities." "Christianization in the Fourth Century: The Example of Roman Women," *Church History* 45(June 1976): 154.

4. Romans 13:1 This section depends heavily on the insights offered in Parvey, "The Theology and Leadership of Women in the New Testament."

5. Romans 13:8-10.

6. I Corinthians 11:3.

7. Ibid. 7:1, 7.

8. Katherine M. Rogers, *The Troublesome Helpmate: A History of Misogyny in Literature* (Seattle: University of Washington Press, 1966), pp. 14-15, argues that this fear of the female as leading to sexual desire often leads to a general misogyny captured in warnings about the dangers of women. Important for our purposes is the recognition of the power of women, however much there may have been attempts to undermine it. Schüssler-Fiorenza, *In Memory of Her*, p. 232, sees in the call for women to be silent in the community of worship a demand for decorum so that the assembled Christians might be distinguished from the orgiastic cults where women with disheveled hair spoke as prophetesses.

9. I Corinthians 7:32-34.

10. Schüssler-Fiorenza, *In Memory of Her*, p. 90.

11. I Corinthians 7:3-4. Schüssler-Fiorenza, *In Memory of Her*, p. 244, warns against extending these sexual obligations to other aspects of the marriage relation.

12. Galatians 3:38.

13. I Corinthians 12:12-27. See further Parvey, "The Theology and Leadership of Women in the New Testament," p. 127; and Schüssler-Fiorenza, *In Memory of Her*, p. 229.

14. Schüssler-Fiorenza, *In Memory of Her*, p. 212, cites a "sayings tradition" that included such pronouncements as God's response to the question of when his kingdom was to come: "When the two shall be one and the outside like the inside, and the male with the female neither male nor female."

15. The following section relies heavily on Jo Ann McNamara, "Sexual Equality and the Cult of Virginity in Early Christian Thought," *Feminist Studies* 3/4 (Spring-Summer 1976): 144-58.

16. Ibid., p. 154.

17. It is interesting to note the contrast here between the Christian and Jewish response to celibacy. In the Jewish tradition only in the unity of male and female, marriage, could one find the image of God. See further Maryanne Cline Horowitz, "The Image of God in Man—Is Woman Included?" *Harvard Theological Review* 72 (July-October 1979): 187.

18. I Corinthians 7:31.

19. Cited in Frances and Joseph Gies, *Women in the Middle Ages* (New York: Harper & Row, 1978), p. 37.

20. Thucydides, *History*, II.44. See Chapter 2 of this volume.

21. Peter Brown, "Saint Augustine," in *Trends in Medieval Political Thought*, ed. Beryl Smalley (Oxford: Basil Blackwell, 1965), p. 1, cites a saying of Isidore of Seville, who wrote: "If anyone told you he had read

all the works of Augustine, he was a liar." To avoid any such accusations of mendacity, I here acknowledge my debt in this section and the next to the thorough and extremely helpful work by Karl Elisabeth Børresen. *Subordination and Equivalence: The Nature and Role of Woman in Augustine and Thomas Aquinas* (Washington, D.C.: University Press of America, 1981).

22. See Horowitz, "The Image of God in Man," for a discussion of the ways in which this passage may be translated.

23. Genesis 2:21-24.

24. Børresen. *Subordination and Equivalence*, pp. 16-17.

25. Ibid., pp. 27-28.

26. *City of God*, 22.4.

27. Peter Brown, *Augustine of Hippo* (Berkeley and Los Angeles: University of California Press, 1967), pp. 50-51.

28. *City of God*, 14.16 (Bettenson translation).

29. Ibid.

30. Ibid.

31. Børresen, *Subordination and Equivalence*, p. 3.

32. Ibid., pp. 119-20.

33. This is not to suggest that there was to be no procreation in the structure of the family. The world created by God was to be populated, but the concern was with God's world and not the state or political community of which a family was a part.

34. Suzanne Fonay Wemple, *Women in Frankish Society: Marriage and the Cloister 500 to 900* (Philadelphia: University of Pennsylvania Press, 1981), p. 147.

35. It is interesting to note that Plato's *Republic*, emphasizing as it does the priority of contemplation over action through the focus on the abstraction from the body and from eros, allows for an unparalleled equality between the sexes in ancient thought; Socrates then has to confront the difficult task of reproduction by developing his fantastic eugenics scheme.

36. Most of the literature on the rise of convents is from the end of the nineteenth century. See, for example, Mary Bateson, "Origin and Early History of Double Monasteries," *Transactions of the Royal Historical Society* n.s. 13 (1899): pp. 137-198; and Lina Eckenstein, *Woman Under Monasticism: Chapters on Saint-Loire and Convent Life between A.D. 500 and A.D. 1500* (Cambridge: Cambridge University Press, 1896). For more recent work, see Jo Ann McNamara and Suzanne F. Wemple, "Sanctity and Power: The Dual Pursuit of Medieval Women," in *Becoming Visible: Women in European History*, ed., Renate Bridenthal and Claudia Koonz (Boston: Houghton Mifflin, 1977), pp. 90-118; and Wemple, *Women in Frankish Society*.

37. McNamara and Wemple, "Sanctity and Power," p. 95.

38. Ruether, "Mothers of the Church," p. 74. Ruether describes how Macrina transformed the family estates into a monastic community of prayer and charitable service.

39. McNamara and Wemple, "Sanctity and Power," p. 99. Wemple, *Women in Frankish Society*, p. 172, comments on the business acumen of abbesses engaged in "aggressive economic policy" during the ninth century.

40. Wemple, *Women in Frankish Society*, p. 183.

41. Eleanor McLaughlin, "Women, Power and the Pursuit of Holiness in Medieval Christianity," in *Women of Spirit: Female Leadership in the Jewish and Christian Traditions*, ed. Rosemary Ruether and Eleanor McLaughlin (New York: Simon and Schuster, 1979), pp. 103-07.

42. Ibid., p. 109.

43. Carolyn Walker Bynum, *Jesus as Mother: Studies in the Spirituality of the High Middle Ages* (Berkeley: University of California Press, 1982), suggests that the increasing importance of clerical authority in the twelfth and thirteenth centuries, as well as the exclusion of women from the priesthood, led to a decline in the openness toward women leaders of any sort. See esp. Chapter 5. The rise of female societies considered heretical, such as the Beguines, needs to be studied and understood in this context.

44. Historians writing about this period suggest a surprising level of involvement of women in political life and in the care of the large feudal manor. The standard work expressing this perspective is Eileen Power, *Medieval Women*, ed. M.M. Postan (Cambridge: Cambridge University Press, 1975). See also Wemple, *Women in Frankish Society*, Chapters 4-6.

45. Bynum, *Jesus as Mother*, Chapter 4.

46. Bynum, ibid., discusses how the feminine images of the divine do not surface in the writings of nuns, but are much more prevalent in the works of the monks.

47. Wemple, *Women in Frankish Society*, for example, traces how, by the eighth century, there was in Frankish society an increasing level of male supervision over the lives of nuns and how the double monasteries that had been founded earlier were gradually disappearing. See also Bateson, "Origin and Early History of Double Monasteries"; and Eckenstein, *Woman Under Monasticism*.

48. *Summa Theologica*. I-II. q.91, a.2. c. Translation by the fathers of the English Dominican Province; all subsequent translations from the *Summa Theologica* are from this edition.

49. Ibid., I-II, q. 91, a.3, c.

50. *On Kingship*, 1.6, as reprinted and translated in *The Political Ideas of St. Thomas Aquinas*, ed. Dino Bigongiari (New York: Hafner, 1953), p. 176.

51. *Summa Theologica*, I. q. 99, a.2, ad. 2.

52. Ibid., I. q. 99, a.2, ad. 1.

53. Børresen. *Subordination and Equivalence*, p. 315.

54. Ibid., p. 172.

55. *Summa Theologica*, I. q. 92, a.1, ad. 1.

56. Børresen. *Subordination and Equivalence*, p. 257.

57. Eleanor Commo McLaughlin, "Equality of Souls, Inequality of

Sexes: Woman in Medieval Theology," in *Religion and Sexism: Images of Woman in the Jewish and Christian Traditions*, ed. Rosemary Radford Ruether (New York: Simon and Schuster, 1974), p. 221.

58. *Summa Theologica*, I, q. 92, a.2. c.

59. Børresen. *Subordination and Equivalence*, p. 253.

60. Ibid., p. 258.

Chapter 7

1. Machiavelli, *The Prince*. Chapter 18.

2. Ibid., Chapter 15.

3. For a discussion of the Phyllis story, see Horowitz, "Aristotle and Woman," pp. 189-91, and the further references in her notes 20 and 21. See also Natalie Zemon Davis, *Society and Culture in Early Modern France* (Stanford: Stanford University Press, 1965), pp. 135-36.

4. Henry Krauss, *The Living Theater of Medieval Art* (Philadelphia: University of Pennsylvania Press, 1967), Chapter 3, esp. p. 42.

5. Angela M. Lucas, *Women in the Middle Ages: Religion, Marriage and Letters* (New York: St. Martin's Press, 1983), p. 15; Joan Ferrante, *Woman as Image in Medieval Literature* (New York: Columbia University Press, 1975), pp. 30-35.

6. McLaughlin, "Equality of Souls," p. 246.

7. Ephesians 5:22-25.

8. In some authors the Church becomes the bride of God through analogy with the bride of the Song of Songs in the Old Testament. Some of those writing on the Song of Songs even asked men "to identify with a woman as the bride represents all of mankind" (Lucas, *Women in the Middle Ages*, p. 17. Ferrante, *Woman as Image*, p. 29, writes about St. Bernard, whose "devotion to the Virgin is such that he can identify himself, through her, with a woman's role, and speak of himself as a mother to his monks." See also Bynum, *Jesus as Mother*, 115-18, and Chapter 4, for a detailed discussion of the attraction of the female image for religious men, especially monks.

9. For a further discussion of Machiavelli's transformation of the meaning of traditional terms, see Clifford Orwin, "Machiavelli's Unchristian Charity," *American Political Science Review* 72 (December 1978): 1217-28.

10. Since this chapter was written, an extremely interesting discussion of Machiavelli and women has appeared: Hanna Fenichel Pitkin, *Fortune Is a Woman: Gender and Politics in the Thought of Niccolo Machiavelli* (Berkeley: University of California Press, 1984). Though the orientation and concerns are quite different from those expressed in this chapter, it illustrates the centrality of women and the feminine for Machiavelli's work.

11. Ferrante, *Woman as Image*, pp. 46-49, has a helpful discussion

of this issue in her treatment of Boethius. His discourse with the feminine Philosophy "makes him see that Fortune is part of the workings of fate and not a separate hostile entity, that it was his perspective that was wrong and not her actions" (p. 47).

12. Quentin Skinner, *The Foundations of Modern Political Thought: The Renaissance* (Cambridge: Cambridge University Press, 1978), I, pp. 176-79, comments on the public-private dimensions of *virtu*. The *virtu* in Machiavelli, he argues, relates to a public excellence, to the virtual exclusion of the private. Attaching the male and female connotations to the public-private dimensions, we can see how Machiavelli's virtue is here masculinized.

13. For the Italians of Machiavelli's time, Moses certainly does not come from the realm of myth; it is part of Machiavelli's heresy to include him in the same category as such characters as Romulus and Theseus.

14. Compare here the highly sexual language of Chaper 26 of *The Prince*, to be discussed below.

15. Chapter 26. The subsequent quotes in this paragraph come from this chapter.

16. *The Discourses*, II.24.

17. Ibid., I, Introduction.

18. Ibid., II.2.

19. Ibid., III.10.

20. Harvey C. Mansfield, Jr., *Machiavelli's New Modes and Orders: A Study of the "Discourses on Livy"* (Ithaca and London: Cornell University Press, 1979), p. 195, n. 12, suggests that *ozio* can also mean the leisure for contemplation. Thus, "the affinity of Christianity and philosophy is again suggested." Elsewhere in his study of *The Discourses*, Mansfield associates philosophy with that which is womanly (pp. 390ff).

21. *The Discourses*, I.21.

22. Ibid., I.19.

23. Ibid., III.46.

24. Ibid., III.36.

25. Ibid., III.5.

26. Ibid., I.40.

27. *The Prince*, Chapter 19.

28. See the discussion of Scipio in *The Discourses*, III.20.

29. Ibid., III.6.

30. Ibid., II.28.

31. Ibid., III.26.

32 As in our discussion of Greek drama in Chapter 2, the analyses will have to be limited, in this case to how the comedies highlight the place of women in Machiavelli's political thought; thus, much of the complexity of the plays' themes and plots will have to be ignored. For discussions of Machiavelli's plays, with a focus on their political implications, see particularly Mera J. Flaumenhaft, "The Comic Remedy: Machiavelli's "Mandragola," *Interpretation* 7 (May 1978): 33-74; and Martin Fleisher, "Trust

and Deceit in Machiavelli's Comedies," *Journal of the History of Ideas* (July 1966): 365-80.

33. *The Prince*, Chapter 23. Here Machiavelli notes that a prince who is not wise in his own right may, by chance, have a counselor who is a very prudent man. This situation, though, does not last long, "since such a governor would in a short time take the state from him."

34. *The Mandragola*, I.3.

35. Ibid., I.1.

36. Ibid.

37. Livy, I.47.

38. *The Mandragola*, V.4.

39. In Plautus' version, the son also hopes to have access to the girl once she is wed to his slave.

40. Fleisher, "Trust and Deceit," notes that in the *Casina* there is no emphasis on the welfare of the family.

41. Nicomaco's impotence is an issue of no small comic interest during the preparations for the wedding night. *Clizia*, IV.2.

42. Ibid., II.4. The allusions to Machiavelli's own role concerning the education of the young are evident here. We might also note the relation of Nicomaco's name to Machiavelli's.

43. Ibid., III.1.

44. Ibid., III.4.

45. Ibid., V.3. See Davis, *Society and Cuture*, pp. 124-51, for the social role of "Women on Top" in transitional societies.

46. *Clizia*, V.3.

47. Ibid., IV.1.

48. Ibid., V.5.

Chapter 8

1. Machiavelli, *Discourses*, I.19.

2. The classic case for Machiavelli is that of the Brutus of the early Republic who pretended to be a fool at the same time that he plotted the overthrow of the tyrannical kings. See *Discourses*, III. One might also see a parallel here with Machiavelli's presentation of himself in the dedicatory epistle of *The Prince*.

3. See Chapter 1 of this volume.

Bibliography

Note: Primary sources are not included unless reference to a particular modern edition was made in the Notes. I have included some works not cited in the Notes that might be helpful for background on the development of themes presented in the text.

Annas, Julia. "Plato's *Republic* and Feminism." *Philosophy* 51 (1976): 307-21.

Adcock, F.E. *Roman Political Ideas.* Ann Arbor: University of Michigan Press, 1959.

Adkins, A. W. H. *Moral Values and Political Behavior in Ancient Greece: From Homer to the End of the Fifth Century.* New York: Norton, 1972.

Aquinas, St. Thomas, *Summa Theologica.* Translated by the Fathers of the English Dominican Province. London: Thomas Baker, 1912.

Arthur, Marylin B. "The Divided World of *Iliad* VI." In *Reflections of Women in Antiquity.* Edited by Helene P. Foley. Pp. 19-44. New York, London, and Paris: Gordon and Breach, 1981.

———. "Liberated Women: The Classical Era." In *Becoming Visible: Women in European History.* Edited by Renate Bridenthal and Claudia Koonz. Boston: Houghton Mifflin, 1974.

———. "Early Greece: The Origins of the Western Attitude Toward Women." *Arethusa* 6 (Spring 1973): 7-58.

Augustine, St. *City of God.* Translated by Henry Bettenson. Harmondsworth: Penguin Books, 1972.

Bateson, Mary. "Origin and Early History of Double Monasteries." *Transactions of the Royal Historical Society* n.s. 13 (1899): 137-98.

Børreson, Kari Elizabeth. *Subordination and Equivalence: The Nature and Role of Women in Augustine and Thomas Aquinas.* Washington, D.C.: University Press of America, 1981.

Brown, Peter. *Augustine of Hippo.* Berkeley and Los Angeles: University of California Press, 1967.

———. "Saint Augustine." In *Trends in Medieval Political Thought.* Edited by Beryl Smalley. Oxford: Basil Blackwell, 1965.

Butler, Melissa. "Early Liberal Roots of Feminism: John Locke and the Attack on Patriarchy." *American Political Science Review* 72 (March 1978): 135-50.

Bynum, Caroline Walker. *Jesus as Mother: Studies in the Spirituality of the High Middle Ages.* Berkeley: University of California Press, 1982.

Clark, S. R. L. "Aristotle's Woman." *History of Political Thought* 3:2 (Summer 1982): 177-91.

Copleston, Frederick. *A History of Philosophy.* Volume I, part II. Garden City, N.Y.: Image Books, 1962.

Cowell, F. R. *Cicero and the Roman Republic.* Baltimore: Penguin Books, 1948.

Davis, Natalie Zemon. *Society and Culture in Early Modern France.* Stanford: Stanford University Press, 1965.

Diels, Hermann and Walther Kranz. *Die Fragmente der Vorsokratiker.* Berlin: Weidman, 1951-52, 3 vols.

Eckenstein, Lina. *Woman Under Monasticism: Chapters on Saint-Loire and Convent Life Between A.D. 500 and A.D. 1500.* Cambridge: Cambridge University Press, 1896.

Edelstein, Ludwig. *The Meaning of Stoicism.* Cambridge, Mass.: Harvard University Press, 1966.

Elshtain, Jean Bethke. *Public Man, Private Woman: Women in Social and Political Thought.* Princeton: Princeton University Press, 1981.

———. "The Feminist Movement and the Question of Equality." *Polity* 7 (Summer 1975): 452-77.

———. "Moral Woman and Immoral Man: A Consideration of the Public-Private Split and Its Political Ramifications." *Politics and Society* 4 (1974): 453-73.

Euben, J. Peter. "Political Equality and the Greek Polis." In *Liberalism and the Modern Polity.* Edited by Michael J. Gargas McGrath. Pp. 207-28. New York and Basel: Marcel Dekker, 1978.

Ferrante, Joan M. *Woman as Image in Medieval Literature.* New York: Columbia University Press, 1975.

Filmer, Robert. *Patriarcha or the Natural Power of Kings.* In John Locke, *Two Treatises of Government.* Edited by Thomas I. Cook. Pp. 249-310. New York: Hafner Press, 1947.

Finley, M. I. *Politics in the Ancient World.* Cambridge: Cambridge University Press, 1983.

———. *Democracy Ancient and Modern.* New Brunswick, N.J.: Rutgers University Press, 1973.

Flaumenhaft, Mera J. "The Comic Remedy: Machiavelli's 'Mandragola.' " *Interpretation* 7 (May 1978): 33-74.

Fleisher, Martin. "Trust and Deceit in Machiavelli's Comedies." *Journal of the History of Ideas* (July 1966): 365-80.

Foley, Helene P. "The Conception of Women in Athenian Drama." In *Reflections of Women in Antiquity*. Edited by Helene P. Foley. Pp. 127-68. New York, London, and Paris: Gordon and Breach, 1981.

Fustel de Coulanges, Numa Denis. *The Ancient City*. Baltimore and London: Johns Hopkins University Press, 1980.

Gies, Frances, and Joseph Gies. *Women in the Middle Ages*. New York: Harper & Row, 1978.

Glotz, Gustave. *The Greek City and Its Institutions*. Translated by N. Malinson. New York: Alfred A. Knopf, 1930.

Gomme, A. W. "The Position of Women in the Fifth and Fourth Century B.C." In *Essays in Greek History and Literature*. Edited by A.W. Gomme. Pp. 89-115. Oxford: Basil Blackwell, 1937.

Hallet, Judith P. "The Role of Women in Roman Elegy." *Arethusa* 6 (Spring 1973): 103-24.

Harrison, A. W. R. *The Law of Athens: The Family and Property*. Oxford: Clarendon Press, 1968.

Hobbes, Thomas. *Leviathan*. Edited by C. B. Macpherson. Harmondsworth: Penguin Books, 1968.

Horowitz, Maryanne Cline. "The Image of God in Man—Is Woman Included?" *Harvard Theological Review* 72 (July-October 1979): 175-206.

———. "Aristotle and Woman." *Journal of the History of Biology* 9 (Fall 1976): 183-213.

Jaeger, Werner. *Five Essays*. Translated by Adele M. Fiske. Montreal: Marco Casalini, 1966.

Kitto, H. D. F. *The Greeks*. Baltimore: Penguin, 1951.

Krauss, Henry. *The Living Theater of Medieval Art*. Philadelphia: University of Pennsylvania Press, 1967.

Lacey, W. K. *The Family in Classical Greece*. Ithaca, N.Y.: Cornell University Press, 1968.

Lange, Lynda. "The Function of Equal Education in Plato's *Republic* and *Laws*." In *The Sexism of Social and Political Theory*. Edited by Lorenne M. G. Clark and Lynda Lange. Pp. 3-15. Toronto: University of Toronto Press, 1979.

Locke, John. *Two Treatises of Civil Government*. Edited by Thomas I. Cook. New York: Hafner Press, 1947.

———. *A Letter Concerning Toleration*. Edited by Patrick Romanell. Indianapolis: Bobbs-Merrill, 1955.

Lord, Carnes. "The Character and Composition of Aristotle's *Politics*." *Political Theory* 9 (November 1981): 459-78.

Lucas, Angela. *Women in the Middle Ages: Religion, Marriage and Letters*. New York: St. Martin's Press, 1983.

McLaughlin, Eleanor Commo. "Women, Power and the Pursuit of Holiness in Medieval Christianity." In *Women of Spirit: Female Leadership in the Jewish and Christian Tradition*. Edited by Rosemary Ruether and Eleanor McLaughlin. Pp. 90-130. New York: Simon and Schuster, 1979.

———. "Equality of Souls, Inequality of Sexes: Woman in Medieval Theology." In *Religion and Sexism: Images of Woman in the Jewish and Christian Traditions*. Edited by Rosemary Radford Ruether. New York: Simon and Schuster, 1974.

McNamara, Jo Ann. "Sexual Equality and the Cult of Virginity in Early Christian Thought." *Feminist Studies* 3/4 (Spring-Summer 1976): 144-58.

McNamara, Jo Ann, and Suzanne F. Wemple. "Sanctity and Power: The Dual Pursuit of Medieval Women." In *Becoming Visible: Women in European History*. Edited by Renate Bridenthal and Claudia Koonz. Pp. 90-118. Boston: Houghton Mifflin, 1974.

Mansfield, Harvey C., Jr. *Machiavelli's New Modes and Orders: A Study of the "Discourses on Livy."* Ithaca, N.Y., and London: Cornell University Press, 1979.

Mill, John Stuart. *On Liberty*. Indianapolis: Bobbs-Merrill, 1956.

Nichols, Mary P. "The Good Life, Slavery, and Acquisition: Aristotle's Introduction to Politics." *Interpretation* 11 (May 1983): 171-83.

———. "Thought and Action in Aristotle's Political Science." Paper read at the Midwest Political Science meetings, Cincinnati, Ohio, April 16-18, 1981. Xerox.

Okin, Susan Moller. *Women in Western Political Thought*. Princeton: Princeton University Press, 1979.

Orwin, Clifford. "Machiavelli's Unchristian Charity." *American Political Science Review* 72 (December 1978): 1217-28.

Pangle, Thomas L. *The Laws of Plato*. New York: Basic Books, 1979.

Parvey, Constance F. "The Theology and Leadership of Women in the New Testament." In *Religion and Sexism: Images of Woman in the Jewish and Christian Traditions*. Edited by Rosemary Radford Ruether. Pp. 117-49. New York: Simon and Schuster, 1974.

Pateman, Carole. "Sublimation and Reification: Locke, Wolin, and the Liberal Conception of Politics." *Politics and Society* 5 (1975): 441-67.

Pierce, Christine. "Equality: *Republic* V." *Monist* 57 (1973): 1-11.

Pitkin, Hanna Fenichel. *Fortune Is a Woman: Gender and Politics in the Thought of Niccolo Machiavelli.* Berkeley: University of California Press, 1984.

Pomeroy, Sarah B. *Goddesses, Whores, Wives and Slaves.* New York: Schocken Books, 1975.

Power, Eileen. *Medieval Women.* Edited by M. M. Postan. Cambridge: Cambridge University Press, 1975.

Redfield, James. *Nature and Culture in the Iliad: The Tragedy of Hector.* Chicago and London: University of Chicago Press, 1975.

Rogers, Katherine M. *The Troublesome Helpmate: A History of Misogyny in Literature.* Seattle: University of Washington Press, 1966.

Ross, David. *Style and Tradition in Catullus.* Cambridge, Mass.: Harvard University Press, 1969.

Ruddick, Sara. "Maternal Thinking." *Feminist Studies* 6 (1980): 343-67.

Ruether, Rosemary. "Mothers of the Church: Ascetic Women in the Late Patristic Age." In *Women of Spirit: Female Leadership in the Jewish and Christian Traditions.* Edited by Rosemary Ruether and Eleanor McLaughlin. Pp. 99-130. New York: Simon and Schuster, 1979.

———. "Virginal Feminism in the Fathers of the Church." In *Religion and Sexism: Images of Woman in the Jewish and Christian Traditions.* Edited by Rosemary Radford Ruether. Pp. 150-83. New York: Simon and Schuster, 1974.

Salkever, Steven G. "Women, Soldiers, Citizens: Plato and Aristotle on the Politics of Virility." Paper read at the annual meetings of the American Political Science Association, Chicago, September 1-4, 1983.

Saxonhouse, Arlene W. "Eros and the Female in Greek Political Thought: An Interpretation of Plato's *Symposium.*" *Political Theory* 12 (February 1984): 5-27.

———. "Classical Greek Conceptions of Public and Private." In *Conceptions of Public and Private in Social Life.* Edited by S. I. Benn and G. R. Gaus. London: Croom-Helm, 1983.

———. "Family, Polity and Unity: Aristotle on Socrates' Community of Wives." *Polity* 15 (Winter 1982): 202-19.

———. "Men, Women, War, and Politics: Family and Polis in Aristophanes and Euripides." *Political Theory* 8 (1980): 65-81.

————. "Comedy in Callipolis: Animal Imagery in the *Republic*." *American Political Science Review* 72 (1978): 888-901.

————. "The Philosopher and the Female in the Political Thought of Plato." *Political Theory* 4 (1976): 195-212.

Schaar, John. "Some Ways of Thinking About Equality." *Journal of Politics* 26 (November 1964): 887-95.

Schapps, David. *Economic Rights of Women in Ancient Greece.* Edinburgh: Edinburgh University Press, 1979.

Schochet, Gordon J. *Patriarchalism in Political Thought.* New York: Basic Books, 1975.

Schüssler-Fiorenza, Elisabeth. *In Memory of Her: A Feminist Theological Reconstruction of Christian Origins.* New York: Crossroads, 1983.

Segal, Charles. *Poetry and Myth in Ancient Pastoral: Essays on Theocritus and Virgil.* Princeton: Princeton University Press, 1981.

Shaw, Michael. "The Female Intruder: Women in Fifth Century Drama." *Classical Philology* 70 (October 1975): 255-66.

Skinner, Quentin. *The Foundations of Modern Political Thought: The Renaissance.* Volume I. Cambridge: Cambridge University Press, 1978.

Spelman, Elizabeth V. "Woman as Body: Ancient and Contemporary Views." *Feminist Studies* 8 (Spring 1982): 109-30.

Wemple, Suzanne Fonay. *Women in Frankish Society: Marriage and the Cloister 500 to 900.* Philadelphia: University of Pennsylvania Press, 1981.

Wolff, Hans Julius. "Marriage Law and Family Organization in Ancient Athens: A Study of the Interrelation of Public and Private Law in the Greek City." *Traditio* 2 (1944): 43-95.

Yarbrough, Ann. "Christianization in the Fourth Century: The Example of Roman Women." *Church History* 45 (June 1976): 149-65.

Zuckert, Catherine. "Aristotle on the Limits and Satisfactions of Political Life." *Interpretation* 11 (May 1983): 185-206.

Index

Achilles, in Homer's *Iliad*, 21
Adam, 137, 148
Aeneas, in Vergil's *Aeneid*, 93,
    119–123
Aeneid (Vergil), 93, 119–123
Aeschylus, *Oresteia*, 25–28
Agamemnon, in Aeschylus'
    Oresteia, 25–28
Amata, in Vergil's *Aeneid*,
    122–123
Amazons, 140, 144
Anchises (father of Aeneas), in
    Vergil's *Aeneid*, 93
Andromache (wife of Hector): in
    Homer's *Iliad*, 21–22; in Euri-
    pides' *Trojan Women*, 31–32
Annals (Tacitus): 113–118; Agrip-
    pina (elder, grandmother of
    Nero), 116–117; Agrippina
    (younger, mother of Nero),
    117–118; Claudius, 117;
    Livia, 115–116; Messalina
    (wife of Claudius), 117;
    Tiberius, 116
Antigone (Sophocles), 28–31
Apollo, in Aeschylus' *Oresteia*,
    26, 27
Apostles, 125–126. *See also*
    Luke, Saint; Paul, Saint
Aristophanes: and Plato, 45–46;
    in Plato's *Symposium*, 53,
    55. Works: *Ecclesiazusae*,
    34–35, 45, 175–177; *Lysis-
    trata*, 32–34
Aristotle: 12–15, 63–92, 128, 177,
    181; *akuron* (definition of),
    akuron (definition of), 74; bi-
    ology of female, 67–68, 71–
    75; on choice, 66–67, 79–80;
    on equality, 86–88; on hierar-

chy, 68–76, 84–88, 181;
    logos, 66, 88; on love of one-
    self, 82–83; nature, concept
    of, in Greek thought (versus
    nomos), 18–19, 36; and
    Phyllis, 153; *physis* (nature),
    64; on Plato's *Republic*, 80–
    85; polis (see also specific
    reference): family as model of,
    71–78, 84–88, ideal, 88–90,
    and law, 65–66, 77–80, and
    stability of, 76, 79–80, 83–86;
    ruler, how to choose, 75–76;
    as student of Plato, 63–64; on
    slavery, 70–71, 75; on Sparta,
    78–80, 85; telos and teleol-
    ogy, 64–69; *to bouleutikon*
    (the deliberative power), 74;
    Works: *Ethics*, 87, 89; *Gener-
    ation of Animals*, 68, 71; *Pol-
    itics*, 10–13, 69–90; *Rhetoric*,
    79
Aspasia (Pericles' mistress): in
    Plato's *Menexenus*, 52, 55–57
Athene, in Aeschylus' *Oresteia*,
    26
Athens: and origins of political
    thought in Greece, 17–18;
    Aristophanes' criticism of,
    176–177; theater in, 24–25
Augustine, Saint: 130, 146; *City
    of God, The* (work), 135–136;
    City of God (spiritual commu-
    nity), 135–140; City of Man,
    136–137; *civitas (dei* versus
    hominum), definition of,
    135–137; and Genesis, 137;
    ius, definition of, 135; and
    marriage, 138–140; and
    Manichaeans, 138; politics, re-

About the Author

Arlene W. Saxonhouse is professor of political science at the University of Michigan, Ann Arbor, and a former director of women's studies there.

Professor Saxonhouse has published widely in the area of Greek political thought, with a special focus on the writings of Plato, Aristotle, and Thucydides. Her articles and reviews have appeared in *American Political Science Review, Ethics, Interpretation, Political Theory, Polity,* and *Women and Politics.*

Professor Saxonhouse received her B.A. from Oberlin College and holds an M.Phil. and Ph.D. from Yale University.

About the Editors

Rita Mae Kelly is a Professor at the School of Public Affairs, Arizona State University, Tempe, Arizona. She holds a Ph.D. in political science from Indiana University, has served on numerous editorial boards, including *Evaluation Quarterly, Journal of Women and Politics, Policy Studies Review*, and was issue editor for *The Journal of Social Issues* symposium, "Productivity and Satisfaction in the Public Sector: A Socio-Psychological Perspective" (Fall 1980, 36,4). She has written several books, including: *Community Control of Economic Development* (Praeger, 1977) and *The Making of Political Women* (with Mary Boutilier; Nelson-Hall, 1978). She currently is editor of the Praeger Series on Women and Politics (with Ruth B. Mandel) and is editor of the *Policy Studies Review* Special Symposium "Productivity, Public Policy, and Societal Well-Being" (February 1985) and the forthcoming anthology *Promoting Productivity in the Public Sector: Problems, Strategies, and Prospects*. She is also editor of the *Journal of Women and Politics* special symposium on Political Socialization, forthcoming 1985.

Ruth B. Mandel, Associate Professor at Rutgers University's Eagleton Institute of Politics, is Director of Eagleton's Center for the American Woman and Politics (CAWP). Established in 1971 as a research, education, and public service center, CAWP studies women's participation in American public life, with special emphasis on candidates, officeholders, and women seeking political leadership roles. Mandel is the author of *In the Running: The New Woman Candidate* (Boston: Beacon Press, 1983).